Joseph Conrad

The popular yet complex work of Joseph Conrad has attracted much critical attention over the years, from the perspectives of post-colonial, modernist, cultural and gender studies.

This guide to Conrad's compelling work offers:

- an accessible introduction to the contexts and many interpretations of Conrad's texts, from publication to the present;
- an introduction to key critical texts and perspectives on Conrad's life and work, situated in a broader critical history;
- cross-references between sections of the guide, in order to suggest links between texts, contexts and criticism;
- suggestions for further reading.

Part of the *Routledge Guides to Literature* series, this volume is essential reading for all those beginning detailed study of Joseph Conrad and seeking not only a guide to his works but also a way through the wealth of contextual and critical material that surrounds them.

Tim Middleton teaches modern and contemporary English and American Literature at Bath Spa University. He has written articles and books on a wide range of authors including Iain Banks, Joseph Conrad, Colm Tóibín and Joseph O'Connor and is a long-standing member of the committee of the Joseph Conrad Society (UK).

Routledge Guides to Literature*

Editorial Advisory Board: Richard Bradford (University of Ulster at Coleraine), Jan Jedrzejewski (University of Ulster at Coleraine), Duncan Wu (St. Catherine's College, University of Oxford).

Routledge Guides to Literature offer clear introductions to the most widely studied authors and literary texts. Each book engages with texts, contexts and criticism, highlighting the range of critical views and contextual factors that need to be taken into consideration in advanced studies of literary works. The series encourages informed but independent readings of texts by ranging as widely as possible across the contextual and critical issues relevant to the works examined and highlighting areas of debate as well as those of critical consensus. Alongside general guides to texts and authors, the series includes 'sourcebooks', which allow access to reprinted contextual and critical materials as well as annotated extracts of primary text.

Available in this series

Geoffrey Chaucer by Gillian Rudd
Ben Jonson by James Loxley
William Shakespeare's The Merchant of Venice: A Sourcebook edited by
    S. P. Cerasano
William Shakespeare's King Lear: A Sourcebook edited by Grace Ioppolo
William Shakespeare's Othello: A Sourcebook edited by Andrew Hadfield
William Shakespeare's Macbeth: A Sourcebook edited by Alexander Leggatt
William Shakespeare's Hamlet: A Sourcebook edited by Sean McEvoy
John Milton by Richard Bradford
John Milton's Paradise Lost: A Sourcebook edited by Margaret Kean
Alexander Pope by Paul Baines
Mary Wollstonecraft's A Vindication of the Rights of Woman: A Sourcebook
    edited by Adriana Craciun
Jonathan Swift's Gulliver's Travels: A Sourcebook edited by Roger D. Lund
Jane Austen by Robert P. Irvine
Jane Austen's Emma: A Sourcebook edited by Paula Byrne
Jane Austen's Pride and Prejudice: A Sourcebook edited by Robert Morrison
Mary Shelley's Frankenstein: A Sourcebook edited by Timothy Morton
The Poems of John Keats: A Sourcebook edited by John Strachan
The Poems of Gerard Manley Hopkins: A Sourcebook Edited by Alice Jenkins
Charles Dickens's David Copperfield: A Sourcebook edited by Richard J. Dunn
Charles Dickens's Bleak House: A Sourcebook edited by Janice M. Allan
Charles Dickens's Oliver Twist: A Sourcebook edited by Juliet John
Charles Dickens's A Tale of Two Cities: A Sourcebook edited by Ruth Glancy
Herman Melville's Moby-Dick: A Sourcebook edited by Michael J. Davey

* Some books in this series were originally published in the Routledge Literary Sourcebooks series, edited by Duncan Wu, or the Complete Critical Guide to English Literature series, edited by Richard Bradford and Jan Jedrzejewski.

Joseph Conrad

Tim Middleton

Routledge
Taylor & Francis Group

LONDON AND NEW YORK

First published 2006
by Routledge
2 Park Square, Milton Park, Abingdon, Oxon OX14 4RN

Simultaneously published in the USA and Canada
by Routledge
270 Madison Ave, New York, NY 10016

Routledge is an imprint of the Taylor and Francis Group, an informa business

© 2006 Tim Middleton

Typeset in Sabon and Gill Sans by RefineCatch Limited, Bungay, Suffolk
Printed and bound in Great Britain by
TJ International Ltd, Padstow, Cornwall

British Library Cataloguing in Publication Data
A catalogue record for this book is available from the British Library.

Library of Congress Cataloging in Publication Data
Middleton, Tim, 1962–
   Joseph Conrad / by Tim Middleton.
      p. cm.—(Routledge guides to literature)
   Includes bibliographical references.
   1. Conrad, Joseph, 1857–1924—Criticism and interpretation.
I. Title.   II. Series.
   PR6005.O4Z7785 2006
   823'.912—dc22

                                          2006009934

ISBN 10: 0–415–26851–6 (hbk)
ISBN 10: 0–415–26852–4 (pbk)

ISBN 13: 0–978–26851–6 (hbk)
ISBN 13: 0–978–26852–3 (pbk)

Contents

3: Criticism   137

Acknowledgements

I'd like to thank Bath Spa University for funding various library visits during which the essential research for this project was undertaken. I'm also grateful to the University for supporting my attendance at conferences on Conrad in the UK, USA, and Poland. Elements of the present work have been aired at these conferences and I'm grateful to Conrad colleagues for feedback and advice.

At Routledge, Liz Thompson has been a patient editor and I must thank her, series editor Dr Jan Jedrzejewski and the readers of the first draft of this book for their helpful and supportive feedback.

A particular debt that I'm pleased to acknowledge is to Dr Keith Carabine, Chairperson of the Joseph Conrad Society (UK). As an undergraduate at the University of Kent in the 1980s I was fortunate to study Conrad's work with Keith and was inspired to undertake postgraduate studies by his passion and insight. I'm delighted to work with him now as a member of the organising committee of the Joseph Conrad Society UK.

My final thanks are to Gaynor for her unstinting support.

Abbreviations, frequently cited works and cross-referencing

Primary texts

All quotations from and references to the works of Joseph Conrad are keyed to the texts of Dent's Uniform Edition (London, Dent, 1923–8).

A Personal Record (1912)

First published in the *English Review* in December 1908–June 1909 as 'Some Reminiscences', this autobiographical work provided period critics with important material on Conrad's early life and it remains an essential text in any account of his life and work. The collection was published in England in 1912 as *Some Reminiscences* and a US edition was published in the same year under the title of *A Personal Record* and this title was then used for the second English edition published in 1916. For simplicity's sake I will refer to the work by its more familiar second title throughout this book.

Conrad's letters

The majority of quotations from Conrad's letters are taken from the texts given in the Cambridge *Collected Letters*. These are attributed by the abbreviation CL and the number of the volume, followed by page reference(s).

Cross-referencing

Cross-referencing between sections is a feature of each volume in the Routledge Guides to Literature series. Cross-references appear in brackets and include section titles as well as the relevant page numbers in bold type, e.g. (see Life and Contexts, pp. 14–15).

Introduction

Józef Teodor Konrad Korzeniowski was born on 3 December 1857 into a family of Polish landowners in a part of the Polish Ukraine that had been annexed by Russia since 1793: known as Joseph Conrad he would die on 3 August 1924 at the age of sixty-six in an English village just outside Canterbury in Kent, having become one of the most celebrated novelists of his age. In between these dates Conrad famously lived 'three lives' – as the son of Polish revolutionaries, as a British merchant seaman, and as one of the greatest novelists of the twentieth century. Referring to his dual Polish and English allegiances he once described himself as 'homo-duplex' (CL3: 89) – the double man. In what follows I will introduce some of the key contexts in relation to which the interpenetration of these varied lives continue to be studied.

Part 1, 'Life and Contexts', provides readers with an overview of his Polish childhood and discusses his sea career in terms of its impact on his fiction, and the coverage here is supplemented by a detailed biographical chronology which outlines key aspects of his pre-writing life (see Chronology, **pp. 168–81**). This section also offers a selective account of his writing life which concentrates upon his stylistic and thematic debts to French and Russian authors and his literary friendships in terms of their influence on his approach to his craft. Part 2, 'Works', provides a detailed account of all of Conrad's completed novels and short stories. Drawing extensively on his revealing letters, this section records his creative struggles when composing his fiction and assesses the development of his work from the early Malay novels of the 1890s through the great works of his middle period to conclude with an account of the often maligned late fiction of the 1920s. In recent years some of the most innovative and insightful work in Conrad studies has been devoted to his late fiction and short stories – see, for example, Hampson's work on the late fiction in *Joseph Conrad: Betrayal and Identity* (1992) or Vulcan's *The Strange Short Fiction of Joseph Conrad* (1999) – and this volume reflects this shift in critical attention by devoting equal space to canonical works and overlooked collections. Thus the present volume does not scruple in giving equal coverage to flawed but fascinating lesser known collections like *A Set of Six* (1908) or the convoluted history of the writing of *The Rescue* (1920) – a work whose composition can tell readers a great deal about Conrad's shifts in technique and artistic ambition from the 1890s to the 1920s – whilst devoting attention to the established classics of his canon such as *Lord Jim* or *Nostromo*. In an introductory work it seems to me essential that readers are helped to make up their own minds about the relative merits of a text and to this end my coverage includes details of the composition and subsequent critical reception of each book along with a concise commentary on its story and plot which highlights key scenes and sequences and reflects on the ways in which these illuminate aspects of Conrad's technique. Discussion of each text concludes with a concise account of its subsequent critical reputation, keyed to representative suggested further reading.

As this is an introductory work I do not seek to offer new interpretations of Conrad's work but, instead, provide a summary of the critical history of each text along with details of current critical perspectives from which readers can commence their own analyses of the work in question. Part 3, 'Criticism', provides a survey of the milestones in the critical study of Conrad's work from the first full-length study in 1914 to the work of today's leading scholars. This section also contains discussion of some key topics in current Conrad studies, offering concise outlines of works dealing with his fiction in terms of its engagement with debates around notions of national identity, post-colonialism, or the politics and poetics of revolution or gender. This section eschews interpretative commentary in favour of concise summaries of the main argument or critical position adopted in the work under discussion, supplemented by remarks on its place in the development of Conrad studies. The work concludes with a detailed contextual chronology, which provides readers with a concise overview of Conrad's life and works and sets this material in the wider cultural context of the epoch in which he lived.

The book as a whole is organised with detailed cross-referencing, a thematic index, and a full bibliography so as to permit the reader to use it as a reference text, pursuing particular topics in the writer's life and works, but also enabling it to be read from cover to cover as a comprehensive introduction to the life and work of Joseph Conrad.

1

Life and contexts

A Polish childhood

Although he was naturalised as a British citizen in 1886, Conrad's own attempt at autobiography, *A Personal Record*, suggested the importance of his Polish childhood for an understanding of his fiction, describing it as 'that inexorable past from which his work of fiction and their personalities are remotely derived' (25). He was born on 3 December 1857 in Berdyczów, a small town in a part of Poland which had been annexed by Russia in 1793 and is today a part of the Ukraine. His parents were active in revolutionary circles working to overthrow the foreign occupation, and his full name – Józef Teodor Konrad Korzeniowski – captures some of their political commitment:

> His first name, given after his maternal grandfather, was connected with a legacy of anti-romanticism, political opportunism, and enlightened conservatism in social opinions. The second name the boy received after his paternal grandfather, ex-captain of the Polish Army and a fervent patriot. But the most heavily loaded with meaning was his third name, which had been made popular in Poland by two heroes of Adam Mickiewicz's poems.
>
> (Najder 1964: 4)

Polish Romantic poet Adam Mickiewicz's *Konrad Wallenrod* (1827) told of a Lithuanian boy raised by Teutonic knights who schemes to overthrow his German captors whilst his *Dziady* (1832) presented the awakening of nationalist sensibilities in a romantic egocentric who adopts the name Konrad as a symbol of his ideological transformation. If these associations were not enough of a burden for the child to live up to, Conrad's father, Apollo, wrote his own poem for his baby son, saturated in his dreams for a renewed nation-state:

> Baby son, tell yourself
> You are without land, without love,
> Without country, without people,
> While *Poland – your Mother* is in her grave.
> For your only *Mother* is dead – and yet

> She is your faith, your palm of martyrdom.
>   Hushaby, my baby son!
>   (Najder 1983b: 33)

When Conrad was only five years old, his father was arrested for his political activity and, after a period of imprisonment, the family were exiled in 1862 to Vologda, some 300 miles north-east of Moscow. The journey was difficult, and the young boy and then his mother fell ill with pneumonia. Vologda was 'a huge quagmire' where there were only 'two seasons', a white winter which 'lasts nine and a half months' and a green winter which persists for 'two and a half'; during the white winter the temperature falls to minus 30 Fahrenheit (Najder 1983b: 67). During this time, Apollo wrote and anonymously published his pamphlet on 'Poland and Muscovy' which examined human history as a conflict between barbarity and civilisation – Poland, unsurprisingly, is on the side of the angels whilst Russia is depicted as 'the plague of humanity' (Najder 1983b: 77). Whilst in exile, Apollo completed translations into Polish of works by Charles Dickens, Victor Hugo and Shakespeare, works which first introduced Conrad to English literature.

In their exile, Conrad's mother, Ewa, suffered from extended periods of illness and, despite brief respites, her health declined and she died in April 1865 when Conrad was seven. He recalled his mother as more 'than a mere loving, wide-browed, silent, protecting presence, whose eyes had a sort of commanding sweetness' (*A Personal Record*, 24). Apollo's few remaining letters from this period catch something of the depths of his despair – he writes of spending 'the greatest part of my days by the grave', of his 'torments' and suffering (Najder 1983b: 94–5). He acknowledged that 'the little mite is growing up as though in a cloister, the grave of our Unforgettable is our *memento mori*' and noted that 'the little one, seeing nobody, burrows too deeply into books' (Najder 1983b: 102, 104). Apollo's own health declined after Ewa's death, but he continued to care for Conrad, overseeing his education and encouraging his reading of Polish Romantic poetry and of those authors he was translating. As several biographers have noted, Conrad had a lonely childhood, nursing a father gripped by despair, psychological and physical illness in an atmosphere of 'mysticism touched with despair' (CL2: 247).

Conrad had little formal education during the years between seven and eleven but he seems to have read widely, wrote patriotic dramas and recited Mickiewicz's poetry (Najder 1964: 10). In 1869, they moved to Kraków where Apollo was to further his journalistic work, but his health rapidly deteriorated and he died on 23 May. His funeral became the occasion for popular protest and the young Conrad led a funeral procession that comprised several thousand people. His account of this experience, for all its after-the-event writerly hyperbole, captured the emotional challenge of this occasion:

> the small boy ... following a hearse; a space kept clear in which I walked alone, conscious of an enormous following, the clumsy swaying of the tall black machine, the chanting of the surpliced clergy at the head, the flames of tapers passing under the low archway of the gate, the rows of bared heads on the pavements with fixed, serious eyes. Half the population has turned out on that fine May afternoon.
>   ('Poland Revisited', *Notes on Life and Letters*, 169)

After the death of his father, Conrad was initially cared for by his father's friend Stefan Buszczyński and then by his devoted maternal grandmother Teofila Bobrowska, who became his official guardian in 1870. Conrad lived with her in Kraków until May 1873, but the management of his education was subject to the influence of his maternal uncle, Tadeusz Bobrowski. Bobrowski had little time for his brother-in-law's politics, and biographers have speculated on the psychological tensions which Conrad might have experienced whilst trying to remain true to his father's memory and accommodate the views of his influential uncle. Conrad was initially placed in a Kraków boarding school, but his lack of prior formal education meant he was behind his year group and the family appointed a personal tutor, a young medical student called Adam Marek Pulman, who also accompanied Conrad on his long summer holidays. His uncle faced many worries as Conrad continued to be not only sickly but also somewhat independently minded. On top of this Conrad was still deemed to be a Russian citizen and could be expected, in future, to be subject to a period of military service – potentially disastrous for the son of a known opponent of the State. To try and prevent this, the family sought Austrian citizenship for Conrad but this was unsuccessful.

It was in late 1872 that Conrad stunned his family by announcing that he wished to have a career at sea – a declaration that 'stirred up a mass of remonstrance, indignation, pitying wonder, bitter irony and downright chaff' (*A Personal Record*, 42). His plans were initially resisted. After a trip to Switzerland for medical treatment in May 1873 and a brief period back in Kraków with his grandmother, Bobrowski decided that Conrad would be best cared for at his cousin Syroczyński's boarding house and school in Lwów. He told Conrad that the move was intended to 'help harden you, which is something that every man needs in his life' (Najder 1983a: 35). This move to stricter environs may have been part of Bobrowski's attempt to put a dampener of his seafaring ambitions but Conrad appears to have been an unruly pupil, fretting under the rules of the boarding house, and in September 1874 he was moved back to Kraków by his uncle, perhaps because of Syroczyński's disapproval of a developing flirtation between Conrad and his cousin Tekla. In October, Conrad, having finally persuaded his uncle of the merits of a sea career, travelled to Marseilles to begin life as a sailor on French ships.

The long-term influence of Polish culture on Conrad's work remains a contested area of scholarly debate. Conrad spent most of his life away from his home country and bereft of his immediate Polish family, and this isolation brought with it a critical distance from the cultural and social concerns of his homeland. It is clear from his letters that he was touchy about suggestions that he had abandoned his country by electing to write in English, and critics have noted a Polish heritage in his syntax and fondness for adverbs (Busza 1966, Morzinski 1994). Through his father, Conrad was exposed to the Romantic nationalism of Mickiewicz and his romantic-nationalist compatriots and imbibed their heady brew of selfless fidelity and obsession with the preservation of honour at an impressionable age. In their works, personal happiness comes very much second to patriotic duty, and critics have seen evidence of these Polish concerns in Conrad's fictions – whether it be in Jim's self-destructive adherence to a code of conduct in *Lord Jim*, or Marlow's choice of nightmares in 'Heart of Darkness' (see Works, **pp. 44–6, 49–52**). Conrad's childhood experience of revolutionary action, filtered by

Bobrowski's disapproval, may have informed his withering account of nationalist ambitions in *Nostromo* and his wry study of bungling revolutionaries in *The Secret Agent*, and is undoubtedly central to his great study of honour and betrayal, *Under Western Eyes* (see Works, **pp. 64–7, 70–2, 83–6**). Whilst his critical view of revolutionary action owes much to the views of his uncle, his ability to capture its idealism owes a debt to the Romantic nationalism of his father. For his leading Polish critic, 'the curse of Conrad's inner life and bitter inspiration for his art' seems to stem from this tension between Polish Romantic idealism and Polish pragmatism (Najder 1964: 19). Polish characters and settings do not, however, feature large in his canon, with the exception of the short story 'Prince Roman' (see Works, **pp. 131–2**). We can see little direct engagement with Polish history and culture in his work aside from some heavily inflected reflections in *A Personal Record* and the essays 'Autocracy and War', 'The Crime of Partition', 'A Note on the Polish Problem', and 'Poland Revisited' collected in *Notes on Life and Letters*. For most commentators, it is the less obvious manifestations of his Polish background that shape his themes. For his most influential Polish critic, it is Conrad's Polish background that makes him 'a man disinherited, lonely, and (for a Western writer of that time) exceptionally conscious of the sinister brutalities hidden behind the richly ornate façade of *bourgeois* political optimism. And these characteristics are precisely what makes Conrad our contemporary' (Najder 1964: 31).

Sea life

Having left his homeland at the age of sixteen, Conrad did not return to it until 1890 when he was thirty-two, and during those sixteen years of travel, sea life and associated personal growth, he added crucial elements to his experience that would shape his fiction just as profoundly as his Polish childhood. It is important to stress that whilst Conrad spent many years working as a merchant mariner, to claim him as a writer of sea stories would be a mistake. To be sure, there are some key works in which the 'wrestle with wind and weather' (CL2: 354) are integral such as 'Youth', *The Nigger of the 'Narcissus'*, 'Typhoon' or *The Shadow Line* (see Works, **pp. 48–9, 32–5, 57–8, 114–16**), and others in which events afloat are a key part of the text – one thinks of Jim's voyage on the *Patna* in *Lord Jim* or Decoud and Nostromo's night voyage in the lighter in *Nostromo*, for example (see Works, **pp. 44–6, 64–7**). In these texts, the sea voyage is figured as part of a rite of passage, a testing ground for a character's beliefs and values. In his reflections on things maritime, Conrad suggested that whilst 'from sixteen to thirty-six cannot be called an age, . . . it is a pretty long stretch of that sort of experience which teaches a man slowly to see and feel' (*The Mirror of the Sea*, xi), and in writing about men and the sea Conrad found a fluid and formidable mirror in which to refract the tensions and predilections of his epoch. 'Twixt land and sea he found not only a title for a collection of short fiction but also a terrain that a marginal outsider in English letters could make his own.

Conrad's first study of men and the sea was *The Nigger of the 'Narcissus'* – a key text in the history of his writing since it marked his turn from the 'exotic' settings of his early fiction and focused on English ships and the passions of those who worked on them. His seafarers in that novel were, by and large, simple men from the age of sail and in this great paean to the English merchant marine he decisively broke away from settings that had begun to pigeonhole him as the Kipling of the Malay Archipelago and firmly aligned himself with his new country's traditions, addressing issues of class conflict and national character in ways designed to chime with the politics of the period. As Jonathan Raban has remarked, in his sea fiction Conrad is

> building a counterworld; a mirror-world of shimmering lucidity, unlighted by the horrors of nineteenth century industrial democratic life. His love for the one is sustained by his hatred of the other, and it is poignantly sharpened by . . . [his] knowledge that he is writing about a dying age in the life of the sea
>
> (1992: 20)

Whilst writing of men and the sea in the age of sail might be seen as part of a reactionary politics – given that the modern diesel engines had been invented some five years earlier and screw-driven steam ships such as Brunel's SS *Great Britain* had been in service since the 1840s – the novel's narrative method was startlingly contemporary (see Works, pp. 32–5).

Conrad's ship-based fictions provided him with settings that offered a social microcosm within which societal and cultural mores could be carefully put into play in ways that challenged and at times debunked his era's dominant ideologies. Although in many of these sea fictions it is the physical challenge of the sea-based world for humanity that his work explores – in 'Typhoon', the examination of the 'disintegrating power of a great wind' (40), the disease-haunted, delay punctuated voyage in *The Shadow Line* or the limping progress of the *Judea* in *Youth* (see Works, pp. 57–8, 114–16, 48–9) – to read these as sea fictions in the tradition of Frederick Marryat's *Mr Midshipman Easy* (1836), Fenimore Cooper's *The Pilot* (1839), or R. H. Dana's *Two Years Before the Mast* (1840) is to overemphasise their settings' significance when compared to their thematic concerns. The great tradition of American writing about the sea is one that celebrates humanity's exploration of the natural world, whilst in Britain the legacy of a Romantic awe when faced by the power of the natural world fed the industrial epoch's sense of the separation of nature from mankind and meant that writers were less concerned to classify and explain the seaborne world than they were interested in evoking its alien, sublime strangeness. In his fictional works about the sea and sailors, Conrad is a writer first and merchant sailor second. This isn't to say that he doesn't pay attention to seamanship but rather to suggest that knowledge of it is not a prerequisite for enjoying his novels. Tests of character and resolve are central themes in Conrad's sea stories, and it is the value of solidarity and collaborative endeavour that is being celebrated in works such as *The Nigger of the 'Narcissus'*, which showed an ethnically disparate crew wedded together by the fellowship of the craft and the rules of merchant sea life despite the provocations of the agitator Donkin and the sentimentalising allure of the dying James Wait (see Works, pp. 32–5). We might take a cue from this novel for a view of the relative importance of things nautical in Conrad's sea fiction for, with one or two exceptions (the vicious killer ship of *The Brute* springs to mind (see Works, p. 76)), Old Singleton's assertion that 'ships are alright. It's the men in them' (*The

Nigger of the 'Narcissus', 24) can be taken as a crude summary of the focus of his novelistic attention.

Detailed biographical and archival research, begun with the pioneering studies of Norman Sherry in *Conrad's Eastern World* (1966) and *Conrad's Western World* (1971), has traced the ways in which Conrad drew upon his sea experiences as a source for stories and incidents and as a basis for particular characters. The following list details some of the ways he drew upon his sea life for the characters, incidents or settings of some of his major works. It is important to stress that in nearly every case he wove these experiences into fictions in ways that adumbrated the basic facts with further material drawn from his prodigious reading or vigorous imagination:

Novel(s)	Example(s) of personal sources and experience drawn upon
Almayer's Folly (1895), *An Outcast of the Islands* (1896), *The Rescue* (1920)	Conrad drew upon the life of William Charles Olmeijer *(1848–1900)* who lived in Berau on Borneo's Pantai River which he visited as first mate of the *Vidar* on trading voyages between August and December 1887. From Olmeijer he heard tales of William Lingard (1829–88), the English adventurer who provides a model for Tom Lingard. For discussion, see Works, **pp. 22–6, 28–30, 124–5**.
'Youth' (1902)	In September 1881 Conrad signed on as second mate on the *Palestine* for its journey to Bangkok from London. The ship's journey is punctuated by delays and ends with its cargo of coal spontaneously combusting when the ship is off Sumatra. These events form the basis of the plot of 'Youth', with the ship being renamed the *Judea*. For discussion, see Works, **pp. 48–9**.
The Nigger of the 'Narcissus' (1897)	Conrad was second mate on the *Narcissus* for its journey from Bombay to Dunkirk in 1884. During this voyage a black sailor, Joseph Barron, died at sea. For discussion, see Works, **pp. 32–5**.
Lord Jim (1900)	Conrad drew upon a well-publicised scandal involving Augustine Podmore Williams (1852–1916) who was first mate on the pilgrim ship *Jeddah* for its voyage from Penang to Jeddah in July 1880. Following a storm, the ship began to leak and its white captain and crew abandoned its pilgrim passengers – Williams was the last to leave ship and was thrown overboard by the pilgrims. Following an inquiry, in which he was reprimanded, Williams worked as a water clerk in Singapore and married a Eurasian woman. Williams's story provided Conrad with a basis for Jim's pre-Patusan life, and Norman Sherry has suggested that the two men met in 1883 whilst Conrad was in Singapore (1971: 299–311). Jim's Patusan life draws upon Conrad's knowledge of the well-known figure James Brooke (1803–68), the so-called White Rajah of Sarawak. For discussion, see Works, **pp. 44–6**.

'Typhoon' (1903)	Captain MacWhirr is based upon Irishman Captain John McWhir, under whom Conrad sailed as first mate in 1887. For discussion, see Works, **pp. 57–8**.
The Shadow Line (1917), 'The Secret Sharer' (1912), 'A Smile of Fortune' (1912)	Conrad draws upon his experience as Captain of the *Otago* and 'A Smile of Fortune' (1912) in 1888 and 1889 in these texts. For discussion, see Works, **pp. 114–16, 93–4**.
'Heart of Darkness' (1902)	Whilst working in the Belgian Congo in 1890, Conrad assisted the captain of the river steamer *Roi des Belges* in the upriver journey from Kinchasa to Stanley Falls and took charge of the ship when its captain became ill during the return journey. For discussion, see Works, **pp. 49–52**.

It seems clear that many of Conrad's fictions draw directly upon a range of experience he amassed during the course of his professional career. Later fictions also continued to draw upon personal experience but when weighing the relative influence of his sea life on his art we should recall his dictum that 'imagination, not invention, is the supreme master of art' (*A Personal Record*, 25). Conrad's preference for imagination over invention might go some way to explain the remarkable ways in which his novels and stories are formed from an amalgamation of sources which are dominated by printed books, newspapers and journals rather than his sea life. In his developing approach to fiction we can see the emergence of the idea of the novel as an assimilative, impression-shaped form – an early move in a direction which James Joyce would push to its extreme in the modernist masterpiece *Ulysses* (1922).

Literary and cultural contexts

For the purposes of the present study we can consider Conrad's relationship to the period's literary culture in three distinct ways. First, there is the legacy for his fiction of his own wide reading and assimilation of sources, styles and methods drawn from works as diverse as Shakespeare's *The Tempest* to the latest mass-market potboilers. Then there are questions about the shaping of his style in the light of the complex patterns of influence or homage arising from his involvement with a discrete group of writers and critics who formed his immediate circles of literary *confrères*. Finally, there is the complex history of his engagement with the period's burgeoning literary publishing industry and his agent's canny playing of that marketplace to his own and his client's ends. Related to this is Conrad's method of composition, which would be exacerbated by the increasing demands of the literary marketplace, and the role of periods of writer's block in the gestation of some his greatest works. These topics are weighty enough to have taken up many book-length studies in their own right, and what follows is simply a sketch designed to provide readers with an overview of some of the main issues in these arenas.

Conrad the reader

Conrad's extensive reading served him in lieu of a formal education as a young child in exile with his father. Studies of his reading habits demonstrate an astonishing breadth, and his letters and the recollections of his friends suggest that this was matched by a detailed recall of much that he read. To get a sense of the scale of his reading, one can turn to critical studies by David Tutien (1990) and Hans van Marle (1991). Tutien's study lists a library of some 686 works and van Marle's notes the existence of a further 200. Conrad not only immersed himself in fiction but also read widely in non-fiction and contemporary journalism and apparently enjoyed reading his son John's *Boy's Own Annual*, fairy stories by the Brothers Grimm and Hans Christian Andersen, and the nonsense poetry of Edward Lear. In some cases, Conrad relied on books to help him devise cultural and environmental details for his fiction. Scholarship has established, for example, the significance of A. R. Wallace's *The Malay Archipelago: The Land of the Orang Utan and the Bird of Paradise* (1869) and other traveller's studies for his work set in that region and in *Nostromo* he famously created the imaginary South American country of Costaguana from extensive reading in the history and culture of Latin America, including G. F. Masterman's *Seven Eventful Years in Paraguay* (1869) and Ramón Paez's *Wild Scenes in South America; or, Life in the Llanos of Venezuela* (1869) (see Works, **pp. 63–8**).

Conrad's boyhood reading included 'Victor Hugo and other Romantics' along with 'history, voyages, novels' (*A Personal Record*, 70–1). He read work by novelists Miguel de Cervantes (1547–1616), Charles Dickens (1812–70), Walter Scott (1771–1832) and William Thackeray (1811–63) in Polish translations and claimed that his first experience of English literature was his father's translation of Shakespeare's *The Two Gentlemen of Verona* (*A Personal Record*, 71), closely followed by Dickens's *Nicholas Nickleby* (1838–9). The latter's work was a particular enthusiasm with Conrad, who declared *Bleak House* (1852–3) amongst his favourite novels and drew upon it in his evocation of London in *The Secret Agent* and *Chance* (Epstein 1997) (see Works, **pp. 69–73, 98–103**). Critics have also traced Shakespearian influences on *Lord Jim* with its Hamlet-like central figure and have seen a rewriting of *The Tempest* in *Victory* (Batchelor 1992).

Detailed scholarly work has shown that it is French and Russian writers who most shape Conrad's craft. As with many late nineteenth-century novelists he was influenced by Gustave Flaubert (1821–80) who brought an impersonal and ironic detachment to the art of fiction. It is in part reading Flaubert that informs the development of Conrad's own narrative strategies which see him withdrawing an omniscient authorial presence from the narration, supplanting it with more or less fallible intermediary narrators. As Yves Hervouet's invaluable study has shown, Conrad also drew upon Flaubert for character groupings, thematic patterning and structural devices (Hervouet 1990). Amongst myriad examples, Hervouet cites the role of parallels and doubles in fictions such as *Under Western Eyes* and the structural function of the opening of *Nostromo* (in which the tale of the two gringos of Azuera acts to prefigure the fate of those who become entangled with the silver of the mine) as strategies adapted from Flaubert (Hervouet 1990: 171, 172, 173). Conrad also drew upon techniques developed by Flaubert's protégé Guy de Maupassant, a debt he acknowledges in his preface to Ada Galsworthy's

1904 translation of *Yvette and Other Stories* (reprinted in *Notes on Life and Letters* (cf. CL3: 52)). The influence of Maupassant's thinking about the novel as a form which stressed 'selection, arrangement and emphasis' (Hervouet 1990: 176) is to be found in Conrad's 'Preface' to *The Nigger of the 'Narcissus'*, with its emphasis on the struggle of the novelist as artist whose appeal to his readers is made 'through the senses' as a result of the writer's 'unswerving devotion to the perfect blending of form and substance' 'Preface', ix). In addition to numerous incidental details in works ranging from 'The Return' to *The Secret Agent*, Maupassant also provided sources for aspects of *Nostromo* (Hervouet 1990: 91–3).

Conrad also drew on work by the Russian authors Ivan Turgenev (1818–83) and, in more guarded ways, Fyodor Dostoevsky (1821–81). Paul Kirschner and Cedric Watts have influentially argued for the importance of Turgenev's 1860 lecture 'Hamlet and Don Quixote: The Two Eternal Human Types' on the characterisation of his heroes, and parallels between the two writers' works have been found in *Lord Jim* and *Under Western Eyes* (Kirschner 1968: 241–52, Watts 1993: 67–74). Conrad wrote a brief preface to a critical book on Turgenev by his friend and early mentor Edward Garnett, using it to distinguish the writer's 'mastery and gentleness' from the 'damned souls knocking themselves to pieces' (*Notes on Life and Letters*, 41) who, in Conrad's view, peopled the work of the then voguish Dostoevsky. The influence of the latter on Conrad is a more vexed subject on which recent textual and critical study has shed much light. Although Conrad made many protestations about his dislike of 'the convulsed, terror-haunted Dostoyewski' (*Notes on Life and Letters*, 42) the complex inter-relationship between *Crime and Punishment* and *Under Western Eyes* is one of literature's most remarkable examples of intertextuality. Keith Carabine has influentially argued that Conrad's attitude towards the great Russian writer can only be understood when we realise the, for Conrad, uncanny similarities between the Russophobic Apollo Korzeniowski and the Pole-hating Dostoevsky: in the latter, Carabine suggests, Conrad confronted both 'a rival, grimacing version of his father's deepest beliefs' and a model of 'the kind of patriot and writer both his father and his race wanted him to be' (Carabine 1996: 83). Conrad may have borrowed aspects of the heroine of *Crime and Punishment* for the character of Natalia Haldin and, whilst there are further links in the role of doubles in both works, critics have demonstrated that Conrad built his own narrative in ways that critiqued and sought to displace Dostoevsky's (Berman 1977, Busza 1976).

Literary friendships and literary culture

Conrad began his writing career at a time when the market for literary work was growing rapidly. In 1891 there were some 6,000 people listed in the UK census returns as authors, editors and journalists. This figure had risen to 11,000 by 1901, and in 1911 it had reached 14,000 (Gross 1973: 220). The 1890s saw the rise of reviews and little magazines and these created a burgeoning literary marketplace where the adaptable author might thrive. The commercially minded novelist Arnold Bennett (1867–1931) offered an insider's take on this field in his *Journalism for Women: A Practical Guide* (1898) when he suggested that the budding writer should not 'disdain to write mere paragraphs. The present is an era of paragraphs, and they form a most marketable commodity' (cited in Gross 1973: 233). The modernist era brought with it a segmented literary marketplace that publishers and the then new literary agents exploited by niche publication designed to appeal to discrete audiences. An ability to read the marketplace was, therefore, essential if one was to tread the path between market-led populism and highbrow obscurity (Wexler 1997: 8). Conrad is often presented as a proto-modernist artist, ill-suited to writing mere paragraphs, yet it should be noted that his first forays into print were clearly pitched for this new mass market – with 'The Black Mate' being written for the popular magazine *Tit Bits*, and *Almayer's Folly* submitted for inclusion in Fisher Unwin's mainstream *Pseudonym Library* (see Works, **pp. 22–7, 133–4**). Through the intercession of advisers such as Edward Garnett (see Life and Contexts, **pp. 11–12**) and, later, his literary agent J. B. Pinker (see Life and Contexts, **pp. 13–14**), Conrad would eventually become adroit at making one story pay several times over via separate deals for UK and US serialisations followed by separate volume publication for each market. This commercial bent is not to be derided as a contaminant of his art since what Conrad's fiction very often did was take the frameworks of popular genre fiction and weave within them tales with deeper and more complex ethical and moral concerns.

Conrad's letters from the time when he begins to see himself as a novelist reveal a scorn for populism – decrying New Woman novelist Sarah Grand's success with *The Heavenly Twins* (1893), 'the book has gone through ten editions and the author has pocketed 50,000 francs', as evidence that '[t]he world is a dirty place' (CL1: 185). Yet his letters also show evidence of a thorough knowledge of the literary marketplace, with schemes for *Almayer's Folly*'s translation jostling with debate about work in progress on *An Outcast of the Islands* (e.g., CL1: 246–8), advice to budding authors and a shrewd awareness of the players in the London literary scene (e.g., CL1: 211, 231). This awareness of market trends was not simply a matter of business-like prudence since, in the flood of material for the marketplace, writers of literary fiction had to be able to present their work in ways that distinguished it from the mass. Writing in 1898, as the author of three novels, Conrad declared:

> I have some – literary – reputation but the future is anything but certain, for I am not a popular author and probably never shall be. That does not sadden me at all, for I have never had the ambition to write for the all-powerful masses. I haven't the taste for democracy – and democracy hasn't the taste for me. I have gained the appreciation of a few select spirits and I do not doubt I shall be able to create a public for myself, limited it is true, but one which will permit me to earn my bread.
>
> (CL1, 390)

Unlike some early modernist writers, Conrad was not part of any of the literary coteries that flourished and died in rapid succession in the literary London of the late nineteenth century. He was part of a loose circle of writers working in the south-east of England, including Ford Madox Ford (1873–1939), Henry James (1843–1916) and H. G. Wells (1866–1946). With Wells there was genuine friendship, lasting for some years (1898–1909), which was initiated when the latter reviewed *An Outcast of the Islands* and came to end as the two men drifted further apart as Wells's politics became more socialist. In the case of James, friendship is the wrong word to describe a relationship that, at least in its public record, seems more formal than friendly. Conrad met James when the American-born novelist was an established author and, whilst there are clear literary affinities in their subtle narrative styles, James's private views suggest that the enthusiasm he professed for Conrad's work was largely superficial.

Conrad enjoyed more straightforward friendships with other authors. He was a close friend of the successful writer John Galsworthy (1867–1933), whom Conrad first met in 1893 as a passenger aboard the *Torrens* whilst he was working as first mate. Letters reveal his close interest in fostering the publishing career of the younger man and bear eloquent testimony to a lifelong friendship which did not wane with Galsworthy's commercial success. Another writer with whom Conrad enjoyed a close friendship was the American novelist Stephen Crane (1871–1900). The two men met via Sydney Pawling, a partner in Heinemann's publishing house and early advocate of Conrad's work, and remained close until Crane's early death from tuberculosis in 1900. Critics have suggested that Crane's novel *The Red Badge of Courage* (1895) influenced Conrad's move from the Malay world of his first novels to the sea life of *The Nigger of the 'Narcissus'*, a work that Crane commented on whilst it was being written (Nettels 1978).

Whilst these writers formed part of Conrad's literary circle, and in some cases commented on his work in progress, none had the impact on his early and major-phase work as his friendships with the publisher's reader and literary journalist Edward Garnett (1868–1937) and the novelist Ford Madox Ford. Garnett was a key figure in turn-of-the-century literary circles, working as a reviewer, publisher's reader, and supporter of a raft of new writers including Galsworthy, the poet Edward Thomas (1878–1917) and, later, poet and novelist D. H. Lawrence (1885–1930). Garnett encountered *Almayer's Folly* whilst working as a reader for the publishers T. Fisher Unwin. His championing of the unknown writer's novel initiated Conrad's literary career and assisted his own reputation as an astute man of letters. The two men worked closely together from 1894 until 1898, with Garnett advising and making editorial suggestions whilst drawing upon his literary contacts to ensure that Conrad's work found suitable outlets for publication. As Cedric Watts puts it,

> Edward Garnett was the sole figure who, in the crucial period which saw the publication of *Almayer's Folly*, could stress the importance of further work based on Conrad's peripatetic experience of the world and, furthermore, could lubricate and sensitively mediate Conrad's always temperamental movement towards sustained relationships with publishers
>
> (Watts 1996: 81–2)

Perhaps the most significant gesture Garnett made was in helping secure a contract with Heinemann for publication of *The Nigger of the 'Narcissus'* and arranging for its serial form to appear in their journal, *The New Review*. Letters note Garnett's role in the novel's significant shift in Conrad's literary concerns –

the book is 'Your book which you try to coax into bloom with such devotion and care' (CL1: 323) – and in general his role was to 'work artistically for art – for the very essence of it' (CL1: 343). Garnett also facilitated the agreement with the prestigious *Blackwood's Magazine* for the publication of 'Karain' and subsequently 'Youth', 'Heart of Darkness', and *Lord Jim*. As Conrad justly commented, '[a]ll the good moments – the real good ones in my new life I owe to you' (CL1: 378).

Garnett may have brought about Conrad's meeting with Ford Madox Ford in autumn 1898, and from this first meeting the two developed plans for collaboration. Conrad may have sought collaboration with Ford as a way out his impasse with *The Rescue* (see Works, **pp. 121–6**) and would have been attracted by his apparent facility for writing (Ford had already produced four books) and by his cultural connections (Batchelor 1994: 80). Conrad moved his young family to the Pent Farm in October, taking over Ford's lease. Ford was Conrad's closest literary friend between 1898 and 1909, working with him as collaborator and scribe, and his role as literary helpmate was undoubtedly significant. Impulsive, generous, and opinionated, Ford was happy to take criticism from an older writer whose talents he had nothing but praise for (Ford was twenty-four to Conrad's forty). Domestically, Ford's easy manners and erratic time-keeping made things difficult for Conrad's wife Jessie who seems to have disliked him at best and, in later life, would loathe him with a passion. Some commentators suggest that Conrad was happy to use Ford, taking his money, occupying his home and happily letting him act as unpaid amanuensis (see, for example, Batchelor 1994: 81), but these views have to be set against the fact that during their period of collaboration Conrad wrote some of his most significant works – including 'Heart of Darkness', *Lord Jim* and *Nostromo*. As Ford's most recent biographer suggests, the collaboration certainly helped Ford become a better writer but what it gave Conrad is, in the final analysis, rather harder to define (Saunders 1996: 114). The collaborations themselves – *The Inheritors* (1901), a clumsy political novel with sci-fi trappings, *Romance* (1903), an overlong romance of Caribbean pirates and Kentish smugglers, and *The Nature of a Crime* (1924) (published in the *English Review* in April and May 1909), a feeble tale of business intrigues and domestic infidelities – are all poor works in comparison with anything that Conrad produced alone. Working with Ford on these collaborations may have helped, psychologically at least, to offset anxieties regarding his own fiction, and most biographers agree that his best work was written whilst at the Pent. Ford had a hand in 'The End of the Tether', *The Mirror of the Sea*, *A Personal Record* and *Nostromo* and provided ideas for 'Amy Foster', 'Tomorrow' and *The Secret Agent*. He wrote powerfully, if rather unreliably, about their friendship and collaboration in *Joseph Conrad: A Personal Remembrance* (1924) (see Criticism, **pp. 140–1**).

Ford's relationship with Conrad foundered in 1909 when, caught up in an extramarital affair, he fell out with his collaborator and a number of their mutual Kentish friends – Conrad wrote sternly of Ford's 'grave failures of discretion' and warned him of finding himself isolated amongst 'only the wrecks of friendship' (CL4: 223). Things came to a head with a faintly comical misunderstanding over a visit from American novelist Willa Cather (1876–1947) in May, and a more serious falling out over Conrad's contribution of instalments of his reminiscences to Ford's journal, *The English Review*. Conrad fell behind with his work and failed to provide what Ford thought was a planned eighth instalment, leading him to publish a note explaining its absence as being due to Conrad's illness. Conrad, already infuriated by Ford's messy domestic affairs, expressed his outrage at Ford's behaviour (CL4: 263) and there was no contact between the two until March 1911 and, thereafter, it was Ford who would initiate correspondence by sending Conrad his latest book – the replies were polite but there was never a rapprochement. Raymond Brebach's *Joseph Conrad, Ford Madox Ford, and the Making of 'Romance'* (1985) offers a detailed study of their most substantial collaborative work. Max Saunders, *Ford Madox Ford: A Dual Life* (1996) is the best biographical work on Ford.

It would establish a false distinction if we were to identify these literary friendships as particularly distinct – in terms of their impact upon his fiction – from those that Conrad enjoyed with writer and socialist politician R. B. Cunninghame-Graham (1852–1936) or gentry Kentish farmer Arthur Marwood (1868–1916). Lack of material evidence means we can only speculate on the extent of Marwood's discussions with Conrad about matters of craft, but we know that Conrad had high regard for his literary judgement. Cunninghame-Graham clearly influenced the thematic and philosophic underpinning of the early work, including 'Heart of Darkness' and *Nostromo*, and their correspondence provides revealing insights into Conrad's philosophical outlook at the time of writing these major works (Watts, 1978). Summing up Conrad's range of influential friendships, one biographer has suggested that the 'people with whom Conrad became most intimate' fell into two distinct categories, being 'either, like Galsworthy or [his agent] Pinker, distinguished by a firm, masculine grasp of everyday experience or else, like Cunninghame Graham and Crane, . . . [men who] resembled him in having had their wayward minds tempered by an unusual diversity of experience' (Baines 1971: 533). It is clear that Conrad found it valuable to have a close, preferably younger, associate with whom he could share work in progress – Edward Garnett (1894–1900), Ford Madox Ford (1898–1909) and Richard Curle (1912–24) all occupied this role.

Whilst these friendships all had an impact on Conrad's literary development, it is arguable that the most significant influence on Conrad's output was that excercised by his literary agent J. B. Pinker (1863–1922). The two men first corresponded in the summer of 1899 when Conrad turned down his offer to act as his agent, but by autumn 1900 Conrad called on Pinker to assist in the sale of the collaborative fiction *Romance*, beginning an association that would, in its final decade, turn into a strong friendship that included collaboration on a screenplay for silent film version of the short story 'Gaspar Ruiz' (see Works, pp. 74–5). The scale and complexity of their relationship has yet to be given expansive critical consideration, but there are important short studies of it by Karl (1976) and Watts (1989). Wexler drew on the archive of over 5,000 items relating to Pinker's work in the period 1900–34 at Northwestern University in Chicago for her study of the economics of modernism (Wexler 1997), but to date there are no book-length studies devoted to the work of this remarkably influential literary agent who represented writers ranging from Oscar Wilde to Arnold Bennett.

Pinker invested in Conrad – financially and emotionally – to an astonishing extent, and the *Collected Letters* are full of the latter's anguished begging letters for additional advances. For the fourteen-year period from the publication of *Lord Jim* to *Chance*, it is Pinker 'who, more than anyone else, ensured the maintenance of Conrad's literary career' (Watts 1989: 85). Watts' short study revealed the extent of Conrad's indebtedness to Pinker, noting that in 1909 he owed his agent £2,250 'at a time when the average earnings of a doctor were less than £400' (Watts 1989: 88), but also outlined the fact that his agent's perseverance paid off once Conrad – thanks to Pinker's shrewd management – started to earn substantial sums. The two men quarrelled many times but relations broke down completely in 1909 when Pinker insisted that Conrad complete *Under Western Eyes* instead of working on essays for the *English Review* (see Works, **pp. 82–7**). An outraged Conrad declared that he would sooner burn the novel's manuscript and, although he was so indebted he could not actually sever his professional relations with Pinker, the two men did not speak for two years. Writing in 1916, Conrad himself summed up Pinker's contribution to his work as follows:

> Our relations are by no means those of client and agent. And I will tell you why. It is because those books which, people say, are an asset of English Literature owe their existence to Mr Pinker as much as to me. For 15 years of my writing life he has seen me through periods of unproductiveness through illnesses through all sorts of troubles. . . . And the fact is that P kept me going as much perhaps by his belief in me as with his money.
>
> (CL5: 619–20)

As Frederic Karl has suggested, in most lights Pinker 'was a saint' (1976: 173) without whose more or less unflagging support Conrad would not have produced such a diverse range of work.

Conrad the writer

Whilst Conrad published comparatively little on his own approach to writing, his letters and the handful of essays that he wrote on other authors bear eloquent testimony to his fascination with his craft. His letters are punctuated by frequent laments over his sense of difficulty in writing which in part stems from a strict commitment to be original, the kind of writer who must reject 'all formulas and dogmas and principles of other people's making. These are only a web of illusions. We are too varied. Another man's truth is only a dismal lie to me' (CL1: 253). Given this attitude, it is not surprising to read letters where Conrad emphasises the anguished mental labour of writing and the stern role of imagination:

> Other writers have some starting point. Something to catch hold of. They start from an anecdote – from a newspaper paragraph . . . They lean on dialect – or on tradition – or on history – or on the prejudice or fad of the hour; they trade upon some tie or some conviction of their time – or upon the absence of these things – which they can abuse or praise. But at any rate they know something to begin with – while I

don't. I have had some impressions, some sensations – in my time: – impressions and sensations of common things. And it's all faded – my very being seems faded and thin like the ghost of a blonde and senti-mental woman, haunting romantic ruins pervaded by rats.

(CL1: 288–9)

Conrad's wrestle with fleeting impressions frequently turned into periods of writer's block – something he first experiences in acute form with *The Rescue* (see Works, **pp. 121–6**):

12 pages written and I sit before them every morning, day after day, for the last 2 months and cannot add a sentence, add a word! I am paralyzed by doubt and have just sense enough to feel the agony but am powerless to invent a way out of it. When I face the fatal manuscript it seems to me that I have forgotten how to think – worse! How to write.

(CL1: 296)

Conrad's habitual way out was, surprisingly, to write something else, and during 1896 he wrote the short story 'The Idiots' (May) (see Works, **p. 38**), returned to 'the stupid' *Rescue* (CL1: 285) only to set it aside to begin *The Nigger of the 'Narcissus'* (June) (see Works, **pp. 31–5**), only to set that aside to write 'An Out-post of Progress' (July) (see Works, **p. 38**), then writing 'The Lagoon' (August) (see Works, **p. 39**), before picking up *The Nigger of the 'Narcissus'* again when he returned to England (September) and completing it in January 1897. So for Conrad an instance of writer's block was actually often the occasion for intense displaced literary production which rehearsed issues of theme or character from the blocked text. The patterns of writing that Conrad established in these early years are ones that often recur, with a period of block being written out of with a new project which often grows from a short fiction into a full-blown novel – as happens with *Lord Jim, Nostromo* and *Under Western Eyes* (see Works, **pp. 43–7, 63–8, 82–7**). It is notable that so many of his longer books grew organically – they were not planned as novels but they expanded into their final form. Increasingly, short fiction, as was the case in these early years with 'Karain' (see Works, **pp. 36–7**), 'The Lagoon' and 'An Outpost of Progress', was something that got written for money whilst Conrad worked on a larger project.

Given his sense of *The Nigger of the 'Narcissus'* marking a significant change in artistic tack, it is not surprising that Conrad felt moved to write what for many remains one of the most significant accounts of his ambitions as a writer in a document which was to become the 'Preface' to novel's US edition, published in 1914 by Doubleday and Page, and which appeared in this guise in the UK in the 1921 edition by Heinemann. The final serial instalment in the *New Review* was followed by this text in the form of an 'Author's Note'. Conrad sent a draft of this document to his early mentor Edward Garnett (see Life and Contexts, **pp. 11–12**) – disingenuously declaring that 'I've no more judgement of what is fitting in the way of literature than a cow' (CL1: 375) – and whilst it would initially only have been read by the relatively small readership of the *New Review*, it is clearly a significant statement of intent by a writer committed to the development of his career as an English novelist.

The 'Preface' is a liberal humanist argument for the sincerity of Conrad's liter-ary endeavour and made a case for the capacity of fiction to outweigh the local and time-bound. For Conrad, a writer:

> appeals to that part of our being which is not dependent on wisdom; to that in us which is a gift and not an acquisition – and, therefore, more permanently enduring. He speaks to our capacity for delight and won-der, to the sense of mystery surrounding our lives; to our sense of pity, and beauty, and pain; to the latent feeling of fellowship with all creation – and to the subtle but invincible conviction of solidarity that knits together the loneliness of innumerable hearts, to the solidarity in dreams, in joy, in sorrow, in aspirations, in illusions, in hope, in fear, which binds men to each other, which binds together all humanity – the dead to the living and the living to the unborn.
>
> ('Preface', viii)

To speak to the reader, the writer must appeal to temperament via 'an impression conveyed through the senses . . . because temperament, whether individual or collective, is not amenable to persuasion' (ix). This requires 'an unremitting never discouraged care for the shape and ring of sentences' (ix) in the writer's attempt:

> by the power of the written word to make you hear, to make you feel – it is, before all, to make you *see*. That – and no more, and it is everything. If I succeed, you shall find there according to you deserts: encourage-ment, consolation, fear, charm – all you demand – and, perhaps, also that glimpse of truth for which you have forgotten to ask.
>
> ('Preface', x)

This emphasis on the words on the page means that the writer cannot be a devotee of a particular approach since such 'temporary formulas' (x) are, in the end, attempts to persuade the reader to see things from a partial point of view whereas Conrad has what George Eliot in another context described as a 'keen vision' (1988: 159) regarding the potential penetration of novelistic inquiry:

> to snatch in a moment of courage, from the remorseless rush of time, a passing phase of life, is only the beginning of the task. The task approached in tenderness and faith is to hold up unquestioningly, without choice and without fear, the rescued fragment before all eyes in the light of a sincere mood. It is to show its vibration, its colour, its form; and through its movement, its form, and its colour, reveal the substance of its truth – disclose its inspiring secret: the stress and passion within the core of each convincing moment. In a single-minded attempt of that kind, if one be deserving and fortunate, one may perchance attain to such clearness of sincerity that at last the presented vision of regret or pity, of terror or mirth, shall awaken in the hearts of the beholders that feeling of unavoidable solidarity; of the solidarity in mysterious origin, in toil, in joy, in hope, in uncertain

fate, which binds men to each other and all mankind to the visible world.

('Preface', x)

As Jacques Berthoud has argued, the 'Preface' is a subtle attempt to explain the difference in Conrad's mind between Realism and his own, much larger, conception of 'fictional truth' (1984: 180). In this it can be placed in a tradition of Romantic defences of the value of literary responses to the human predicament in which:

> Literature embodied kinds of humanly necessary truths or values which were not attainable elsewhere; it therefore had a higher kind of utility than the material and the quantitative; and it was produced by, and communicated to, constituents of the human personality, usually described as the imagination or sensibility, which were not available to scientific psychological study but were nevertheless necessary to explain not only man's aesthetic impulse but the grounds of his religious, moral and social life.
>
> (Watt 1979: 154)

As Watt goes on to note, Conrad's manifesto lacked the dismissive contempt for the general reader that was a feature of the manifestos of later modernists but shared something of their sense of the superiority of the artist who, in Conrad's terms, will 'awaken' the latent feelings of solidarity in 'the hearts of the beholders' ('Preface', x). There was, as is the case in so much of Conrad's work, a careful alertness to the context in which the 'Preface' was initially being read – its dismissal of European aesthetic critics in preference for plain old English words on the page was designed to appeal to the *New Review*'s peculiarly *fin-de-siècle* mix of aestheticism and reactionary politics (Willy 1985, McDonald 1996).

The emphasis in the 'Preface' on 'the translation of the artist's sense perceptions into vivid and evocative language' (Watt 1979: 160) has led many commentators to claim that Conrad was an impressionist writer. Impressionism was a term applied to the new art of the 1870s and 1880s associated with the work of French painter Claude Monet. Yet it was soon applied to writers whose work seemed to possess the qualities commonly associated with impressionist art, 'to works that were spontaneous and rapidly executed, that were vivid sketches rather than detailed, finished, and premeditated compositions' (Watt 1979: 172). In art it was the painter's subjective vision that provided the subject of these artworks whilst in literature it was the individual perceptions of the characters which became a central concern of texts produced in this mode. In literary impressionism, the stress upon the confused understanding of the individual and the related emphasis on the psychological as opposed to the social marked an important divergence from realism (Watt 1979: 171). Watt suggests that Conrad is an impressionist only to the extent that 'he is primarily interested in presenting the subjective aspects of individual experience' (1979: 160) but notes that whilst his approach works through the senses it has the ultimate aim of providing readers with 'that glimpse of truth for which you have forgotten to ask' ('Preface', x).

By emphasising fiction as a product of imagination – of impressions made on the author by experience – Conrad began to develop an approach that saw a novel as 'a form of imagined life clearer than reality and whose accumulated verisimilitude of selected episodes puts to shame the pride of documentary history' (*A Personal Record*, 15). This was a bold statement for a novelist to make in 1908 – the date of the work's first appearance in its serial form (see Works, **pp. 88–92**) – suggesting as it does that fiction was 'clearer than reality' because it works via selection as opposed to the strict chronology of a 'documentary history'. This is an aesthetic position which shapes the narrative structure of Conrad's proto-modernist masterpieces *Lord Jim* and *Nostromo*, with their artfully disrupted chronologies and the dazzling juxtapositions of character and event that these disruptions enable (see Works, **pp. 43–7, 63–8**). It is this emphasis on selection and the related relegating of documentary-like chronicling which means that Conrad's prose technique feeds directly into the modernism of Virginia Woolf (1882–1941) and James Joyce (1882–1941).

Englishness

Whilst Conrad began his life in Poland, he ended it as a naturalised Englishman, with an abiding commitment to his new country born of sixteen years service in its merchant marine and two decades of involvement in its cultural life. Yet Conrad's relationship to his adopted country was a complex one and it is clear that he retained a keen sense of being regarded as an outsider. Whilst he was not averse to playing to the prejudices of the readers of the conservative magazines in which some of his fictions appeared – think of 'Heart of Darkness' and its harping on the 'efficiency' and 'real work' that goes on under British imperialism (50, 55) – the dominant note in his depiction of Englishmen is wryly critical, as is the case with Jim and Captain Brierly from *Lord Jim*, the old language teacher in *Under Western Eyes*, fussy Joe Mitchell in *Nostromo*, the dreadful Fynes in *Chance*, or the cruel villagers of 'Amy Foster' (see Works, **pp. 44–5, 83–5, 64–6, 99–101, 58–9**). In his personal relations with the English, Conrad was self-conscious about his inflected spoken English.

It is not only from his sea career that Conrad came into close contact with English beliefs and values. He married an Englishwoman and this gave him further insights into the working of his adopted country's class system. In 1896, he married Jessie George (1873–1936), an English girl of lower middle-class origins from south London, and supported the younger members of her large extended family (Conrad 1970: 13). There are elements of Conrad's distaste for his mother-in-law in the portrait of Winnie Verloc's mother in *The Secret Agent* (1907) (see Works, **pp. 70–1**). The Conrads had two children, Borys (1898–1978) and John (1906–82), and, despite precarious finances, they attempted to live a bourgeois English life; the children's memoirs present an affectionate account of life with an unpredictable but loving father (Conrad 1970, Conrad 1981). His writing brought him into cultured circles and he may have been alert to the rather low opinion in which some of his friends (for example, Edward Garnett) held his wife. What may have seemed to more class-ridden English minds a rather odd alliance between a cultured and well-travelled Pole and a pretty but unintellectual lower-middle-class English girl might in fact be viewed as a facet in Conrad's modernity.

He entered English life in the 1880s, at a time when the values and beliefs which had seemingly welded together the nation during the nineteenth century were being questioned and rejected. The ideas and ideals of Englishness imagined and evoked at this time very often rested upon a nostalgic yoking together of past and present in ways that sought to establish a continuity of tradition and cultural aspiration between contemporary England and the nation's past. The Englishness which was created in the latter part of the nineteenth century was, as is the case with all notions of national identity, largely an invented, imaginary affair – a product of a desire to bring together an increasingly disparate people in ways that sought to paper over the social and cultural differences which, by the later 1900s, had become starkly visible to any dispassionate observer of the English scene (Giles and Middleton 1995).

Conrad's early writing career developed whilst the country dealt with the débâcle of the Boer War (1899–1902), came to terms with the development of an organised working-class political party (the Labour Party was founded in 1900) and an organised nationalist party in British-held Ireland (Sinn Féin was founded in 1905), nervously witnessed workers' attempted revolution in Russia (1905) and the increasingly vociferous demands for women's suffrage (from 1906) at home. It is tempting to argue that Conrad's sardonic perspective on England and the English bears the traces of the profound social and cultural changes – the much discussed 'Edwardian crisis' – that Britain was experiencing in the early years of the twentieth century. Benita Parry, following Najder, has argued that Conrad's identification with England's dominant culture was based upon his perception of its 'respect for order and tradition, . . . cohesive civil society and . . . widely disseminated stance of self-assurance which the politically volatile continent lacked' (Parry 1989: 190). Whilst Conrad's characters often assert the kind of respect for tradition that Parry outlines, they are at the same time often flawed or comprised in ways that undercut their presentation of the values they espouse. Conrad's artful literary technique is a kind of sly civility, a means of weaving critique into apparently positive accounts of the culture. At the level of textuality, even his positive presentations of Englishness may be viewed as an example of what Homi K. Bhabha termed the 'menace of mimicry', and can be read as texts which mimic the values of his adopted culture in order to critique them. As Bhabha puts it:

> mimicry . . . problematizes the signs of racial and cultural priority so that the 'national' is no longer naturalizable. What emerges between mimesis and mimicry is a *writing*, a mode of representation, that marginalizes the monumentality of history, quite simply mocks its power to be a model . . . The *menace* of mimicry is its *double* vision which in disclosing the ambivalence of colonial discourse also disrupts its authority . . . [mimicry] articulates those disturbances of cultural, racial and historical difference that menace the narcissistic demand of colonial authority
>
> (Bhabha 1994: 87–8)

Whilst Conrad's fiction was shaped by his difficult childhood, his sea life and his literary friendships and predilections, the works of his major phase (1899–1915) seem to me to be triumphant syntheses of this diverse and often contradictory raw material which he arranged in a 'spirit of scrupulous abnegation' in accordance with an exacting credo which held that 'the only legitimate basis of creative work lies in the courageous recognition of all the irreconcilable antagonisms that make our life so enigmatic, so burdensome, so fascinating, so dangerous – so full of hope' (CL2: 348).

2

Works

Joseph Conrad wrote thirteen complete novels, twenty-nine novellas and short stories, two stage plays, two major works of reminiscence and over forty essays. His most widely studied works today, however, represent only a tiny portion of this output. Fictions such as the novella 'Heart of Darkness' (see Works, pp. 49–52), the novels Lord Jim (see Works, pp. 43–7) and The Secret Agent (see Works, pp. 69–73), and the short story 'The Secret Sharer' (see Works, pp. 94–5) contain much that is characteristically Conradian, but a critical view of the author based on these works alone is hardly likely to be accurate. Drawing extensively on Conrad's letters, this section provides the reader with an overview of the major works via a concise commentary on each text along with factual information about its composition, reception and place in the larger canon of his works. To avoid expansive plot summary or a plethora of notes, however, I have assumed that readers will have some familiarity with the work in question. My summary account of each work's major thematic and stylistic feature is followed by a concise discussion of its reception along with an overview of the later critical reception, which provides readers with the secure starting point of generally accepted critical opinion from which to move on to their own more detailed engagement with the text or to proceed to the more complex and at times controversial analyses discussed in Part 3. I make no apology for placing an emphasis on the initial reception of each text, since the work of period reviewers is both crucial to any understanding of how Conrad came to be central to English letters and indispensable when tracking the wider impact of modernist aesthetics within mass culture.

Given space constraints and the intended readership of the present work I have not included commentary on Conrad's volume of nautical reminiscences, The Mirror of the Sea: Memories and Impressions (1906), his non-fiction collected in Notes on Life and Letters (1921) and the posthumous Last Essays (1926). The likely readership of this book are unlikely to be seeking material on the unfinished posthumously published novel Suspense (1925), the unfinished fragment of a novel The Sisters, or the dramatisations One Day More (1919) and Laughing Anne (1923), and these works will be given limited coverage here. Conrad also collaborated with Ford Madox Ford on three novels, but the first collaboration, The Inheritors (1901) and their final work, The Nature of a Crime (1924 [written in 1906 and serialised in the English Review, April and May 1909]), are almost entirely Ford's work and have so little of Conrad's hand in them as to be of no importance to those who are beginning their study of Conrad (and of limited appeal to those who are well versed in either author's work). *Romance* (1903), begun as *Seraphina*, was summed up by an early reader as 'Hueffer's story and Conrad's telling', but modern critical opinion suggests that Conrad only wrote one of the novel's five parts (Knowles and Moore 2000: 315). Conrad told Richard Curle, the first critic to write a full-length study of his works, that consideration of his uncollected prose works 'would bring a needless complication into your general view of J.C.' (CL6: 275), and in this book I have been guided by Conrad's sentiment as I believe that discussion of the collaborative and uncollected works is not essential in a one-volume introduction to his work.

Almayer's Folly (1895)

Conrad's first novel was written during the final years of his sea career. It formed the final text of a trilogy in reverse, with *An Outcast of the Islands* (1896) and *The Rescue* (1920) being chronologically the second and first respectively (see Works, pp. 28–31, 121–6). In *A Personal Record*, Conrad noted that he began writing *Almayer's Folly* in 1889 at his London lodgings in Pimlico in order to fill in time whilst waiting for his next position at sea, but at this stage he did not envisage a career as a writer and '[t]here was no vision of a printed book before me as I sat writing at that table, situated in a decayed part of Belgravia' (9–10). The manuscript went with him on his final sea journeys and even accompanied him during his time in the Congo (see Chronology, p. 173). He completed the novel on 24 April 1894 and sent the manuscript to the publisher T. Fisher Unwin under the pseudonym of Kamudi (the Malay word for rudder), and his letters over the summer of 1894 revealed a growing anxiety over his book's fate. By August, however, he was already at work on what was to become his second novel, *An Outcast of the Islands*; it was not until October that he finally heard from Unwin that the novel was to be published. He was paid £20 for the copyright of his first novel and noted that he took this comparatively small sum 'because, really, the mere fact of publication is of great importance' (CL1: 178). The novel was to be accompanied by a 'Preface' which Conrad duly wrote in December 1894 but it was not used until the Doubleday, Page 'Sun Dial' edition of 1921 (Higdon 1975). Conrad was also asked to contribute to the publicity and suggested that the book be billed as a 'civilised story in savage surroundings' (CL1: 199). The novel appeared on 29 April 1895 in the UK and was published in the USA by Macmillan on 3 May.

Commentary

The novel begins with Almayer daydreaming of the success of a treasure-seeking venture that he has launched on the proceeds of gunpowder smuggling and mulling over the failures of his past. As with so many of Conrad's narratives, it is left to the reader to see the gap between Almayer's dreams and what he has actually achieved. For rather creaky plot reasons (or is this Conrad's lack of interest in cause but fascination with effect?) Captain Lingard – 'a hero in Almayer's eyes' (8) – adopts him as his clerk, persuades him to marry the Malay girl he 'rescued' from pirates and settles a large dowry on him. Almayer agrees to the arranged marriage on the grounds that it will lead him to the 'indolent ease of life' for which he feels 'so well fitted' (10). His sense of shame at the idea of marrying a Malay and assumption that it is 'easy enough to dispose of a Malay woman, a slave after all' (10–11) do not bode well for the relationship. There is much in this first chapter, in terms of handling of narrative point of view and evocation of setting, to explain why this novel proved attractive to a shrewd literary judge such as Edward Garnett (see Life and Contexts, **pp. 11–12**).

Chapters 2–5 move us back in time to the early days of Almayer's marriage and then even further back to the scene of Lingard's defeat of Mrs Almayer's piratical relations. Having established the origins of her dissatisfaction, we learn that her future prospects soured as Almayer's hopes of establishing a strong trading post were soon frustrated. Lingard's banker fails and he takes Almayer's child Nina off to Singapore to be educated whilst he searches for money to support his plans. This leaves Almayer alone with the wife who despises him. The narrative glosses over the intervening years – again suggestive of Conrad's concern with the 'why' and not the 'superficial how' (*Lord Jim*, 56). We do learn briefly about Nina's time in Singapore, where she was marginalised by women and preyed upon by men because of her mixed-race origin. Nina is shown to be fascinated by Mrs Almayer's tales of Sulu violence, suggesting a further distance from Western culture that will inform her later rejection of Almayer:

> [a]nd now she had lived on the river for three years with a savage mother and a father walking about amongst pitfalls, with his head in the clouds, weak, irresolute, and unhappy. She had lived a life devoid of all the decencies of civilization, in miserable domestic conditions; she had breathed the atmosphere of sordid plotting for gain, of the no less disgusting intrigues and crimes for lust or money; and those things, together with the domestic quarrels, were the only events of her three years' existence.
>
> (42)

It's worth noting that Conrad's presentation of Nina seeks to improve upon the stock exotic temptress figure from popular fiction; her rejection of her father's feckless capitalism and embrace of the culture of her mother's people deliberately sets up questions about the value of 'white' civilisation and its mores in colonial endeavour. Chapter 4 introduces the piratical prince and trader Dain Maroola who, in Mrs Almayer's eyes, would be a highly suitable partner for Nina. Dain wants to use Almayer in a gunpowder-trading scheme since he can give him access to an English vessel unlikely to be searched by the Dutch authorities. Dain is dazzled by Nina's beauty and forgets 'the object of his visit and all things else, in his overpowering desire to prolong the contemplation of so much loveliness' (55). This complication of men's scheming by the eruption of sexual desire is something that we will see in much of Conrad's Malay fiction – featuring in the short stories 'Karain' and 'The Lagoon' as well as in *An Outcast of the Islands* (see Works, **pp. 36–7, 39, 28–31**).

The sequence from Chapter 6 to the opening of Chapter 12 covers a twenty-four hour period in which Dain's attempts to deceive his Dutch pursuers have unintended consequences. We learn that he has also been scheming with Rajah Lakamba, who agrees to help him hide from the Dutch. Dain departs for one last tryst with Nina whilst the Rajah and his adviser, Babalatchi, discuss Dain's chances of safely negotiating the swollen river. Chapter 7 opens with Almayer awakening to an apparently deserted Sambir – deserted because all are at the riverside looking at what appears to be the body of Dain because of its distinctive jewellery but, since the face is pulped, the true identity cannot be ascertained. We approach this scene from Almayer's point of view and, once again, Conrad makes good use of his limited grasp of events. As readers we are probably alerted to the deception by Nina's lack of emotion but, of course, Almayer does not know of her feelings for Dain and so he is not alerted. Conrad's positioning of the reader is adroit, making Almayer's outburst to Nina deliciously ironic since he accuses her of not caring about the failure of his plans when, if it were really Dain, we know that she would care intimately. There is a powerful scene of father–daughter conflict in which Nina's silence regarding Dain's true fate is presented as marking the victory of her Malay self. Almayer is unable to see the outwards signs of her inner conflict because he is wracked with 'self-pity, . . . anger, and by despair' (103). The chapter ends with the arrival of the Dutch.

Chapter 8 opens with village gossip about Dain's death spreading as Babalatchi and Nina clearly intended. Chapter 9 begins with Babalatchi's revelation of the role of Nina's mother in creating the deception by battering the body so that its features could not be recognised. Babalatchi and Mrs Almayer listen to Almayer's conversation with the Dutch officers who are seeking the gunpowder smugglers. Almayer is very drunk and the officers ask Nina if she can help persuade him to show them Dain's corpse. The officers are taken aback by Nina's hostility towards whites – 'I hate the sound of your gentle voices' (140). The Dutch find the body and hold a court of inquiry in Almayer's Folly to help them determine if it is Dain's. Chapter 10 sees mother and daughter planning for the future. Mrs Almayer advises Nina on the right way to treat a Malay man and the facts of Malay married life. Of Nina we are told '[s]he had little belief and no sympathy for her father's dreams; but the savage ravings of her mother chanced to strike a responsive chord' (151). With Dain, 'she thought she could read in his eyes the answer to all the questionings of her heart' (152). Almayer awakens from a drunken stupor to an empty house to find the slave girl Taminah watching him and she reveals to him what is actually happening. Dain, alone in the forest, is shown to conceive of himself as an heroic warrior and the narrative here evokes the myth of the dark forest and Dain's fantasies of glorious violence. After a period of waiting, Nina arrives and Conrad gives Romance its head as the two lovers meet and Dain is greeted by her surrender (171–2):

> never before had he felt so proud as now, when at the feet of that woman that half belonged to his enemies. . . . The thing was done. Her mother was right. The man was a slave. As she glanced down at his kneeling form she felt a great pity and tenderness for that man she was used to call—even in her thoughts—the master of life (172)

The narrator is critical of Nina, noting that it is 'the sublime vanity' of a woman that makes her 'be thinking already of moulding a god from the clay at her feet' (ibid.). This criticism appears to be echoed by the land itself for 'the heavens were suddenly hushed up in the mournful contemplation of human love and human blindness' (173).The rather overblown feel continues with the arrival of a gun-toting Almayer. He tries to warn Nina against a liaison with Dain on the grounds of racial incompatibility – '[b]etween him and you there is a barrier that nothing can remove (178)' – but she rejects him and the white world:

> No two human beings understand each other. They can understand but their own voices. You wanted me to dream your dreams, to see your own visions – the visions of life amongst the white faces of those who cast me out from their midst in angry contempt. But while you spoke I listened to the voice of my own self; then this man came, and all was still; there was only the murmur of his love. You call him a savage! What do you call my mother, your wife?
>
> (179)

With the Dutch closing in, Dain has to leave and Nina's decision to accompany him prompts Almayer into the heartfelt declaration that he has no daughter (184). By ceasing to treat her as his child, Almayer is, however, able to reconcile himself to helping Dain and 'that woman' (184) escape capture. Chapter 12 begins with Nina's tearful response to her father's rejection and this prompts Dain to reflect on their difference, '[h]e felt something invisible stood between them, something that would let him approach her so far, but no further' (187); he concludes that this barrier is her whiteness – '[m]y Rance smiles when looking at the man she loves. It is the white woman that is crying now' (188). As the lovers wait on the beach for the canoe that will take them away, there is a final scene between Almayer and Nina which, for all its overwrought emotion, is a key moment in understanding Almayer's situation and the nature of his folly. The narrative shows us a divided self – expressionless and cold externally but internally in desperate turmoil (191). He imagines going with his daughter but his civilised sense of propriety prevents him, making him shout out his rejection of Nina. The narrative works for pathos here, showing Almayer as following a line of 'proper' behaviour that his heart opposes and, in a touching representation of his feelings, he literally erases her trace from his presence by wiping out her footprints from the beach. The corrosive power of 'civilised' values is something that Conrad will examine in later works such as 'Heart of Darkness' and, triumphantly, *Lord Jim* (see Works, **pp. 49–52, 43–7**). Almayer returns to his home like an automaton, destroys his business papers and the remains of his office and then sets the house on fire. The narrative then moves a few months on to reveal a further decline: Almayer has now moved into his folly and turned to opium on hearing that Nina has had a child with Dain. He dies alone.

Almayer's Folly dramatised the clash between West and East in the person of the failed trader Kaspar Almayer and his idealistic dreams for his mixed-race daughter, Nina. The novel's concern is with questions of duty and fidelity; ties of blood and nation are set against ties of love and filiation. In its depiction of Nina it explored the fate of hybrid colonial subjects but is perhaps tainted by its adherence to nineteenth-century notions of racial hierarchies – hierarchies which, admittedly, the novel goes some way to challenge in its depiction of the passive and dream-ridden Almayer and his active, practical wife and daughter. The novel can thus be read as offering an account of the failings of Western civilisation when faced with the complexities of life in the East.

The novel's structure is quite complex, involving the use of a disrupted chronology and extensive narrative focalisation which, at times, borders upon stream of consciousness. As with so many of Conrad's novels, it requires a second reading to fully appreciate the extent to which the narrative point of view is often shaped by Almayer's idealistic dreams. The narrative also makes much use of ironic juxtaposition, retelling scenes from the viewpoints of different characters to create a relativising perspective on character and motive. As so often in Conrad, these carefully wrought stratagems mean that the reader sees more than Almayer can – the narrative strategy ensures that the reader has fuller knowledge than the character so as to allow us to enjoy the ironies of his situation and to appreciate the extent of his folly. Written in the vein of the popular exotic stories of the 1890s, Conrad improved upon his populist original through his subtle use of narrative focalisation. The romance plot, involving Dain and Nina, introduced the love between races in a way that was perhaps too carefully framed to allow it shock period Western readers – her falling in love with Dain is presented as a product of her natural 'barbarity'.

Early reviews

The *Daily News* suggested that the novel revealed that a 'merely sensitive European has no business among the semi-savages of Borneo' but commented favourably on the 'picturesque' qualities of the novel's setting and highlighted Nina's rejection of Almayer as 'an atavistic fit' (Sherry 1973: 47). The *Daily Chronicle* punningly declared that Conrad 'is a man who can write of Borneo and never bore' and praised 'his finely conceived and simply executed love scenes' and his subtle depiction of 'the emasculating and despair breeding effect of the tired but scheming East upon a weak neurotic Western organisation'. The reviewer concluded with the prescient suggestion that 'Mr Conrad may go on' to find a public (Sherry 1973: 49–50). *The World* was less enthusiastic, dismissing the novel as

> a dreary record of the still more dreary existence of a solitary Dutchman doomed to vegetate in a small village in Borneo ... [t]he life is monotonous and sordid, and the recital thereof is almost as wearisome, unrelieved by one touch of pathos or humour. Altogether the book is as dull as it well could be
>
> (Sherry 1973: 51)

In a letter to his publisher Conrad commented, 'the poor old "World" kicks at me (in 15 lines) like a vicious donkey. It is severe blame (perhaps deserved) but, I think, no criticism in the true sense of the word' (CL1: 219). *The Athenaeum* suggested the influence of French naturalistic novelist Émile Zola (1840–1902) and declared the novel 'a genuine piece of work [that] ... in spite of several crudities and awkwardnesses, shows considerable promise' (Sherry 1973: 52). British novelist H. G. Wells (1866–1946), in an unsigned piece in the *Saturday Review*, declared the novel to be 'a very powerful story indeed . . . well imagined and well written, and it will certainly secure Mr Conrad a high place among contemporary story-tellers (Sherry 1973: 53).

Later critical response

The novel has been studied in terms of its biographical origins, its depiction of imperialism, its representation of race and gender and its narrative organisation. It initially received coverage as evidence of an apprentice phase that Conrad had to go through before he could write his major fiction and much of the criticism of the novel has examined the ways in which the story anticipated themes of later works. Paul Wiley's *Conrad's Measure of Man* (1954) presents Almayer as the prototype of Conrad's hermit heroes, a precursor of men such as Lord Jim or *Victory*'s Axel Heyst who withdraw from the world of action (see Works, pp. 43–7, 107–13). Thomas Moser's *Joseph Conrad: Achievement and Decline* (1957) finds the Nina–Dain love story unconvincing and sees the narrative's interest in this theme as the novel's central weakness. John Hicks, 'Conrad's *Almayer's Folly*: Structure, Theme, and Critics' (1964) offers a critical reading of Lingard's role and an account of the Nina–Dain relationship which suggests that it showed inter-racial relationships to be based upon a fidelity absent from Almayer's commercial deal-ings. Edward Voytovich provides an early study of the role of women, which included discussion of Mrs Almayer and Nina, in his 'The Problems of Identity for Conrad's Women' (1974). Ian Watt's '*Almayer's Folly*: Memories and Models' (1974) draws on biographical material and examines the influence of Flaubert on the novel's narrative organisation (see Life and Contexts, pp. 8–9). This work is drawn on in Watt's later coverage of the novel in *Conrad in the Nineteenth Century* (1979). Peter O'Connor's 'The Function of Nina in *Almayer's Folly*' (1975) pro-vides a study of the relationship between the theme of isolation and the imagery of light and darkness used in the presentation of Nina and Almayer. William Slight's 'Anagram, Myth, and Structure of *Almayer's Folly* (1980) also focuses on father and daughter in his analysis of the novel's triangular relationships.

More recent work, focusing upon the novels engagement with imperialist activ-ity includes chapters in Andrea White's *Joseph Conrad and the Adventure Trad-ition: Constructing and Deconstructing the Imperial Subject* (1993), Christopher GoGwilt's, *The Invention of the West: Joseph Conrad and the Double-Mapping of Europe and Empire* (1995), Linda Dryden's *Joseph Conrad and the Imperial Romance* (2000) and Robert Hampson's *Cross-Cultural Encounters in Joseph Conrad's Malay Fiction* (2000) (see Criticism, pp. 160–3). Also see James M. Johnson, 'The "Unnatural Rigidity" of Almayer's Ethnocentrism' (2001) and Anne Tagge, ' "A Glimpse of Paradise": Feminine Impulse and Ego in Conrad's Malay World' (1997). Allan Simmons has written on questions of the novel's narrative organisation in 'Ambiguity as Meaning: The Subversion of Suspense in *Almayer's Folly*' (1989) and his later essay, ' "Conflicting Impulses": Focalization and the Presentation of Culture in *Almayer's Folly*' (1997).

An Outcast of the Islands (1896)

The middle book in the Malay trilogy (see Works, **p. 22**) and Conrad's second novel, *An Outcast of the Islands* is a work which critics have tended to see as little more than a variation on the themes of interracial love and Western degeneration that Conrad took up in his first fiction. The critical mainstream have taken their approach from Conrad himself who, in his 1919 'Author's Note', stressed that the book was 'second in conception, second in execution, second as it were in its essence' (vii). Conrad began work on the novel in the summer of 1895, writing to his 'aunt' Marguerite Poradowska, that 'I have begun to write' something 'very short' called 'Two Vagabonds':

> I want to describe in broad strokes, without shading or details, two human outcasts such as one finds in the lost corners of the world. A white man and a Malay. . . . What bothers me most is that my characters are so true. I know them so well they shackle the imagination.
>
> (CL1: 171)

Conrad was also concerned that his original conception may have lacked interest because it contained no female characters (CL1: 171). In a process that we will see Conrad repeat many times in his writing life, the original short story grew as he wrote and turned into a novel of over 100,000 words. Also typical was the fact that, after an initial burst of enthusiasm, Conrad soon found himself blocked: by October he is lamenting that ' "The Two Vagabonds" are idle' (CL1: 178). At this stage in his career Conrad was still seeking work at sea and this was slowing his writing. By the year-end he was enthusiastic again, writing to his 'aunt' that the story was now a novel called *An Outcast of the Islands* (CL1: 193). Conrad described its main theme as:

> the unrestrained, fierce vanity of an ignorant man who has had some success but neither principles nor any other line of conduct than the satisfaction of his vanity. In addition he is not even faithful to himself. Whence a fall, a sudden descent to physical enslavement by an absolutely untamed woman. . . . The catastrophe will be brought about by the intrigues of a little Malay state where poisoning has the last word. The dénouement is: suicide, again because of the vanity.
>
> (CL1: 185)

The novel was published by Fisher Unwin on March 4 1896 and appeared in the USA with D. Appleton on 15 August.

Commentary

The action of the novel occurs some fifteen years prior to the events of *Almayer's Folly*. Peter Willems comes to the East as a young boy serving on a Dutch ship that he leaves out of 'an instinctive contempt for the honest simplicity of that work which led to nothing he cared for' (17); in short he is, in modern parlance, a slacker. He is taken into the employ of Tom Lingard who eventually places him with the merchant Hudig as his confidential clerk. The novel begins with Willem's being drunk on the day of his thirtieth birthday, reflecting on his future prospects in the most idealistic fashion. Willems has been stealing from Hudig to pay off gambling debts and although he has almost paid back all of the money, he is caught out and sacked by his employer and thrown out by his long-suffering wife. Lingard comes across his protégé as he contemplates suicide and offers him a haven in his trading post on Sambir. The trading post is run by Almayer, whose precarious position there is only secured by the reputation of Lingard, but Willems's arrival is soon seen as a means of undermining the status quo by the scheming Babalatchi. Willems weakness is his love for Aissa, the daughter of blind Omar el Badavi, one-time pirate leader. Omar strongly disapproves of Aissa's liaison with Willems and, at Babalatchi's suggestion, takes his daughter down-river to another village. Babalatchi then reveals Aissa's location to the distraught Willems who pursues her and encounters the Arab trader Syed Abdulla whom he agrees to pilot upriver, thus opening Almayer's trading post to competition and weakening the white influence in Sambir.

The novel mixes a rather overwrought adventure plot driven by Babalatchi's scheming with an equally hackneyed romance plot centred on Willems's over-whelming desire for Aissa. The tensions arising from his passion for her are reasonably well drawn – 'all his sensations, his personality – all this seemed to be lost in the abominable desire, in the priceless promise of that woman' (100). Yet Aissa is little more than a stereotypical femme fatale, alluringly sensual and mys-teriously exotic, and, in making him believe that '[s]cruples were for imbeciles. His clear duty was to make himself happy' (110), her effect on Willems is con-ventionally portrayed as both morally corrupting and mentally destabilising. Aissa saves him from her father's attempt on his life but refuses to leave Sambir, insisting that he work with Abdulla to overthrow Almayer and Lingard, freeing the island of white domination. In the unravelling of the action we do not follow Willems's machinations at first hand, hearing them via Almayer's disgruntled report to Lingard on the changes that have occurred. We learn that Willems is now living in the forest with Aissa and that he is planning to work as Abdulla's agent in trade. By giving the narrative of Abdulla's arrival from Almayer's point of view, we have events filtered through his biased and pompously aggrieved perspective. After Almayer has poured out his woes, Lingard goes to find Willems but discovers he has left. Babalatchi suggests that Lingard revenge himself by killing Willems but he refuses, to Babalatchi's disgust, and goes to meet his one-time protégé and, in a powerful scene, focalised through Lingard, we see the older man's anger and disgust as he lashes out at Willems's betrayal. The two men talk and Willems reveals his fear and mistrust of Aissa's obsessive love, dismissing her as 'a savage . . . a damned mongrel, half-Arab, half Malay' (209). In some rather clumsy symbolism, a thunderstorm breaks, mocking Willems's passionate declar-ation of his fidelity to his white race. Lingard condemns Willems to remain on Sambir as the most fitting punishment for his behaviour. Willems is left to reflect on his folly and ponders his life's shortcomings in a tropical downpour, attended by the bewildered Aissa, before retreating to his hut in gloomy isolation.

The novel's final section deals, from Almayer's perspective, with Willems's estranged wife whom Lingard has brought to Sambir in the hope of effecting a reconciliation. Almayer tells her some of what has happened to Willems and seeks to persuade her to take her husband away from Sambir. He arranges for her to be taken to Willems's camp where she discovers his relationship with Aissa even as Aissa discovers that Willems had a wife and child. In her despair, Aissa kills Willems with his revolver. The narrative concludes with an epilogue in which Almayer tells a visiting trader the 'story of the great revolution in Sambir' (275) and of Aissa's fate: she has become one of his servants and is now a 'doubled-up crone' (279).

The novel continued to develop themes of racial difference, colonialism and commerce broached in *Almayer's Folly*. In his depiction of Willems and his rival Almayer, Conrad expands upon his first novel's representation of white Europeans in the Malay Archipelago as corrupt and deluded. This is not to suggest that Conrad painted his Malay characters particularly sympathetically – the blind Omar el Badavi and the one-eyed Babalatchi, if more successful schemers than the white men, are no less greedy or amoral. They are, however, at least one remove from the feeble and easily defeated natives of much colonial fiction. Conrad's depiction of the ageing adventurer Lingard chimes with this anti-imperialistic note. Lingard has viewed Sambir as his fiefdom but Willems's treachery exposes the arrogance of his paternalistic claim to know what's best for the inhabitants of 'his' river. What was new here, as was the case in *Almayer's Folly*, was Conrad's refusal to adhere to the era's dominant conceptions of white authority.

Early reviews

The *Daily Chronicle* described it as 'a work of extraordinary force and charm', comparing Conrad's description of tropical islands to those of American novelist Herman Melville's (1819–91) Pacific fictions and suggested that his study of white 'degradation' was on a par with that of Robert Louis Stevenson's (1850–94) Pacific tales (Sherry 1973: 63). The *Illustrated London News* suggested that the story was 'a little disjointed' but praised its characterisation and descriptions (Sherry 1973: 66). The *National Observer* felt that the style was 'diffuse' and lamented that Conrad 'spreads his story over a wilderness of chapters and pages . . . his narrative wanders aimlessly through seas of trivial detail'. It also criticised the characterisation as not 'particularly effective', suggesting that it was like one of Stevenson's South Sea stories 'grown miraculously long and miraculously tedious' (Sherry 1973: 69). H. G. Wells, in an unsigned review in the *Saturday Review*, concurred, calling the book 'a remarkably fine romance' but noting that 'Mr Conrad is wordy; his story is not so much told as seen intermittently through a haze of sentences' (Sherry 1973: 73–4). Wells lamented that Conrad had yet to learn 'the great half of his art, the art of leaving things unwritten' (Sherry 1973: 75). Wells was critical but also declared that the novel was 'the finest piece of fiction published this year' and that only 'greatness could make books of which the detailed workmanship was so copiously bad, so well worth reading, so convincing, and so stimulating' (Sherry 1973: 75, 76). Conrad was 'on the whole' satisfied with the novel's reception (CL1: 271) and moved by the *Saturday Review*'s piece to write to its unnamed reviewer in thanks (CL1: 278–9). He was delighted to discover that the reviewer was Wells and wrote to thank him for his review (CL1: 282): the correspondence initiated a friendship (see Life and Contexts, **pp. 10–11**).

Later critical response

Criticism of the novel has tended to lump it with *Almayer's Folly* and until recently there have been relatively few studies of the work in its own right. Carlisle Moore's 'Conrad and the Novel as Ordeal' (1963) is a study of *Lord Jim* but contains suggestive analysis of the ways in which themes in the early Malay fiction mirrored Conrad's own struggles with authorship. Paul Kirschner's 'Conrad and Maupassant' (1965) examines Conrad's debt to the French writer's *Bel Ami*, whilst Harold Davis's 'Shifting Rents in a Thick Fog: Point of View in the Novels of Joseph Conrad' (1969) sees the novel as a failed attempt to utilise a Flaubertian narrative point of view. Rick Gekoski's '*An Outcast of the Islands*: A New Reading' (1969) argues that the central figure of the novel was not Willems but Lingard.

More recently, as post-colonial studies have influenced Conrad criticism, there have been a range of works which offer accounts of the novel's engagement with imperialism. Heliéna Krenn's study, *Conrad's Lingard Trilogy: Empire, Race, and Women in the Malay Novels* (1990) offers a pioneering account of all three works. Andrea White's *Joseph Conrad and the Adventure Tradition* (1993) reads Willems as 'not just a symptom of the disease imperialism proliferates, he is a contributing cause' (1993: 137) and she sees the novel as 'one that denounced the European endeavour in tropical outposts' (1993: 149). Linda Dryden's *Joseph Conrad and the Imperial Romance* (2000), in a complementary study to White's, offered an insightful account of the ways in which Conrad draws on adventure fiction paradigms in a novel which she reads as subverting 'the heroic code' (2000: 109). Robert Hampson's *Cross-Cultural Encounters in Joseph Conrad's Malay Fiction* (2000) examines the novel's representation of cultural diversity and traces the ways in which its narrative is 'constructed around the figures of Willems and Babalatchi' (2000: 108), with the latter's 'adaptability' contrasted with the former's 'inability to adapt' (2000: 109). Hampson also comments on the ways in which 'gender constructions seem to reinforce "racial" barriers' and suggests that the novel relies overmuch on fixed notions of racial and sexual difference in ways that made it far less radical than *Almayer's Folly* (2000: 115).

The Nigger of the 'Narcissus' (1897)

Conrad's first novel to deal with predominantly English concerns, this tale drew upon the author's own sea experience and was carefully positioned for the English literary market. Unlike his first two novels, *The Nigger of the 'Narcissus'* was written with an initial serial publication in mind, appearing in the influential pro-imperialist journal the *New Review* between August and December 1897. In what will become a familiar lament, Conrad wrote to a friend, warning him to wait for the novel to appear in book form since 'the instalment plan ruins it' (CL1: 372). In the USA, the novel was serialised in *Country Life* and the

Illustrated Buffalo Express. In writing this novel of men and the sea Conrad was consciously turning away from the Malay scenes of his early work, prompted in part by Edward Garnett's recommendation that he write a sea story (CL1: 268) (see Life and Contexts, **pp. 11–12**). The work he began as a result of Garnett's prompting, *The Rescue* (see Works, **pp. 121–6**), was not completed until 1920 and in turning away from its familiar Malay settings Conrad may have been consciously embracing his immediate cultural milieu – writing a novel about English sailors returning home for the *New Review* being a way of aligning himself with a particular literary circle with an appetite for tales of men and empire. Conrad certainly saw the shift as part of his maturation as an artist, commenting in the novel's US preface, 'after writing the last words of that book, in the revulsion of feeling before the accomplished task, I understood that I had done with the sea, and that henceforth I had to be a writer' (Kimborough 1979: 168).

The novel is an account of the voyage of the *Narcissus* from Bombay to London, partly based on Conrad's own experience as second mate on the real ship which sailed from Bombay in June 1884, arriving at Dunkirk in October. During this voyage, a crew member, an African-American called Joseph Barron, died. Conrad should not be thought of as simply transcribing a slice of his seafaring life since his fictionalised crew was more homogenously English than the actual crew as he reduced the number of foreign sailors for his fictional account (Najder 1983a: 82). Conrad's letters made it clear that he was consciously trying for something new in *The Nigger of the 'Narcissus'*. Writing to Garnett, he declared that the novel's lack of incident was true to life, noting that only in 'a boy's book of adventures' does one get completed episodes whereas in life '[e]vents crowd and push and nothing happens' (CL1: 321). Given his sense of changing artistic tack, it was not surprising that Conrad felt moved to write what for many remains one of the most significant justifications of his art in a document that would become the novel's 'Preface' in the US edition published in 1914 and then in the UK in 1921. The final serial instalment in the *New Review* was followed by a shorter version of this text in the guise of an 'Author's Note'. Conrad had the full text published as a privately circulated pamphlet in 1902, and it appeared under the title of 'The Art of Fiction' in the US journal *Harper's Weekly* in May 1905. The 'Preface' is significant as a statement of intent by a writer committed to the development of his career as an English novelist (see Life and Contexts, **pp. 15–18** for a discussion of this work). Seven copyright-securing editions of the complete novel (without the 'Preface') were 'published' in July 1897 by Heinemann with full publication following in December 1897. The novel was first published in the USA by Dodd, Mead and Company in November 1897 as *The Children of the Sea: A Tale of the Forecastle* – a title, which Conrad later described as 'absurdly sweet' (CL5: 257).

Commentary

The novel begins with a crew muster and evokes the rough camaraderie of the sailors. We are introduced to the key characters – the old helmsman Singleton, the argumentative Belfast, the lazy and carping Cockney agitator Donkin, the gruff first mate Mr Baker, the homesick second mate Creighton and the enigmatic

James Wait, the 'nigger' of the title. Via its artfully focalised narration, the novel plays off these men in various pairings and oppositional groupings; notably the 'sentimental' friendship which the hard man Belfast develops with Wait and the contrast established between the hooligan Donkin and the unthinkingly reliable Old Singleton. Our first register of the crew's companionable solidarity comes when they rally round Donkin, who has abandoned an American ship without his few belongings, despite their sense that he is a shirker. Wait is marked as different not only for his skin colour but also for his 'disdainful' (18) diction, sonorous voice and wracking cough. The narrator is careful to point up the difference between the seamen of Singleton's generation – 'inarticulate' but 'indispensable' – and the modern seafarers who, like Donkin, 'have learned how to whine' (25).

The ship sets sail, and life aboard amongst the crew is initially presented as gossipy and almost domestic, with the crewmen shown as anxious about Wait's developing illness. The narrator suggests that the men 'hesitated between pity and mistrust', unsure whether his illness is 'reality' or 'sham' and that they are frightened by the idea of a 'stalking death' (36). Gradually, Wait 'made himself master of every moment of our existence': he is felt to have cast 'an infernal spell . . . upon our guileless manhood' (37). The mood on board changes as the crew's first priority shifts from ministering to the ship to caring for 'our incomprehensible invalid' (40). Meantime, Donkin becomes more isolated as he is brought in line by the mate, Mr Baker, who punches him for his insubordination, knocking out one of his teeth. Anxiety over how to respond to Wait's illness leaves the crew gripped by a sense of 'weird servitude' (43). The narrator suggests that Wait 'coughed when it suited his purpose' and implies that he is malingering; in the interests of discipline the Captain has him moved to the deckhouse but his presence continues to 'overshadow the ship' (47).

Rounding Cape Horn, the *Narcissus* runs through heavy weather and, thirty-two days out from Bombay, is caught in a fierce storm in which she is swamped and rolls onto her side. Coping with the aftermath of the storm brings the crew together, symbolised by their sharing of water and their rescue of Wait who is trapped in his deckhouse cabin. Restored by coffee made by the sanctimonious cook, the crew begin the task of righting the ship; revealing grit and determination when held to the task by the injunctions of the officers. Conrad's narrative emphasises the key role of the mate and captain in controlling and shaping the work of the crew. Once the ship is under way, the men restore order to the forecastle, 'arranging to "worry through somehow" as clothes, gear and bedding have been ruined by the sea' (95). Singleton, as befits a relic of the heroic days of sail, has steered with care for the full thirty hours of the storm but now feels the weight of his age, believing himself to be 'broken at last' (99). As the weather settles the men become complacent 'and conveniently forgot our horrible scare . . . decried our officers . . . and listened to the fascinating Donkin' (100); despite their dislike of him, the crew find his words persuasive. Wait continues to appear ill but tells Donkin that he is not sick and asks him not to 'let on too much' (111). The overbearingly religious cook tries to make Wait pray for his life and the resulting row attracts the crew and officers. Wait insists he is now fit for duty but the Captain declares that he has been 'shamming sick' and refuses to allow him on deck (120). The crew, already restless thanks to Donkin's carping, protest and talk of striking. In the confusion, Donkin lobs an iron belaying pin at the officers and the crew recoil amidst cries of '[w]e ain't that kind' (123). The ship's needs break up the confrontation and the Captain shrugs the failed uprising off. Singleton prophesies that Wait will die in sight of land.

The next day, the Captain faces down the crew, declaring that they only know half their work and do half their duty (134). Wait continues to exert a hold on them, and Singleton declares that he is the cause of the head winds which are slowing the ship's progress. Once Wait succumbs to his illness, a 'common bond was gone; the strong, effective and respectable bond of a sentimental lie' (155). He is buried at sea and, as Singleton prophesied, the weather changes, enabling the ship to reach the English Channel within a week. The return to England is the occasion for an evocation of national pride, with the country viewed, somewhat conventionally, as a 'great ship' and 'mother of fleets and nations' (163). Taken in tow, she travels up the Thames and enters harbour and, once docked, the crew depart. Seen through the shore's eyes, the sailors are diminished figures but, tellingly, Donkin is viewed as 'an intelligent man' (169) and declares that he has given up the sea for a job on land. The narrator leaves the crew on London's Tower Hill, with the simple accolade that they 'were a good crowd' (173).

What made this tale of men and the sea so powerful was its exploration of the group psychology of men *in extremis*. In this it was aided by a subtle and artfully unstable narrative point of view which modulated between third-person omniscience and first-person intimacy. The novel also drew very pointedly on debates about English masculinity which were very much in the public mind in the later 1890s. Donkin is a type of man who appeared frequently in the popular press of the period when the urban worker became the focus of a great many cultural anxieties, not least of which was the Darwinian-inspired notion that their apparent 'degeneracy' was evidence of a fatal weakness in the race. Donkin is the 'independent offspring of the ignoble freedom of the slums full of disdain and hate for the austere servitude of the sea' (11) and in this he is readily to be equated with the fin-de-siècle figure of the hooligan, who was being sensationally figured in the popular press of the day. James Wait's self-absorption and its impact on the crew linked him with another problematic late nineteenth-century figure of masculinity, that of the dandy. In the minds of Conrad's readers in 1897, the dandy – par excellence – was the recently disgraced Oscar Wilde. Wait's impact on the *Narcissus* is to make its crew 'sentimental' – a word with period connotations of effeminacy – and at this time the effeminate dandy and the degenerate working-class male represented two sides of the same coin in terms of the threat they were popularly seen as posing to the social order (Middleton 2000). These male types were being read as 'the empty and negative symbol[s] at once of civic enfeeblement' and of a 'monstrous self-absorption that . . . begins to prevail against . . . public welfare' (Bristow 1995: 4–5). Monstrous self-absorption is, of course, what is central to narcissism and Conrad's novel showed how narcissism disrupted a culture's apparently clear-cut social hierarchies. It revealed the threat to public welfare posed by the narcissistic trait of addressing selfish needs over and above those of one's social milieu. Through the impact of Wait's illness and Donkin's complaints, we are presented with a story that details narcissism's corrosive power to destabilise socially cohesive patterns of behaviour.

Early reviews

What struck many early reviewers was the extent to which Conrad had avoided the clichés of sea fiction – no stranded 'beautiful but athletic young ladies, no burning ships, uninhabited islands, pirates or hidden treasure' according to the reviews in the *Glasgow Herald* and *Daily Chronicle* (Sherry 1973: 88–91). The narrative strategy of the novel has long been a source of critical debate, and early readers, such as the novelist Arnold Bennett (1867–1931) noted the powerful effect of the chosen style, 'that *synthetic* way of gathering up a general impression and flinging it at you' (Sherry 1973: 82) whilst, in a letter to Conrad, Constance Garnett wrote of the 'extraordinary reality and great beauty' of the style (Stape and Knowles 1996: 28). The *Daily Chronicle* claimed that 'the value of the book lies in the telling' (Sherry 1973: 90) whilst *The Spectator* noted the 'uncompromising nature' of its author's methods (Sherry 1973: 93). For *The Academy*, however, the narrator was a failure since his language was deemed inappropriately poetic for 'one of the common sailors' (Sherry 1973: 96).

Later critical response

There is a wide range of secondary criticism available on both *The Nigger of the 'Narcissus'* and its 'Preface'. Important early studies included Marvin Mudrick's 'The Artist's Conscience and *The Nigger of the "Narcissus"*' (1957), which offers a critique of Conrad's handling of narrative point of view. Leo Gurko's *Joseph Conrad: Giant in Exile* (1965) examines the theme of death in the novel and claims that Conrad's handling of it underpinned the work's status as his 'earliest masterpiece' (1965: 93). Paul Levine's 'Joseph Conrad's Blackness' (1964), explores Wait's narcissism and sees the novel as a study in initiation. A number of influential articles from the 1950s and 1960s are reprinted in John Palmer (ed.) *Twentieth Century Interpretations of The Nigger of the 'Narcissus': A Collection of Critical Essays* (1969).

Ian Watt's *Conrad in the Nineteenth Century* (1979) offers a detailed study of the novel and its 'Preface'. William Bonney's *Thorns and Arabesques: Contexts for Conrad's Fiction* (1980) gives an account of the function of narrative 'discontinuity in characterological presentation' (1980: 162). A key study of the work's textual history is provided by Kenneth Davis and Donald Rude in their essay on 'The Transmission of the Text of *The Nigger of the "Narcissus"*', (1973). H. M. Daleski's *Joseph Conrad: The Way of Dispossession* (1977) argues that 'the metaphysical emptiness that is asserted in *The Nigger of the "Narcissus"* is also ... the basis of the individual nullity and the moral nihilism pervading whole societies that preoccupy Conrad in the period from *Nostromo* to *Under Western Eyes*' (1977: 30). Theo Steinmann, 'The Perverted Pattern of *Billy Budd* in *The Nigger of the "Narcissus"*' (1974) examines the thematic similarities between Herman Melville's story and Conrad's novel.

Todd Willy's 'The Conquest of the Commodore: Conrad's Rigging of "The Nigger" for the Henley Regatta' (1985) and Peter McDonald, 'Men of Letters and Children of the Sea: Conrad and the Henley Circle Revisited' (1996) examine the ways in which Conrad pitched the serial version of the novel for the predilections of the editor of the *New Review*. Michael Levenson's *A Genealogy of Modernism* (1984) argues that the novel's 'Preface' and the story's narrative organisation are characteristic of early modernism in their apparent mistrust of omniscience. Narrative concerns are central to David Manicom's 'True Lies/False Truths: Narrative Perspective and the Control of Ambiguity in *The Nigger of the "Narcissus"*' (1986) and in Bruce Henricksen's *Nomadic Voices: Conrad and the Subject of Narrative* (1992), whose Bakhtinian reading concludes that the 'wavering point of view . . . is a structural element' of the novel that reveals Conrad to be working in a dialogic mode (1992: 46). Jeremy Hawthorn's *Joseph Conrad: Narrative Technique and Ideological Commitment* (1990) notes the ways in which shifting Victorian conceptions of a racial other were drawn on in the characterisation of Wait. Miriam Marcus examines the treatment of race and class in the depiction of Wait in her essay 'Writing, Race, and Illness in *The Nigger of the "Narcissus"*' (1998). In my essay 'From Mimicry to Menace: Conrad and Late Victorian Masculinity' (Middleton 2000), I examine Conrad's representation of Wait in the light of the figure of the dandy and Donkin in relation to the figure of the hooligan. Allan Simmons has recently discussed the novel in terms of its engagement with notions of Englishness in his 'The Art of Englishness: Identity and Representation in Conrad's Early Career' (2004).

Tales of Unrest (1898)

This was Conrad's first published collection of short stories and it contained five tales, all but one of which had been previously serialised. The stories comprising this collection were the Malay tales 'Karain – A Memory', which first appeared in *Blackwood's Magazine* in November 1897, and 'The Lagoon' which was published in the *Cornhill Magazine* in January 1897. Also included were the African tale 'An Outpost of Progress' which had appeared in the June–July 1897 number of *Cosmopolis*, the previously unpublished tale of middle-class marital break-up 'The Return', and the Brittany-set story of 'The Idiots', which had appeared in *The Savoy* for October 1896. The collection was published in March in the USA by Scribner's and in April in the UK by T. Fisher Unwin. Conrad's short fiction tended to be written when he couldn't make progress on a novel but, as Lawrence Graver has argued, Conrad's interest in short stories grew as it became apparent that they could earn him as much if not more than a novel. At just under 10,000 words, 'Outpost of Progress' earned him as much as the 107,000 words of *An Outcast of the Islands* (Graver 1969: 25). The collection is rather uneven, with powerful works such as 'Karain' and weaker pieces such as 'The Return'.

Commentary

'Karain – A Memory'

'Karain – A Memory' was written in 1897 and published in the same year in the influential pro-imperialist *Blackwood's Magazine*. Whilst superficially similar to 'The Lagoon', which Conrad had written earlier in the same year, in terms of setting and theme the tale marked an advance both for its use of a frame narrative whose narrator is both a participant and recounter of events, and its sympathetic portrayal of a non-white character. Unlike 'The Lagoon', which foregrounded Arsat's story with minimal interference from the frame narrator, the more complex narrative structure of 'Karain' works to establish complexities and ambiguities that unsettle the fixed binary oppositions regarding race which may well have underpinned the mind-set of *Blackwood's* conservative readers.

The story begins with its unnamed frame narrator recalling how he and his fellow gunrunners met Karain, the native ruler of 'an insignificant foothold' in the Eastern Archipelago (4). Memory is foregrounded as the narrator impressionistically recalls his experience of the East in a riot of 'variegated colours of checkered sarongs, red turbans, white jackets, embroideries; with the gleam of scabbards, gold rings, charms' (4). Karain and his fiefdom are figured through a series of theatrical metaphors which work to offer the Western narrator's sense of the fantastic unreality of the place in which some 'petty chief' (7) is treated with 'a solemn respect accorded in the irreverent West only to the monarchs of the stage' (6). Karain appears inviolable in his command of his territory but, in the privacy of the white men's ship, reveals his private fears. He also questions his visitors about Queen Victoria whom he 'called Great, Invincible, Pious, and Fortunate' (13), naively believing these gunrunners to be 'emissaries of Government' (12). Karain, we learn, is an exile and for some, at this stage unspecified, reason he has never returned to his homeland.

After two years, the plans for Karain's local war near fruition and the gunrunners make their final smuggling trip. They discover that Karain's ever – present bodyguard has recently died and that Karain has been absent from his encampment for five days. He arrives on their ship unexpectedly 'looking over his shoulder like a man pursued' (21) – what pursues him is his guilt, in the form of the ghost of his best friend, Matara. In a sequence narrated in part by Karain, it is revealed that in his youth his friend's sister had brought shame on her people by running off with a Dutch trader. Matara swore to restore the lost honour of his family by tracking them down and killing her. Karain accompanied him and after a two-year quest they find their quarry but by this time Karain had secretly become obsessed by the girl whose image has become his 'companion of troubled years' (37). When it comes to the moment of retribution, he cannot allow Matara to kill her and he shoots his friend to save her life. Karain believed that he was haunted by Matara's aggrieved spirit until he met an old man who gave him a charm that kept the ghost at bay. This man then became his bodyguard and it is his recent death which has brought about the changes in Karain, as he believes that he is now haunted once more. He begs his white friends for some charm that will protect him and they concoct one out of a Jubilee sixpence and piece of ribbon (49). Karain believes that this token, with its 'image of the Great Queen' has driven the ghost away 'forever' (51). The story ends with a coda in which the narrator recalls meeting his fellow gunrunner, Jackson, in London's Strand in a sequence that works to evoke the unreality of the city and the questionable power of memory.

'The Idiots'

'The Idiots', written whilst the Conrads were on honeymoon, is the story of a farmer who hoped for children to work his land but could only produce simpletons. Conrad's narrator describes the tale as 'formidable and sad' in its disclosure of the 'obscure trials endured by ignorant hearts' (59). The tale is unremittingly bleak and ends with the wife murdering her husband and then drowning herself. Conrad told his publisher that the story was 'Not for babies' (CL1: 279) but confided to Edward Garnett that it was only fit for the 'twilight of a popular magazine' (CL1: 284). The story appeared in *The Savoy* of October 1896. The *Daily Telegraph* suggested that 'for sheer morbid horror the story ... would be bad to beat in the whole range of fiction' (Sherry 1973: 102).

'An Outpost of Progress'

'An Outpost of Progress' offers a sardonic tale of white degeneration in Africa which is a precursor to Conrad's profound meditation on the colonial encounter in 'Heart of Darkness'. It was written during the Conrad's honeymoon in Brittany in July 1896 and first appeared in *Cosmopolis* for July 1897. Its central characters, Kayerts and Carlier, run a trading post with the support of an African servant known as Makola, who despises his feckless white 'masters'. The white men are the enfeebled products of European civilisation, 'insignificant and incapable' away from 'the high organization of civilised crowds' (89). These are white men in the mould of Almayer and Willems (see Works, **pp. 22–7, 28–31**), ill suited to the challenges of life away from the culture that created them:

> Society, not from any tenderness, but because of its strange needs, had taken care of those two men, forbidding them all independent thought, all initiative, all departure from routine.... They could only live on condition of being machines. And now, released from the fostering care of men with pens behind the ears ... they were like those life-long prisoners who, liberated after many years, do not know what use to make of their faculties.
>
> (91)

These men are incapable of understanding the culture in which they have been deposited since they cannot interact with it as they have not bothered to learn the language – they are said to be like 'blind men in a large room, aware only of what came in contact with them (and of that only imperfectly), but unable to see the general aspect of things' (92). In a playful dig at his readers, Conrad has these men pass their time reading adventure fictions and old newspapers. After a slave-trading gang takes the workers from the station as well as several men from the local village, Kayerts and Carlier become even more isolated and, as their supplies dwindle, their health fails. Eventually the two argue over a cup of sugar and Kayerts shoots and kills Carlier. The next morning, the company steamer arrives with new supplies and Kayerts takes his own life rather than face justice. Conrad concurred with Edward Garnett's view that the 'construction is bad' (CL1: 300) but would later declare this story to be amongst his favourites.

'The Return'

Conrad wrote this story in the summer of 1897 after completing work on *The Nigger of the 'Narcissus'*. He met with no success when attempting to place it with a magazine, perhaps because it was so different from anything he had written prior to it. 'The Return' is an attempt at an urban, domestic drama. Set in London, this tale of middle-class marital discord begins with the smug Alan Hervey returning home only to discover that his wife has left him. She returns and they argue until Hervey declares that 'morality is not a method of happiness' (167) and leaves her. Conrad wrote that he had 'a physical horror' of the story which had 'embittered five months of my life' (CL1: 386), stating that 'I wanted the truth to be first dimly seen through the fabulous untruth of that man's convictions' but had come to believe that the story's shortcomings suggested 'that my fate is to be descriptive and descriptive only' (CL1: 387).

'The Lagoon'

The story was written during Conrad's honeymoon in Brittany in the summer of 1896 and was published in the *Cornhill Magazine* in January 1897. 'The Lagoon' was Conrad's first published short story and is very much a product of his early style, reliant upon lush descriptions of 'exotic' locations. The text is notable for the early use of a frame narrator and has been read as evidence of Conrad experimenting with the ways in which an 'introspective and meditative' (Schwarz 1980: 27) narrative voice could bring an ironic modulation to a fiction's narrative – an approach which is put to great effect with the creation of Marlow's narration in 'Heart of Darkness' and *Lord Jim*. Conrad himself saw the story as apprentice work, and even at the time of writing felt it verged upon self-parody – he described it to Garnett as being full of 'secondhand Conradese' (CL1: 301).

The tale is of interest for its use of a Malay narrator – surely something which Conrad's audience, many of whom doubtless shared the objectionable and ingrained assumption of racial superiority of its white frame narrator, would have been at least a little surprised by. Yet the evocation of place is very much of its era – the forests are 'impenetrable' and ooze darkness and the only active thing in the opening sequence is the white man's canoe. Arsat's narrative, whilst continuing in the vein of exotic stories of the period, nonetheless holds his white guest and, thus, the white readers of the *Cornhill Magazine*, for the duration of his tale; Arsat also suggests that the Malays and white races are similar in that both 'take what they want' (30). Doubtless Conrad's readers also shared the tale's view of the dangerous power of love to undermine fidelity and masculine values. Ultimately, the story remains true to type – focusing upon Arsat's betrayal rather than his love, its narrative works to suggests that the Malay character is ultimately incapable of fidelity.

Early reviews

The reviews of *Tales of Unrest* were mixed – the *Daily Mail* preferred 'The Return' to the 'monotonous' Malay tales (Sherry 1973: 103). Edward Garnett, in a major review for *The Academy*, praised the 'feminine insight' (Sherry 1973: 107) of 'The Return' and highlighted the 'extreme delicacy and great breadth of vision' (1973: 106) of Conrad's work, arguing that his

> power of making us *see* a constant succession of changing pictures is what dominates the reader and leaves him no possible way of escaping from the author's subtle and vivid world . . . His technique is modern in the sense that Flaubert and Turgenev are modern, but he develops at times a luxuriance, and to English people an extravagance of phrase which leads us towards the East
>
> (Sherry 1973: 107)

The Academy went on to award Conrad a 50-guinea prize in 1899 for *Tales of Unrest* 'as one of the best books of the previous year'.

Later critical response

Whilst many book-length studies include discussion of his short fiction, there are several major studies of the short stories which treat them in their own right as a significant aspect of Conrad's work. The works, in order of publication, are Lawrence Graver's *Conrad's Short Fiction* (1969), Ted Billy's *A Wilderness of Words: Closure and Disclosure in Conrad's Short-Fiction* (1997), Daphna Erdinast-Vulcan's *The Strange Short Fiction of Joseph Conrad: Writing, Culture, and Subjectivity* (1999) and Erdinast-Vulcan et al. (eds) *Joseph Conrad: The Short Fiction* (2004). Readers interested in tracing Conrad's work in the short-story form are recommended to start with either Graver or Billy's accessible and comprehensive accounts.

'Karain: A Memory'

Bruce Johnson examines 'Karain' as a precursor to *Lord Jim* in 'Conrad's "Karain" and *Lord Jim*' (1963). André Busza traces some Polish literary models for the tale in 'Conrad's Polish Literary Background and Some Illustrations of the Influence of Polish Literature on his Work' (1966). Wendell Harris's 'English Short Fiction in the Nineteenth Century', (1968), suggests 'Karain' as typical of the late nineteenth-century exotic story which appeared in *Blackwood's*, arguing that Conrad's work marked an important transition point between nineteenth- and twentieth-century short-fiction methods. Graver suggests that 'Karain' 'in many formal ways is the most accomplished piece in *Tales of Unrest*' (1969: 29) and examines its use of frame narration and the role of the narrator who 'for the first time in a Conrad story . . . has moved forward to share the stage with the central character in the drama' (1969: 31). Although Graver notes limitations, he concludes that 'there is something admirably experimental about the story, something of the artist's testing things out in an effort to discover some of the possibilities of his material' (1969: 34). Mark Conroy offers a supernatural reading in 'Ghostwriting (in) "Karain"', (1994). Ted Billy examines the ways in which the story reflect on the processes whereby memory 'falsifies past experiences and warps anticipations of the future' (1997: 128). Daphna Erdinast Vulcan has read 'Karain' 'as a literary assassination of its own prototype ["The Lagoon"], and as a transitional point in the psycho-textual dynamics of Conrad's work' (1999: 55). Reading it as a story about storytelling, she argues that it turned on 'the unresolved tension between two perceptual sets or spheres: the island and the schooner; the stage and the real world; superstition and rationality; East and West' (1999: 62). In this schema, the 'narrator's attempt to privilege his own perceptual system, to contain the other within the realm of the exotic, the mythical, or the theatrical, is constantly thwarted as his Western, rational, realistic, perceptual orbit is constantly breached' (1999: 62). Robert Hampson's *Cross-Cultural Encounters in Joseph Conrad's Malay Fiction* (2000), considers the story in terms of its problematising of cross-cultural and cross-racial male bonding and for its involvement of the reader 'in the various implications of the narrative' (2000: 127). Linda Dryden's *Joseph Conrad and the Imperial Romance* (2000), also reflects on the story's representation of male bonding along with its reworking of other staples of adventure fiction in what she presents as Conrad's conscious 'courting [of] an audience of imperial romance enthusiasts' (2000: 111). David Adams's '"Remorse and Power": Conrad's "Karain" and the Queen', (2001), examines the function of the tale's representation of Queen Victoria, and Cedric Watts touches on similar material in his subtle examination of the significance of the sixpence that Hollis gives to Karain, in the essay 'Fraudulent Signifiers: Saussure and the Sixpence in "Karain"'.

'The Lagoon'

Albert Guerard, in 'Conrad's "The Lagoon"' (1963) dismisses the tale as inferior work but sees in it the seed of Conrad's interest in participant narrators which would lead to the creation of Marlow. Graver, following Conrad, sees 'The Lagoon' as verging on self-parody and traces the way in which 'the setting is the protagonist', commenting on the role of the white listener as a precursor to the engaged audience of listeners figured in later fiction (1969: 28–9). Ted Billy suggests that the story examined the ways in which 'the dream of possession leads to a petrification of selfhood' (1997: 171). He reads the white man as 'a cultural stereotype' (172), unprepared to 'deal with the incomprehensible' (173), and as 'a representative of pernicious colonial influence, which promoted turmoil and unrest, even in peaceful times (175). Hampson examines the role of the Malay narrator in objectifying European perspectives (2000: 120).

'An Outpost of Progress'

'An Outpost of Progress' tends to be studied as a precursor to 'Heart of Darkness' rather than as a story in its own right. D. C. R. A. Goonetilleke's 'Conrad's African Tales: Ironies of Progress', (1971), being a typical example in its view of the story's limitations when compared to the longer work. There is coverage of the sources for the story in Sherry's *Conrad's Western World* (1971), which concludes that 'while it is based firmly on the Congo Conrad knew and that the setting is realistic enough the story itself and its details are invented' (1971: 125). Graver argues for the story to be read as 'an ironical study of human vulnerability' driven by a narrator of 'ruthless belligerence' (1969: 10, 11). Graver suggests that the story's debt to Kipling's 'The Man who Would Be King' is evident in the narrator's reliance on 'euphemistic substitution to mask the ugly facts of life' (1969: 13). He concludes that the story 'reveals a writer handling materials that he has not yet made his own' (1969: 14). Jakob Lothe, in *Conrad's Narrative Method* (1989), analyses the role of the authorial narrator and carefully elucidated its 'surprisingly complex' (1989: 45) contribution to the work. Andrea White's *Joseph Conrad and the Adventure Tradition* (1993) suggests that the story offers an account of Conrad's disillusion at the 'real incompetence and lunacy he encountered on his trip up the Congo' and in this guise 'effectively counters the fictions constructed so persuasively by the dominant discourse of the day' (1993: 166). Ted Billy sums the story up as 'a pantomime dramatizing the emptiness of civilized values' (1997: 68). Lissa Schneider, in *Conrad's Narratives of Difference* (2003) adopts a gender-studies perspective to argue that 'Kayerts and Carlier are feminized caricatures' of white colonialists whilst Price is constructed as 'a more masculine, powerful figure' (2003: 68, 70).

'The Return'

Robert Morris has examined parallels between 'The Return' and aspects of T. S. Eliot's *The Waste Land* in 'Eliot's "Game of Chess" and Conrad's "The Return"' (1950). Edward Said's *Joseph Conrad and the Fiction of Autobiography* (1966) regards it as amongst Conrad's most powerful and philosophically most interesting early stories for its account of 'emotional responses to shame' (1966: 104, 105). Lawrence Graver describes the story as one of 'the strangest works in the Conrad canon' and pondered the extent to which it was a conscious attempt to branch out into new territory (1969: 34). For Graver, the key to the story's failure lies in its narrative method, and he suggests that Conrad's difficulties in writing it could be taken as evidence that he found 'a straightforward, analytical method . . . uncongenial' (1969: 38). Dale Kramer's 'Conrad's Experiments with Language and Narrative in "The Return"' (1988) and William Bonney's 'Contextualizing and Comprehending Joseph Conrad's "The Return"' (1996) seek to make a more positive case for the text. Ted Billy, whilst noting the tale's flaws, also offers some positive comments, suggesting that 'Conrad dramatizes the vacuous heart of darkness that lies at the core of many conventional marriages once profit has replaced passion' (1997: 178). He examines the story's satire of bourgeois culture in terms of its modernist revelation of the instability of meaning and its undermining of a conventionally 'stable sense of self-hood' (1997: 179).

'The Idiots'

Milton Chaikin, 'Zola and Conrad's "The Idiots"', (1955) identifies debts to Émile Zola's *La Terre* and *La Joie de vivre*. Richard Herndon's 'The Genesis of "Amy Foster"' (1960) suggests that 'The Idiots' inform the plot pattern of the later story (see Works, pp. 58–9). Edward Said examines 'The Idiots' as part of a group of works which demonstrate that nothing could be rescued from the past.

In the recollecting narrator's inability to understand his narrative, Said sees evidence of Conrad's characteristic interest in the failure of 'reflective description' to 'adequately grasp impulsive, and hence obscure, action' (1966: 97). Lawrence Graver argues for the influence of Maupassant in Conrad's characterisation, narration and theme, but suggests that after a competent opening, 'creditable imitation turns into a pretentious and implausible melodrama' (1969: 8) (see Life and Contexts, pp. 8–9). Daniel Schwarz's *Conrad: Almayer's Folly to Under Western Eyes* (1980) argues that the true focus of the tale is the 'moral idiocy' of the adults (1980: 25). Ted Billy seeks to save the story from dismissal as 'borrowed melodrama' by arguing that 'Conrad's narrative is a satirical fable of Western culture in which medieval feudalism evolves into modern "futilism"' (1997: 163, 171). Vulcan describes it as 'one of Conrad's most pointless stories' because it is 'a narrative without a proper ending, without a moral' (1999: 83, 84). She suggests that 'all the conventional idealizations of peasant life – Nature, Community, Tradition – are demolished in the telling' and that all we are left with is 'an "idiot reality", a reality which resists narrativization with the indifferent force of brute matter' (1999: 85, 86).

Lord Jim (1900)

Lord Jim was begun as a short story entitled 'Tuan Jim – A Sketch' in early summer 1898; a sample was sent to Blackwood's literary adviser in June and Conrad was given £5 'on account' by Blackwood (CL2: 65, 67). He was stalled with *The Rescue* (see Works, pp. 121–6) and seems to have turned to the new project both as means of securing cash and as a way of unlocking his blocked creativity. He seems to have worked on 'Youth' (see Works, pp. 48–9), which also features Marlow as a narrator, at the same time as making his early notes on Jim, and through the simultaneous early development of these texts we can see that Conrad was honing the narrative voice that was to shape two of his greatest works – *Lord Jim* and 'Heart of Darkness' (see Works, pp. 49–52). 'Youth' was completed by early June and Conrad returned to his main project, *The Rescue*, only to be beset with difficulties. By August 1898 he was in despair over this novel since, with serial publication proposed for October, his publishers were demanding copy and he was in 'an inextricable mess' (CL2: 90). He renewed his efforts to find a command at sea – 'to get to sea would be salvation' (CL2: 88) – but, nurtured by Edward Garnett's letters and visits, kept writing. House moves and plans for collaboration with Ford Madox Ford intervened (see Life and Contexts, p. 12) and it was not until June of the following year that he picked up *Lord Jim* again, but by early July he had sent three chapters to Blackwood's (CL2: 184). At this point Conrad believed that the work would amount to 40,000 words and by early August he was prematurely discussing serialisation, believing that the text would amount to only four instalments – in fact it ran for fourteen instalments from October 1899 to November 1900, with Conrad only completing the text of the serial version in July 1900 (CL2: 191, 281).

Conrad tended to play down the artistic dimension of *Lord Jim*'s organisation – disingenuously stating that the 'structure is a little loose' (CL2: 193). Working to the demands of serial publication clearly made Conrad carry on writing, but he tended to fret over the emerging text – the 'beginning wobbles a good deal' (CL2: 213); the second instalment is 'too wretched for words' (CL2: 221) – but by the end of its development he felt, at least in letters to his publisher, more bullish about its merits – 'the story *is* good' (CL2: 274). To Garnett, however, he was more pessimistic: 'What is fundamentally wrong with the book . . . is want of power. . . . I mean the want of *illuminating* imagination. I wanted to obtain a sort of lurid light out the very events . . . alas! I haven't been strong enough to breathe the right sort of life into it' (CL2: 302).

Lord Jim: A Tale was published by Blackwood on 9 October 1900 and was published in the USA by Doubleday, McClure on 31 October as *Lord Jim: A Romance*. There are some marked variations between the serial and first UK edition, totalling around 400 changes:

> The most sizeable revisions occur in the first half of the novel: Conrad made seventeen drastic cuts (passages from five to fifty-seven lines in length) and well over fifty cuts of one to three lines. Of these major cuts and changes, perhaps the most significant have to do with Jim's psychology. Apparently Conrad felt that he had been too explicit in the periodical version, that later in the novel he had sufficiently dramatized his conceptions, and that therefore explicit statements ought to go. Conrad also lowered Jim's age from twenty-six to twenty four, made Cornelius into Jewel's stepfather rather than her real father, and . . . humanized Gentleman Brown.
>
> (Moser 1996: 249)

Lord Jim is an early modernist masterpiece, whose dazzling narrative arrangement not only enables Conrad to record the psychological tensions that shape Jim's dereliction of duty but also allows him to reveal the coruscating power of Jim's guilty conscience. Marlow's narration is a *tour de force* of storytelling which tells us as much about the motivations of a middle-aged English sea captain as it does about experience's withering impact on Jim's youthful idealism. The novel is both an imperial romance, a profound critique of that genre and an artful meditation on the 'dark places of psychology' (Woolf 1938: 151).

Commentary

The tale begins in the world of the imperial romance, with Jim's training for a life at sea. Even here there is a discrepancy between his deeds and the self-image he has derived from his reading in 'light holiday literature' (5). Whilst he dreams of 'a stirring life in the world of adventure' (6), the chance for some youthful glory, when the trainees are called upon to rescue a stricken ship, eludes him as he is paralysed by fear over the apparent hostility of the weather. Jim's sea career is 'strangely barren of adventure' (10) and, after being injured by a falling spar (an injury which echoes the one that Conrad experienced whilst first mate of the *Highland Forrest* in 1887), he has to spend time ashore where he falls in with a crowd of sailors united by 'the determination to lounge safely through existence' (13). Jim is keen to work, however, and signs on as first mate on the *Patna* – a ship 'eaten up with rust worse than a condemned water tank' (13–14) – which is taking Muslim pilgrims from Singapore to Jeddah. The ship hits some underwater debris and its terrified self-serving crew abandon her, leaving the pilgrims to their fate. A passing steamer picks them up, but the *Patna* does not sink and is towed into port by a French gunboat. Confronted by their shameful actions, the rest of the crew disappear, leaving Jim to stand trial. The first five chapters are presented via third-person omniscient narration, but Marlow's narration carries most of the story. The context for his tale-telling is an after-dinner yarn to a circle of listeners and his narrative (Chapters 5–35), which draws upon interpolations based on conversations with various people who met or know of Jim's case, moves between his mature reflections and recreations of his experience of Jim at the time of the inquiry and after.

At the hearing Marlow becomes fascinated by the case and decides to help Jim, who is stripped of his mate's certificate and, in consequence, is unable to pursue his sea career. He sets him up with various posts, but at each one some imagined rumour of the *Patna* case pricks Jim's conscience and causes him to leave. Eventually Marlow arranges through his old friend Stein for Jim to be placed in an out-of-the-way trading post he controls on the island of Patusan. Here, for a little while, he achieves some of his youthful dreams as he leads the native people against the Arab traders and establishes a safe society. He is loved by Jewel, the stepdaughter of Cornelius, his displaced predecessor at the trading post. He also finds friendship with Dain Waris, son of Doramin, the local chief, and for his work in bring peace to the island he is given the title Tuan (Lord). The idyll is destroyed when a disreputable trader, a gunrunner ironically called Gentleman Brown, stumbles across the island, and this unwelcome arrival from the wider world puts Jim in another dilemma – should he remain true to his island friends and kill Brown to stave off the threat of further unwelcome intrusion or should he acknowledge his duty to another white man and offer succour to Brown and his reprobate followers. The novel's final chapters (36–45) take the form of a long written narrative in which Marlow pieces together the last days of Jim's life on Patusan for a 'privileged man' (337) from amongst his circle of listeners who had shown a particular interest in Jim's case. Brown's men launch an attack upon the village that, in Jim's absence, is repulsed by Dain Waris and his men, but when Jim returns to confront Brown his conscience is pricked once more by Brown's presumption of a common bond between them. For Brown this is simply a matter of ethnicity, but for Jim the assumption brings with it 'a sickening suggestion of common guilt, of secret knowledge that was like a bond of their minds and of their hearts' (387). Jim stakes his authority with the villagers on his claim that the best course of action is to let these white men go, but Brown and his gang, led by the malign Cornelius, massacre Dain Waris and his followers. Brown escapes but news soon comes to the village and Jim finds that once again he has 'lost [. . .] all men's confidence' (409), and he goes to Doramin to accept his fate. He is shot in retribution for Dain's death, in a gesture that Marlow calls a 'pitiless wedding with a shadowy idea of conduct' (416).

Marlow's narrative, unlike the official inquiry, is interested in the 'fundamental why' (56) of Jim's case. The novel makes use of a cast of supporting characters whose function is to shed further light on Jim's motivations. The seemingly impervious Captain Brierly who conducts the inquiry into the *Patna* case and then takes his own life 'very soon after' (58); the meditative French lieutenant who declares that 'the honour . . . that is real' (148), or the mournful Jewel who knows Jim has some secret that he can never share with her and so taints their love. The narrative also drew on historical events, which some of Conrad's readers would have been aware of:

> The *Patna* episode appropriates from the pages of the news the *Jeddah* incident of 1880, which was widely discussed in the British press precisely in terms of issues of conduct and Western ideals, and Jim resembles the first mate of the *Jeddah*, Augustine Podmore Williams. Williams, like Jim, was the son of an English clergyman, and Conrad and Williams were both in Singapore in 1883, where they could have met. Captain Brierly's suicide was apparently suggested by the suicide of Captain Wallace of the *Cutty Sark*.
>
> (Henricksen 1992: 85)

The novel's complex strands are held together in Marlow's narrative and, because Marlow is a participant narrator, we have to be alert to the ways in which his prejudices inform the text. *Lord Jim* is Marlow's version – his *tale* – of Jim's life, and it includes perspectives ranging from simple recounting of the case to more meditative reflections upon it. This means that 'Jim is both the object of Marlow's narration and a figure in the narration of others, including those who knew very little of him' and because of this 'multiplicity of virtuoso narrative techniques that sometimes alienate the reader, Jim, [. . .] is both at the novel's centre and on its periphery' (Stape 1996: 63). Whilst the novel begins with third-person omniscience, this tale is not one in which factual pronouncements will help much – 'as if facts could explain anything!' (29) – and the shift to Marlow's narrative facilitates a move to a more probing and at the same time ambiguous presentation of Jim – a shift that enables the novel to engage with philosophical questions. At one point Marlow remarks that 'the less I understood the more I was bound to him in the name of that doubt which is the inseparable part of our knowledge' (221) – the problematic of knowing and the basis of our knowledge of 'how to be' is a central concern in this profoundly philosophical novel.

Early reviews

The novel met with many favourable reviews, although most commentators felt that this was not a work that would meet with popular success, and several disputed the notion that Marlow's oral narrative could be told in one night. The *Manchester Guardian* described the novel as a work of 'remarkable originality' and praised its 'deep energy' (Sherry 1973: 111, 113), but the *Daily Telegraph* was more critical, focusing on 'the method of storytelling' and lamenting the 'constant wandering from the point, the recurrent introductions of incidents' were 'distinctly weakening' (Sherry 1973: 115). *The Academy* was seemingly more alert to the rationale informing the narrative style, noting the subsidiary characters as successful 'solely by virtue of their relation to Jim' and praising Conrad as both 'a reader's and novelist's novelist' (Sherry 1973: 116). *The*

Speaker declared the novel a 'profound' psychological study (Sherry 1973: 120) and noted that 'the arrangement of the book is original and effective; it seems to have solved one of the great difficulties of the philosophical romance' (Sherry 1973: 121). The *Pall Mall Gazette* sounded what was to become, in later years, a standard note in criticism when it argued that the novel suffered from a 'very broken backed narrative . . . although here is a kind of weak backed unity in the tale, the various fragments of narrative do not hold interest, or, rather, pass from point to point' (Sherry 1973: 123).

Later critical response

Since a reasonably comprehensive list of further reading for the novel would take up several pages, I have limited my recommendations to what are generally agreed to be amongst the most significant studies of the novel. Readers coming to the novel for the first time might want to start their engagement with secondary sources with those gathered by Thomas Moser for his second Norton Critical Edition of *Lord Jim* (1996) as this work offers a full account of the historical background to the text along with a selection from the key criticism, including substantial extracts from seminal works by Albert Guerard, Ian Watt, Fredric Jameson and Edward Said. The selection of essays on the novel reprinted in Keith Carabine (ed.) *Joseph Conrad: Critical Assessment: Volume 2: The Critical Response: Almayer's Folly to The Mirror of the Sea* (1992) are a useful supplement to those featured in Moser's edition. Those interested in the novel's narrative strategy might wish to draw on the perspectives offered in Harold Bloom (ed.) *Marlow* (1992), which contains a good selection of short extracts from the major critical studies along with full text reprints of important essays by Benita Parry and Mark Conroy.

Whilst there are a number of studies of the novel written before the late 1950s, readers new to the study of Conrad's novel might want to restrict themselves to Albert Guerard's still compelling evaluation of the novel in *Conrad: The Novelist* (1958) where he examines the work's innovative use of impressionistic techniques. Ian Watt's chapter on the novel in *Conrad in the Nineteenth Century* (1979) also offers an assessment of Conrad's narrative strategy, along with helpful discussion of Marlow's relationship with Jim and reflection on the handling of the novel's ending. Jakob Lothe's *Conrad's Narrative Method* provides a careful study of the 'thematic authority' of Marlow's role in his narrative's framing of Jim's experiences (1989: 174). In *Nomadic Voices: Conrad and the Subject of Narrative*, Bruce Henricksen examines the tension between heroic and romantic modes of discourse in accounting for Jim's action, arguing that 'the Patusan episode exists as an evocation and critique of the romantic, self-congratulatory myths produced by early capitalism in its narrating of its own encounter with other cultures (1992: 98). Henricksen suggests that Conrad's shift to the codes of romance and his playful 'stopping and starting' of the novel's 'highly mannered' ending were strategies designed to provoke a realisation of the ways in which 'conventions structure our notions of where we have been and are going, creating fictions of who we are and how to be' (1992: 100) – devices that pointed up for period readers the debilitating effects of Jim's adherence to 'the spirit of his illusion' (*Lord Jim*, 109) whilst challenging them to move beyond their habitual ways of seeing. Daphna Erdinast-Vulcan's *Joseph Conrad and the Modern Temper* (1991) argues that the book offers an account of 'an active, if desperate' attempt to defeat 'the spiritual and ethical malaise of modernity' by 'a regression to a mythical mode of discourse' (1991: 35). Robert Hampson's *Cross-Cultural Encounters in Conrad's Malay Fictions*, examines the role of gossip and other oral forms in the development of the novel's narrative, noting the way in which the 'circulation of the Patna story among the larger colonial community ironically serves to undermine the European position of authority' (2000: 131). Hampson analyses the competing narratives generated by Jim, emphasising the ways in which Marlow's narrative is one that is 'ideologically shaped' (2000: 142) and pointing up the fact that differences between 'different indigenous groups are as important for the outcome as the differences between Europeans and non-Europeans' (2000: 144). Allan Simmons and John Stape gather a number of contemporary perspectives on the novel in their collection *Lord Jim: Centennial Essays* (2000).

Youth: A Narrative and Two Other Stories (1902)

Both 'Youth' and 'Heart of Darkness' were planned as part of a trilogy in which *Lord Jim* would have been the third text under the title of *Three Tales of Land and Sea*: '[*Lord Jim*] has not been planned to stand-alone. 'Heart of Darkness' was meant in my mind as a foil, and *Youth* was supposed to give the note. All this is foolishness – no doubt. The public does not care – cannot possibly care – for foils and notes' (CL2: 271).

As *Lord Jim* turned into a major novel, Conrad realised that his plans would have to change, and he wrote 'The End of the Tether' with the collection in mind. The collection was published in November 1902 by Blackwood's and in the USA by McClure Phillips in February 1903.

Commentary

'Youth'

'Youth' was written between May and June of 1898 and appeared in *Blackwood's Magazine* in September 1898. It is notable as the first published text to use Marlow as a narrator and also for its reliance on autobiographical material. The voyage of the fictional *Judea* has several parallels with that of the *Palestine* on which Conrad sailed as second mate between 1881 and 1883; including delays in Falmouth and the spontaneous combustion of the cargo (see Chronology, pp. 171–2). 'Youth' is presented as Marlow's recollections of his first voyage to 'the Eastern Seas' (3). Marlow is forty-two at the time of telling the events of his voyage as a twenty-year-old whereas Conrad was twenty-four when he sailed on the *Palestine* and forty-one when he wrote the story.

The brief frame narrative presents the context for narration – a group of men, similar to the grouping who will appear in the frame narrative of 'Heart of Darkness', who have all served as merchant seamen in their youth, meet for supper. The frame narrator describes the tale, rather disingenuously, as a 'chronicle' rather than a 'story' (3) – the former is defined as a 'detailed and continuous register of events in time' (*OED*) but Marlow's narrative is neither of these things. As his narrative unfolds, Marlow punctuates his reminiscences with apostrophes to youth and consumes a good deal of claret – the phrase 'pass the bottle' become a refrain. The story of the struggle to get 'a wretched 600 ton cargo of coal to its destination' (4), 'Youth' follows the *Judea*'s delay-punctuated voyage from London to Bangkok. Three months after departure from London the ship finally begins its voyage only to get caught in a gale that causes it to spring a leak, necessitating a return to port and a further delay in Falmouth whilst the ship is repaired: ominously, just before they set off, rats are seen leaving the ship. The newly watertight ship makes slow progress before, in the midst of the Indian Ocean, the cargo of coal catches fire; as Marlow sardonically comments, 'after keeping water out of her to save ourselves from being drowned, we frantically poured water into her to save ourselves from being burnt' (20). The cargo then explodes, bursting the deck, but miraculously no one is harmed. The *Judea* is taken in tow by a steamer but 'the speed of the towing . . . fanned the smouldering destruction' (29) and the ship is abandoned – the captain turning down the offer of being transported by steamer whilst he and the crew wait to see 'the last of the ship' (ibid.). After several nights at sea in an open boat they make the coast of Java where Marlow has his first encounter with the East, 'I saw brown, bronze, yellow faces, the black eyes, the glitter, the colour of an Eastern crowd' (41). The tale ends with Marlow offering a slightly sozzled paean to youth – 'the best time' (42) – which is somewhat undermined by the frame narrator's concluding account of the teller and his audience as men 'looking anxiously for something out of life, that [. . .] is already gone – has passed unseen, in a sigh, in a flash – together with youth, with the strength, with the romance of illusions' (ibid.).

'Heart of Darkness'

The novella was written between autumn 1898 and February 1899 whilst Conrad was working on *Lord Jim* and blocked on *The Rescue*. The story seems to have been begun in part for pecuniary reasons – he told Garnett that he must write it 'for the sake of the shekels' (CL2: 132). Conrad glossed the novella as follows:

> It is a narrative after the manner of *youth* told by the same man dealing with his experiences on a river in Central Africa. The *idea* in it is not as obvious as in *youth* – or at least not so obviously presented. I tell you all this, for tho' I have no doubts as to the *workmanship* I do not know whether the *subject* will commend it to you . . .
>   The title I am thinking of is 'The Heart of Darkness' but the narrative is not gloomy. The criminality of inefficiency and pure selfishness when tackling the civilising work in Africa is a justifiable idea. The subject is of our time distinc[t]ly – though not topically treated.
>
> (CL2: 139–40)

The tale was finished in February and the serial version appeared in the conservative *Blackwood's Magazine* between February and April 1899. The serial was less explicitly a critique of the Belgian Congo than the manuscript version and there were no major changes between it and the to the first UK edition, although Conrad toned down some descriptions of the Africans. Kimborough's Norton Critical Edition of 'Heart of Darkness' (1988) reprints as footnotes some of the manuscript and magazine passages that were cut.

The story begins with a frame narration in which Marlow and his middle-class professional friends await the turn of the tide aboard the yawl *Nellie* at the mouth of the Thames. Marlow's yarn begins portentously with him declaring 'And this also . . . has been one of the dark places of the earth' (48). We are warned that his stories are not typical seamen's yarns since 'To him the meaning of an episode was not inside like a kernel but outside, enveloping the tale which brought it out only as a glow brings out a haze, in the likeness of one of those misty halos that sometimes are made visible by the spectral illumination of moonshine' (48).

Marlow begins with some reflections on the Roman invasion of Britain, comparing their imperial activity with the more recent British kind that for him is characterised by 'the devotion to efficiency' (50). Marlow's remarks promote comparisons between historically disparate epochs of imperial activity and his suggestion that the 'conquest of the earth . . . mostly means the taking it away from those who have a different complexion or slightly flatter noses than ourselves' (50) relies on sardonic understatement whilst avoiding the obvious importance of economic motives for imperialist activity. Marlow describes his tale as an account of 'the culminating point in my experience' (51) and he proceeds to narrate, with asides which reflect on that experience, the details of his journey to Africa. As he prepares to leave, he meets up with his aunt who was instrumental in getting him the position as captain on a riverboat working for a trading society in an unnamed African country. Marlow's aunt spouts conventional platitudes about the aims of colonial trade, which she memorably glosses as 'weaning those ignorant millions from their horrid ways' (59). Marlow takes this naïve remark as an opportunity to lament over the ignorance of women, declaring them to be 'out of touch with truth' (59). This misogynist note is struck at several key points in the narrative.

En route to Africa, Marlow witnesses the futility of imperialist war when he observes the French navy 'shelling the bush' (61), and during his voyage a 'general sense of vague and oppressive wonder grew upon me. It was like a weary pilgrimage amongst hints for nightmares' (62). Arriving at the Company's lower station on the river Marlow is greeted a 'scene of inhabited devastation' (63), with 'decaying machinery' and 'unhappy savages' (64). Marlow suggests that the Company's endeavours are driven by 'a flabby, pretending, weak-eyed devil of a rapacious and pitiless folly' (65). He encounters a group of sick natives, reduced to silence and 'contorted collapse' by their work for the Company (67). In stark contrast to these broken workers is the chief accountant he meets a few minutes later, a man who is meticulously dressed and seems to represent the only point of order in the 'muddle' of the station (68). It is from this man that he first hears of Mr Kurtz, ' a very remarkable person' (68) and the most successful trader who is destined for great things in the Company. Marlow sets out on the 200-mile walk to the central station and, on arrival, he immediately concludes that this place too is in the grip of the flabby devil and learns that the steamer he is to command has been sunk. Meeting the manager of the station Marlow hears again of Kurtz's importance to the company and of the rumour that he is ill. The manager judges that it will take three months for the steamer to be made ready to travel and the narrating Marlow darkly comments that it was startling 'with what extreme nicety he had estimated the time requisite for the "affair" ' (75), hinting with hindsight that the delay is part of the manager's scheme to frustrate the relief of Kurtz. Whilst waiting at the central station, Marlow learns more of Kurtz, his progressive vision for the company's trading posts and of the intrigues that surround him.

Once the ship has been repaired, Marlow sets off on the two-month journey up river with a crew of cannibals and a group of company men including the manager. As they approach Kurtz's compound they are attacked and Marlow witnesses the death of his helmsman when a spear is thrown through the open windows of the pilothouse. The attack and death of the helmsman are masterfully written examples of impressionist writing, using what Ian Watt has influentially termed 'delayed decoding' to evoke the experience of witnessing events before they are fully understood (1979: 175–9). Shortly after this attack, Marlow breaks off from his narrative to express his frustration at his inability to present the story effectively, describing Kurtz as merely a voice amongst voices and hinting at the novella's ending in an allusion to Kurtz's fiancé, which provokes a further misogynist assertion that 'the women . . . are out of it' (115). During this passage of reflection, the narrating Marlow reveals more about Kurtz, offering a more critical account than we have heard hitherto. Conrad's narrative strategy here allows him to juxtapose the views of the younger and older Marlow. The narrating Marlow reveals that one of his aims in the story is to 'account to myself for – Mr Kurtz' and he goes on to describe Kurtz's family background – '[a]ll Europe went into the making of Mr Kurtz' – and the breakdown of his idealism after 'his nerves went wrong' (117). As evidence of this change of heart, Marlow cites a note Kurtz added to his pamphlet for the International Society for the Suppression of Savage Customs which, after seventeen pages, 'vibrating with eloquence' (117) 'blazed at you, luminous and terrifying, like a flash of lightning in a serene sky: the note simply states "Exterminate all the brutes!" ' (118).

Marlow finds Kurtz broken by illness, cared for alternately by his native mistress and a freelance Russian trader. The Russian tells of Kurtz's involvement in native rites and declares that he was 'shamefully abandoned' (132) by the Company. The dying Kurtz is brought aboard the steamer and his African mistress is seen walking to the riverbank where she makes a defiant gesture. Conrad is careful to present this women solely through the perceptions of the white European men who observe her – she is 'savage and superb, wild eyed and magnificent' (135–6) but, unlike Kurtz's other followers, she returns the European's gaze with 'unswerving steadiness' (136). That night, Kurtz escapes from the ship and is followed into the jungle by Marlow who, in an encounter which is presented in somewhat metaphysical terms, has to persuade him to return. The next day, the ship prepares to leave and some of the native people, including Kurtz's lover, congregate to witness his departure and are killed by the jittery company men in an act of random slaughter. Kurtz himself dies on the journey downriver and at the point of death, in what Marlow suggests may have been 'a moment of complete knowledge', enigmatically calls out 'The horror! The horror!' (149).

Marlow suggests that this cry represents a moment of self-revelation and 'a moral victory' and sees it as marking Kurtz's return to humanity after indulging in 'abominable terrors' and 'abominable satisfactions' (151).

Shortly thereafter, Marlow himself falls ill and leaves Africa. On returning to Europe he is irritated by the untroubled existence of its citizens 'because I felt sure they could not possibly know the things I knew ... I had some difficulty in restraining myself from laughing in their faces' (152). Gradually he gives away Kurtz's papers, offering to the company representative the 'report of the "suppression of Savage Customs", but with the postscriptum torn off' (153); they refuse it. To Kurtz's cousin he gives some family letters and to a journalist he gives 'the famous Report for publication, if he thought fit' (154) – though without Kurtz's final note. These encounters give him – and the reader – further perspectives on Kurtz which casting him as a musician, journalist or potential populist politician. His final meeting is with Kurtz's fiancé and during their encounter Marlow is haunted by the grim reality of Kurtz's final days whilst he talks with the 'guileless' girl in terms which seek to preserve her simplistic worldview (157). As his earlier asides suggested, he is unable to tell her the true story of Kurtz's last words, preferring instead the tritely romantic lie that the 'last word he pronounced was – your name' (161). The story ends enigmatically with the frame narrator describing an 'overcast sky' and the Thames as 'a tranquil waterway' but one that 'seemed to lead into the heart of an immense darkness' (162).

'The End of the Tether'

In March of 1902 Conrad began work on 'The End of the Song', the tale that would become 'The End of the Tether' (CL2: 393). In April he was still at work, glossing the tale as 'rather sentimental' (CL2: 407), and by June, as the serial version of the story was appearing in *Blackwood's*, where it ran until December. He described it to Garnett as 'heartbreaking bosh' (CL2: 424). In late June disaster struck when an oil lamp exploded whilst Conrad was working on copy for the second serial instalment, and he worked with Ford to rewrite lost portions of manuscript. He did not complete the tale until October and worked on proofs into November (CL2: 450).

The story is concerned with the last years of Captain Whalley – once renowned for his daring exploits as a clipper captain but now reduced to working for the disagreeable shipowner Massy as captain of the *Sofala* in order to support his daughter Ivy and her invalid and unlucky husband. Whalley is losing his sight but if he retires early he will not be able to reclaim the savings he invested in the *Sofala*. Meanwhile, Massy's gambling debts drive him to plot the wrecking of the ship so that he can claim the insurance money. He hangs a jacket laden with iron near the ship's compass to make it run off course and Whalley unknowingly steers it onto a reef: too late he discovers Massy's scheme:

> 'Well, you have nothing at all now. The ship's lost, and the insurance won't be paid.'
> Captain Whalley did not move. True! Ivy's money. Gone in this wreck. Again he had a flash of insight. He was indeed at the end of his tether.
> (332)

Whalley stays aboard and goes down with his ship whilst Massy escapes any blame and departs for Manila with the insurance money. A year later, Ivy receives a letter telling her of her father's death and the novella ends with her final recognition of her love for her father.

Early reviews

'Youth'

Many of the initial reviews of the collection focused only on the title story. Edward Garnett, writing in *The Academy*, suggested that for the period's general reader 'Youth' and 'The End of the Tether' were likely to 'be more popular' than 'Heart of Darkness', glossing 'Youth' as 'a modern English epic of the sea (Sherry 1973: 132). The *Manchester Guardian* noted the story's 'surprising humour' (Sherry 1973: 134) and declared that it 'does something to enlarge our conception of heroism' (Sherry 1973: 135), concluding that, along with 'Heart of Darkness', it was one of 'the finest expositions of the modern spirit' (Sherry 1973: 135). The *Athenaeum* suggested that the story was a 'stirring . . . epic in little of the life of those who use the sea' (Sherry 1973: 139).

'Heart of Darkness'

The early reviews tended to be respectful but bewildered. The unsigned review which appeared in the *Daily Mail* concentrated upon questions of style, declaring that Conrad's prose is full of 'aggravating mannerisms': 'as often as not [he] prefers to use jumpy, staccato English, and often verbless and sometimes nounless sentences' (*Daily Mail*, 25 November 1902, p. 2).

Conrad was classified as a verbal Manet; his account of the mind's engagement with events regarded as a presentation of 'infinite detail' working via 'a confusion of strokes' to become 'a beautiful scheme from a little distance' (*Daily Mail*, 25 November 1902, p. 2): ' "The Heart of Darkness" is a wonderful impression. It is, however, the application of the methods of Mr Henry James to Central Africa! The association is incongruous but the result strangely interesting' (ibid.).

In the review in *The Graphic* for 3 January 1903, the reviewer argued that: ' "Heart of Darkness" [is] a lurid study . . . of one of those demonic personalities which have more than once, found scope beyond the utmost borders of civilization for lust of wealth, of power, of freedom' (ibid.).

Hugh Clifford's long review of the *Youth* volume in the 29 November 1902 issue of *The Spectator* saw the volume as the work of an author guided by impressionist notions of textual practice. Conrad's prose style was said to generate texts which are the literary equivalent of a mosaic (1902: 827), but Clifford argued that the subtlety of characterisation and related presentation of events occasioned by Conrad's mosaic technique made his fiction unacceptably complicated for the average reader.

Edward Garnett's review, in the long-established and influential *Academy*, set the tone for later response. Whilst the title story and 'The End of the Tether' were seen as more generally accessible, 'Heart of Darkness' was characterised as 'the high water mark of the author's talent' (606). Garnett described the novella as 'a consummate piece of artistic *diablerie*' which works for a psychological realism and the art of the tale lies is said to lie in its ability to show the relation: 'of the things of the spirit to the things of the flesh, of the invisible life to the visible, of the sub-conscious life within us, our obscure motives and instincts, to our conscious actions, feelings and outlooks' (606).

Garnett classified the novella as a 'psychological masterpiece' and went on to argue that it caught the 'infinite shades of the white man's uneasy, disconcerted and fantastic relations with the exploited barbarism of Africa; it implies the acutest analysis of the deterioration of the white man's morale, when he is let loose from European restraint' ('Mr Conrad's New Book', 606).

This experience is felt to be 'too strong meat for the ordinary reader' because of what Garnett defines as the complexity of the narrative technique – 'which calls for close attention on the reader's part' – but also because of the 'subtlety of its criticism of life' (606).

The unsigned review in the *Manchester Guardian* on 10 December 1902 initially appeared untroubled by Conradian technique, arguing that 'Youth' and 'Heart of Darkness' 'follow Mr Conrad's particular convention; they are the outpourings of Marlow's experience' (3). Yet it is clearly his sense of Conrad's 'particular convention' which leads the critic to suggest that neither text will be accessible to the general reader – 'it would be useless to pretend that they can be very widely read' (3) since 'Even to those who are most impressed an excitement so sustained and prolonged, in which we are braced to encounter so much that menaces and appals, must be something of a strain' (3).

'Heart of Darkness' is characterised as 'a destructive experience' (3), only lightened by the ending which is said to bring 'us back to the familiar, reassuring region of common emotions' (3). The reviewer stresses those aspects of Conrad which enabled critics to link him with Stevenson and Kipling as some sort of adventure novelist, with comments claiming that he offers 'a great expression of the world's mystery and romance' (3) or that 'he is the greatest of sea-writers' (3). An authoritative rejection of Conrad's impressionistic prose technique came in Arthur Quiller-Couch's (or 'Q.' as he was known) review, 'Recent Fiction: Some Stories by Joseph Conrad'. Whilst Q. accepted that Conrad's technique provides a certain rhetorical vigour, he argued that much of his prose is little more than 'wordy underbrush' (1903: 224) which detracted from the true business of fiction. Q. lamented that Conrad's narrative technique was too often thwarted by what he terms 'attacks of analytic meditation' (1903: 224) and he commented that the 'entanglement of psychological with external phenomena' was 'more or less wearying' (1903: 224). Like many early reviewers, Q. was most troubled by those aspects of Conradian textual practice which were to inform what was to become modernism.

'The End of the Tether'

The *Manchester Guardian* felt that the story was the weakest part of the *Youth* collection, declaring that 'it is not of the amazing quality of Mr Conrad at his best' (Sherry 1973: 134). By contrast, the *Times Literary Supplement* felt that the story was the best thing in the collection, believing that it should have formed 'the forefront of the book' (Sherry 1973: 137). *The Athenaeum* concurred, suggesting that the tale was 'fascinating: '[a] more deeply moving story it would be hard

to find, vivid, full of movement, even of stirring incident, yet piercingly analytic'
(Sherry 1973: 139).

Later critical response

'Youth'

Whilst a minor work, 'Youth' tends to be looked on fondly by the critics and has
received much coverage as an exemplary short story. Much early criticism has
now dated but John Howard Willis's essay 'A Neglected Masterpiece: Conrad's
"Youth"' (1963) is worth consulting for its concise comparative reading of the
role of Marlow and the narrative point of view of *The Nigger of the 'Narcissus'*.
Norman Sherry's *Conrad's Eastern World* (1966) provides a transcript of the
inquiry into the loss of the *Palestine* (1966: 297–8). Lawrence Graver argues that
'the dominant feature of Marlow's narration was the careful alternation between
realism and romance, a movement which 'eventually establishes the delicate and
distinctive tone of the story' (1969: 72–3). He also studies the 'thematic as well as
technical advantages to be gained from using Marlow', suggesting that the gap in
time between experience and narration enabled Conrad to dramatise 'the conflict
between egoism and altruism' (1969: 75). Alan Freidman has examined the
development of Marlow in 'Conrad's Picaresque Narrator: Marlow's Journey
from "Youth" through *Chance*' (1974), whilst James Matthews examines the
older and younger Marlow and 'Ironic Symbolism in Conrad's "Youth", (1974).
Similar material is covered in John Howard Weston's ' "Youth": Conrad's Irony
and Time's Darkness' (1974). Juliet McLauchlan offers a study of all three stories
in 'Conrad's "Three Ages of Man": The *Youth* Volume' (1975). Pierre Vitoux
examines Marlow's development as a storyteller in 'Marlow: The Changing Narrator of Conrad's Fiction' (1975). Todd Willy has studied the relationship
between text and context in 'The Call to Imperialism in Conrad's "Youth": An
Historical Reconstruction' (1980). Kenneth Simons *The Ludic Imagination: A
Reading of Joseph Conrad* (1985), commences his study with an analysis of
'Youth'. Hugh Epstein examines contextual matters in his 'The Duality of
"Youth": Some Literary Contexts' (1996). Douglas Kerr offers a further perspec-
tive on 'Conrad and the "Three Ages of Man": "Youth", *The Shadow Line*, "The
End of the Tether"' (1998). The topic is also studied in Richard Niland's 'Ageing
and Individual Experience in "Youth" and "Heart of Darkness"' (2004).

'Heart of Darkness'

'Heart of Darkness' has become one of the most widely read works by Conrad. It
has provoked controversy for its depiction of Africa and Africans and its perspective on women. Its sources in Conrad's own experience have been exhaustively
studied and its literary antecedents have been relentlessly hunted out. It has also
proved a creative stimulus to other artists, inspiring John Powell's composition
for piano and orchestra *Rhapsodie Nègre* (1917); T. S. Eliot's poems *The Waste
Land* (1922) and 'The Hollow Men' (1925); Graham Greene's *A Burnt Out Case*
(1961), and V. S. Naipaul's *A Bend in the River* (1979). Francis Ford Coppola
drew on the novella for his Vietnam film *Apocalypse Now* (1979).

The bewildering variety of critical approaches that the novel has generated can be confusing for first-time readers. Among the best starting points is Ian Watt's chapter in *Conrad in the Nineteenth Century* (1979) which offers an overview of the story's origins, aesthetic, and political concerns. Norman Sherry's *Conrad's Western World* (1971) provides detail on the historical background, with eleven of the book's thirty-two chapters devoted to contexts for the novella covering each phase of the journey and examining the raw material which Conrad drew upon for the text. Robert Kimborough's Norton Critical Edition (1988) includes a wealth of extracts from background and source information along with material from major critical studies. There are useful surveys of the early critical responses to the story in Bruce Harkness (ed.) *Conrad's 'Heart of Darkness' and the Critics* (1960) whilst Robert Burden's *Heart of Darkness: An Introduction to the Variety of Criticism* (1991) provides a concise survey of the novella's critical fortunes from publication to the late 1980s. This work is complemented by the fuller but less readable study by Nicolas Tredell, *Joseph Conrad: Heart of Darkness* (1998). Harold Bloom (ed.) *Joseph Conrad's 'Heart of Darkness'* (1987b) provides extracts from the major studies along with a selection of modern responses. Ross Murfin (ed.) *Joseph Conrad: 'Heart of Darkness': A Case Study in Contemporary Criticism* (1989) outlines some major literary theoretical approaches to the text. Keith Carabine (ed.) *Joseph Conrad: Critical Assessments*, Vol. II (1992) provides full text reprints of some major essays from the 1970s to 1990s, with a particular focus on post-colonial issues.

In a 1975 lecture, the African writer Chinua Achebe famously denounced the novella, arguing that in its depiction of Africa and Africans Conrad was revealed as 'a thoroughgoing racist' (reprinted in Carabine 1992: II, 393–404 [399]). The essay provoked much debate, including responses by Cedric Watts (available in Carabine 1992: II, 405–18), Wilson Harris and Francis B. Singh (reprinted in part in Kimborough 1988: 262–8, 268–85). There is a concise and coherent rebuttal of Achebe's arguments by Robert Hampson in his 'Introduction' to his Penguin Classics edition of the novel (Hampson 1995: xxx–xxxviii). For a more detailed account of Conrad's representation of inter-ethnic tensions arising from imperialism see, among others, Benita Parry's *Conrad and Imperialism* (1983) and Andrea White's *Joseph Conrad and the Adventure Tradition* (1993).

The novella's place in the development of English modernism has been another fruitful topic for critical debate. Burden (1991: 35–44) provides a concise survey of work in this field and Kenneth Graham's essay on 'Conrad and Modernism' and his study *Indirections of the Novel: James, Conrad and Forster* (1990) offers helpful overviews of this topic. Other recommended work on this subject includes Ian Watt's *Conrad in the Nineteenth Century* (1979), Allon White's *The Uses of Obscurity: The Fictions of Early Modernism* (1981), J. Hillis-Miller's *Poets of Reality* (1985), Edward Said's *The World, the Text and the Critic* (1983), Michael Levenson's *Modernism and the Fate of Individuality* (1991), Daphna Erdinast-Vulcan's *Joseph Conrad and the Modern Temper* (1991), and Con Coroneos's *Space, Conrad and Modernity* (2002).

Questions arising from the novella's representation of women are forcefully raised by Nina Pelikan Strauss in 'The Exclusion of the Intended from Secret Sharing in "Heart of Darkness"' (1987). Strauss examines the ways in which the text excludes female readers and panders to male readers' identification with notions of heroic action. Strauss's reading explores the implications for literary studies of its ongoing celebration of a narrative in which women are excluded as audience. This powerful reading generated a new vein of critical inquiry, further opened up by Peter Hyland, 'The Little Woman in "Heart of Darkness"' (1988); Joanna Smith, '"Too Beautiful Altogether": Patriarchal Ideology in "Heart of Darkness"', (1989); Ruth Nadelhaft *Joseph Conrad* (1991) and Rita Bode '"They . . . Should Be out of It": The Women of "Heart of Darkness"' (1994).

'The End of the Tether'

An early critical study, focusing on Captain Whalley, is offered by William Moynihan in 'Conrad's "The End of the Tether": A New Reading' (1958). Edward Said's *Joseph Conrad and the Fiction of Autobiography* (1966) offers a suggestive account of the philosophical ingenuity of the tale, noting that Whalley represents a doomed attempt to 'create a kind of self consistency' within which 'the blinder he becomes the more he clings to an outmoded code of action' (1966: 116). Lawrence Graver suggests that the tale was overlong because of contractual requirements relating to its serialisation and argued that Conrad's main interest lay in probing 'the weakness that led so inexorably to . . . [Whalley's] criminal act' (1969: 117). He claims that Conrad 'spent far too much energy building up Whalley as an heroic figure and not nearly enough establishing his culpability and justifying his punishment in dramatic terms' (1969: 118). Sanford Pinsker examines Whalley's moral blindness and its affinities with Arthur Miller's Willy Loman in the punningly titled '"The End of the Tether": Joseph Conrad's Death of A Sailsman' (1971–2). Daniel Schwarz '"A Lonely Figure Walking Purposefully": The Significance of Captain Whalley in Conrad's "The End of the Tether"' (1975) examines the story as a study of ageing.

Typhoon and Other Stories (1903)

The volume comprised the stories 'Typhoon', 'Amy Foster', 'Falk: A Reminiscence' and 'To-morrow'. It was published by Heinemann in the UK but in the USA, 'Typhoon' had already been published as a single volume by Putnam in 1902, and in that market the other stories appeared in a separate volume entitled *Falk, Amy Foster, To-morrow: Three Stories*, published by McClure Phillips in 1903. Conrad was unhappy about the separate publication of 'Typhoon', since he had given careful thought to the volume's organisation. All of the stories bar 'Falk' had been previously serialised: 'Typhoon' in *Pall Mall Magazine* (January–March 1902), 'Amy Foster' in the *Illustrated London News* (December 1903) and 'To-morrow' in *Pall Mall Magazine* (August 1902).

Commentary

'Typhoon'

'Typhoon', one of Conrad's most celebrated sea pieces, tells the tale of the steamship *Nan Shan's* voyage from an unnamed Eastern port (Singapore is suggested in the Author's Note) for Fu Chau in southern China. Begun as a short story in October 1900 it grew to a 28,000-word novella by its completion in early January 1901.

The story opens with a portrait of the self-assured Captain MacWhirr – a man who appears to have no imagination and cannot understand metaphorical language but is nonetheless an accomplished sailor with an eye for detail. The *Nan Shan* is taking Chinese labourers back to their homes, but once at sea the ship runs into unexpectedly bad weather. The Captain insists on remaining on course, dismissing first mate Jukes's suggestion of altering direction on the grounds that 'there's just so much dirty weather knocking about the world and the proper thing is to go through it' (34). Yet the storm breaks with such fury 'that it appeared incompatible with the existence of any ship whatever' (41). Whilst Jukes is temporarily overwhelmed with despair, the stolid MacWhirr remains composed. In the midst of the storm, the Bosun struggles up to the bridge to report that the Chinamen 'had broken adrift with their boxes' (59) and are fighting in the ship's hold over money that has spilt out of their trunks. Jukes is despatched to restore order below deck and, with the help of the crew, manages to stop the conflict. Whilst there is a lull in the weather, MacWhirr consults his barometer again and realises that 'the worst was to come' (84). The narrative does not show us the full horror of the storm, leaving it occur 'off stage' between Chapters 5 and 6. Chapter 6 moves us further away from the storm by offering the perspectives contained in three separate accounts of its impact, filtered via the perceptions of their individual readers. We are given Mrs MacWhirr's bored reading of her husband's letter, the engineer's wife's reading of his letter, and Jukes's jolly letter to his friend working on a liner. Jukes's concluding judgement, that MacWhirr is a 'stupid man', has not been borne out by the narrative – MacWhirr successfully sailed the ship through the typhoon, bringing it and all hands to shore again in safety and equitably redistributes the money that caused the Chinamen to fight.

Despite its serious subject, the story is, at times, a deeply comic tale. Much humour derives from MacWhirr's inability to engage imaginatively with his world but, by the end of the story, this humour has been dissipated and there is an attempt to evoke sympathy for him when we see the disinterested way in which his wife responds to his letter. In its closure, the narrative confidently deploys multiple perspectives, but there is no meditative engagement with the psychology of action here and Conrad's working titles ('An Equitable Division' and 'A Skittish Cargo' (CL2: 169, 237) seem to place the emphasis squarely on the 'superficial how' (*Lord Jim*, 56) rather than the fundamental why of this particular affair. Perhaps, as Conrad wrote to Blackwood, the story derives its interest from the morality of action: 'A wrestle with wind and weather has a moral value like the primitive acts of faith on which may be built a doctrine of salvation and a rule of life' (26 August 1901, CL2: 354).

'Amy Foster'

The story was written in the summer of 1901, whilst Conrad was working with Ford Madox Ford on their jointly authored novel *Romance* (see Life and Contexts, pp. 12–13). Tentative early titles included 'A Castaway' and 'A Husband' (CL2: 330) and Conrad described it as a 'dismal story' whose theme was 'the essential difference between the races' (CL2: 402). In this short fiction, written ostensibly for cash from the magazine market, we can see Conrad deploying a simplified version of the techniques he was using in his more self-consciously artistic works.

Conrad glossed the action as follows:

> Story of an Austro-Polish highlander emigrating to America who is shipwrecked on the English coast. He roams around the countryside. No one understands him. He is tracked down like a wild beast. A farmer takes him in. He marries a good fool of a girl, a villager. But he persists in speaking his language to her and their child. That annoys his wife. She begins to fear him. He falls ill. She watches over him. He is thirsty and asks for a drink – but in his own language rather than hers. She doesn't understand. He can no longer understand why she doesn't stir. He becomes angry, he gets up – his alien noises frighten her and she runs away, carrying the child. He dies without ever understanding.
>
> (CL2: 401–2)

What Conrad leaves out here is the role of Dr Kennedy whose narration makes this story, in technical terms, a miniature of the major fiction. Kennedy is fascinated by Yanko, claiming at one point that only he and Amy 'alone in all the land . . . could see his very real beauty' (134). He tells the story of Yanko's life based on what he learnt 'fragmentarily in the course of two years' (117), pointing up his early mistreatment by the villagers to offer a critique of their insular Englishness. Yanko is said to find the people of Colebrook 'hardhearted' (128) and at times would not have known that 'whether he was in a Christian country at all' (129). His experience is implicitly contrasted with Kennedy's, who has come to the region 'from choice' in an act that is seen as evidence of a 'destroyed' ambition (106). Kennedy is described as a man of 'corrosive' intelligence, with 'an investigating habit' and an 'unappeasable curiosity which believes that there is a particle of general truth in every mystery' (ibid.). He tells Yanko's story as a narrative of tragic poignancy which arises from 'irreconcilable differences and from the fear of the incomprehensible' (108). Conrad is careful to alert readers to the gaps in Kennedy's knowledge and the fact that he 'can't follow step by step' the history of Yanko's 'development' (131). Indeed he can be accused of playing on his own ambiguous social position in Colebrook and of overemphasising Amy's simplicity and plainness. Tim Willcocks's script for the 1997 film adaptation of the story emphasised this aspect of Kennedy (Willcocks 1998: ix).

'Falk – A Reminiscence'

The story was written between January and March 1901. 'Falk' is a convoluted tale of courtship, spiced with a little cannibalism, and although Conrad felt that serial publication was refused because of the cannibalism, it seems more likely that the rich vein of sexual references meant the story got nowhere with magazine editors. The object of this sexual focus is Captain Hermann's niece whose 'physical personality' transfixes the narrator and the tug-owning Falk (151).

The narrative begins with a frame narrative in which a group of old friends meet for a supper that turns out to be 'execrable' (145) and they seek consolation by turning to yarning over wine. One of the company tells the story of Falk, the sole tugboat operator at an Eastern port who felt that the narrator was his rival for the affections of Hermann's voluptuous niece.

Hermann and the narrator's vessels are both ready to leave and the narrator is booked as the first to depart, but Falk impetuously decides to tow Hermann out first. In consequence, the narrator has to spend another day in port and goes to Schomberg's hotel for tiffin where he learns of Falk's aversion to meat and his failures with women. The narrator eventually encounters Falk, and in their conversation he puts him to rights regarding his feelings for Hermann's niece. In order to gain Falk's services, the narrator agrees to act as go-between and secure the niece for Falk. Hermann is minded to accept the proposal, but first Falk wishes to make a confession of his past cannibalistic deed, and this revelation outrages the family minded Hermann. Falk explains the grim circumstances of his cannibalism to the narrator and his despair that this incident now appears to be preventing him from marrying. Hermann, however, soon comes to terms with the idea and, despite his dislike of Falk, agrees to the marriage on the grounds that it saves him the expense of taking his niece home with the rest of the family.

The tale relies on Falk's secret to achieve its initial effects but repays rereading as, once known, the hidden motivation for Falk's actions add a rich irony to the early parts of the tale. Conrad explained his intention as 'contrast of commonplace sentimentality with the uncorrupted view of an almost primitive man (Falk himself) who regards the preservation of life as the supreme moral law' (CL2: 402).

'To-morrow'

'To-morrow' was written in January 1902 and tells the story of widowed old Captain Hagberd who plays out his days obsessively awaiting the return of his long-lost son Harry. Set in the same region as 'Amy Foster', it shares something of that story's mood. Conrad told his agent that the story was 'Conrad adapted down to the needs of a magazine' but that it was 'by no means a potboiler' (CL2: 373). Its central twist is that when Harry finally returns, his father refuses to believe that it is him and the feckless son departs. The real focus of the tale is not so much Hagberd's obsession but the effect it has on his brutal neighbour's long-suffering daughter Bessie who, in his fantasy, Hagberd had planned to marry off to his son. When Harry returns, he styles himself as a 'Gambucino', a restless man of the type he has encountered whilst prospecting for gold in Mexico who 'never stopped long where there were houses; they had no wife, no chick, no home, never a chum. You couldn't be friends with a Gambucino, they were too restless' (271). Bessie is embarrassed to have old Hagberd's plans revealed to Harry and equally disappointed that his fantasy has no basis in reality – she gives Harry money to leave and he expresses his gratitude in a cynical kiss. Bessie is overwhelmed by this and is left 'to totter silently back towards her stuffy little inferno of a cottage' (276). Bessie's predicament is sensitively handled and some commentators have suggested that Conrad achieved a more sympathetic portrayal of young womanhood here than he did with Amy Foster.

Early reviews

The reviews of the collection tended to concentrate upon the title story. The *Morning Post* declared that 'Mr Conrad has no equal on the seas' and praised the depiction of MacWhirr (Sherry 1973: 143), noted the 'subtlety' of the depiction of Falk (144), and suggested that 'Amy Foster' was a glimpse 'of pain and terror' (144). 'To-morrow' was described as 'a little masterpiece' and 'these four stories are sufficient in themselves to place the author in the first rank of living writers' (Sherry 1973: 144). The *Daily Mail* argued for Conrad as a sea writer and praised 'Typhoon' as 'the most elaborate storm piece one can recall in English Literature' (Sherry 1973: 146). After reflecting briefly on 'Amy Foster' and 'Falk', the reviewer asserted that 'one of the most remarkable of Mr Conrad's qualities . . . is his treatment of the passion of love' (Sherry 1973: 147). *The Academy* suggested that 'we never question the truth of Mr Conrad's characters. We may sometimes dislike his method, we may find fault with his construction, but the essential human element of his dramas stands beyond cavil. In a word, his psychology has the accuracy of brilliant diagnosis' (Sherry 1973: 153). The reviewer went on to identify a key facet of Conrad's technique: 'This indirectness, this returning upon himself, this effect, often disconcerting, of an abruptly introduced outside comment, are inherent parts of the extraordinary subjectivity of Mr Conrad's method' (Sherry 1973: 153).

The focus on technique led the reviewer to praise 'Falk' as 'architectural, or, rather, like a mosaic, built up out of infinite fragments' and to suggest that 'the apparent diffuseness of his method' indicated the 'eager searching of a masterful mind' (Sherry 1973: 154). 'Amy Foster' was praised as 'bare life, handled with extraordinary skill – life free from any kind of sentimentality, bare to the nerve' (Sherry 1973: 154). Quiller-Couch in *The Bookman* offered a genial overview of what by now was becoming accepted as the Conradian style in which the narration weaves 'A situation round with emotions, scruples, doubts, hesitancies. Misunderstandings, understandings, half-understandings; cutting the web sometimes with the fiercest of strokes; anon patiently spinning it again for another slice' (Sherry 1973: 156).

His review highlighted 'To-morrow' as the finest of the four stories, but he also praised the depiction of MacWhirr. The unnamed reviewer in *The Speaker* was less enthusiastic about 'To-morrow' but noted that it was 'saved from the mere cleverness of the good magazine tale by the fine interview between the girl . . . and the young roving sailor' (Sherry 1973: 158). 'Amy Foster' was declared 'one of the most perfect short stories' (Sherry 1973: 157) whilst 'Falk' and 'Typhoon' were praised for their capacity to hold the imagination.

Later critical response

'Typhoon'

F. R. Leavis is an influential champion of 'Typhoon' in *The Great Tradition* (1948), where he praises it above *Lord Jim*, highlighting the presentation of men rather than the evocation of the storm as central to its achievements. Lawrence Graver outlines the background to the collection's composition and its serialisation and argues that the story revealed 'the comic triumph of a naïve, unimaginative hero' but remains 'one of Conrad's least problematical works' (1969: 95, 98). William R. Hussey examines the strategies of characterisation in the story in 'He Was Spared that Annoyance' (1971). Dennis Walsh reads Jukes in the light of the biblical myth of the Fall in 'Conrad's "Typhoon" and the Book of Genesis' (1974). Charles Schuster examines the tale's comic aspects in his 'Comedy and the Limits of Language in Conrad's "Typhoon"' (1984). Language is also the focus of Joseph Kolupke's 'Elephants, Empires, and Blind Men: A Reading of the Figurative Language in Conrad's "Typhoon"' (1988), and Amar Acheraïou continues to mine this productive seam in his recent essay 'Floating Words: Sea as Metaphor of Style in "Typhoon"' (2004).

'Amy Foster'

Robert Andreach examines the role of Dr Kennedy as one of 'The Two Narrators of "Amy Foster"' (1965). Lawrence Graver also considers Kennedy's role, suggesting that he is 'sometimes strained and unconvincing' (1969: 107–8). Gail Fraser studies 'Conrad's Revisions to "Amy Foster"' (1992), noting that there were over 700 changes between manuscript and serial publication and a further 100 between serial and published volume. The thrust of these was to 'involve the reader more deeply in Yanko's isolation' (1992: 515). More recent work on the story includes Hugh Epstein '"Where He Is Not Wanted": Impression and Articulation in "The Idiots" and "Amy Foster"' (1991); Richard Ruppel's 'Yanko Goorall in the Heart of Darkness: "Amy Foster" as Colonialist Text' (1996) and Jurgen Kramer, 'What the Country Doctor "Did Not See": The Limits of the Imagination in "Amy Foster"' (2003). The story has often been studied for its perspective on England and Englishness (see Life and Contexts, pp. 18–20).

'Falk – A Reminiscence'

Bruce Johnson's 'Conrad's "Falk": Manuscript and Meaning' (1965) remains a useful account of the characterisation of Falk. Lawrence Graver classes it as one of Conrad's major stories and suggests that the tale is, at its heart, about 'how a young, inexperienced captain learns that there are critical moments in life when the codes of society are useless against the elemental pressures of instinctive egoism' (1969: 100). Daniel Schwarz examines 'The Significance of the Narrator in Conrad's "Falk"' (1971) and Joe Kehler looks at the tensions between the experiencing and experienced narrative points of view in 'The Centrality of the Narrator in Conrad's "Falk"' (1974). Tony Tanner argues that Falk is worthy of comparison with 'Heart of Darkness's Kurtz or Victory's Axel Heyst as a social outcast and pariah in his '"Gnawed Bones" and "Artless Tales": Eating and Narrative in Conrad' (1976). Unlike these figures, Falk 'was not guilty of a moment's weakness' and Tanner's persuasive reading goes on to unpack the links between hunger and sexual desire as well as drawing in anthropological material to conclude that in this tale of the eating of 'the uneatable' the narrator has to 'speak the unspeakable' (1976: 36). David Gill includes the story in his larger study of 'The Fascination of the Abomination: Conrad and Cannibalism' (1999).

'To-morrow'

The story has received very little critical coverage, with recent works on the short fiction neglecting it entirely. Often seen as a companion piece to 'Amy Foster', Lawrence Graver suggests that whilst it had the kernel of a typical Conrad story – 'an obsessive egoist', a 'simple minded altruist' and 'a man who acts from obsessive self interest' (1969: 110) – neither Bessie nor her father are sufficiently realised to act as foils to Harry. Daniel Schwarz classes the tale as 'underrated', suggesting that it was in fact sharply 'ironic about conventional turn-of-the-century morality that requires a woman to devote herself to the care of a barbaric father' (1980: 119). Ted Billy suggests that the story's 'melodramatic conclusion . . . anticipates the "madness and despair" refrain associated with Winnie Verloc's predicament in *The Secret Agent*' (1997: 224) (see Works, **pp. 69–73**).

Nostromo (1904)

Nostromo was begun in December 1902, and by January 1903 Conrad wrote to his friend Ford Madox Ford (see Life and Contexts, **pp. 12–13**) pessimistically asserting that 'I believe it will end in something silly and saleable' (CL3: 3–4). The novel was completed in August 1904 and, as with *Lord Jim*, Conrad burdened himself with serialisation prior to the work's completion – the novel ran in *T.P.'s Weekly* from 29 January to 7 October 1904. Like *Lord Jim*, the novel grew from Conrad's original conception, and a host of external circumstances conspired to delay progress. In part, the delay was temperamental, as Conrad wrote slowly but, as the year passed, he and Jessie were afflicted with health problems and then his bankers failed, which forced him to fall back on his agent and his friends for funds. One consequence of these domestic illnesses was that Conrad began to use professional typists, and some of *Nostromo* was dictated (CL3: 128). Ford's support during the writing of the novel was also important – at a point when continued serialisation looked in jeopardy, Conrad told his anxious agent that his friend was 'in possession of my innermost mind (and of my notes) on that story [and] is confident of his ability to finish it should something unforeseen occur' (CL3: 24). Ford did write a few pages of the novel (a section of Part 2, Chapter 5) whilst Conrad was unwell.

Conrad's 'Author's Note', written in 1917, made the unsubstantiated claim that the germ of the story came from a tale he heard when he sailed to the West Indies or the Gulf of Mexico and read of again in a book of sea journeys. The 'Note' goes on to detail the people from his own life on whom he drew for characters in the novel: the French sailor Dominic Cervoni whom he met as a young man in Marseilles was a prototype for Nostromo and the (unknown) Polish girl – 'my first love' (xlvi) – on whom he claims to have based Antonia Avellanos. Some critics have suggested that aspects of Decoud's character drew upon Conrad himself, and others have read the troubled history of Costaguana as an imaginative reworking of Poland's nineteenth-century upheavals. Whatever its origins in Conrad's private experience, the novel itself is a complex work which deploys an artful narrative organisation to tell the events of the turbulent history of the fictional South American republic of Costaguana. Whilst much of the action is focused in a three-week period, with many of the events occurring over just four days, the novel dealt with the republic's history over a seventy-year sweep of time, producing a text of rich complexity and astonishing ambition. Many first-time readers struggle with the novel because of its complex layering of events, but those who persevere are rewarded with one of twentieth-century English literature's finest novels.

Commentary

A simple summary might frame the novel as the story of the consequences of Charles Gould's attempt to revive his father's silver mine. An exile returning to an endeavour and country which claimed the lives of his forebears, Gould brings with him to Costaguana emotional support in the guise of his English wife and financial backing from American capitalist Holroyd. The mine becomes successful and Gould declares his support for the progressive government of Ribiera, but a military coup, lead by the Montero brothers Pedrito and Sotillo, sees Ribiera flee for his life over the mountains, bringing the insurrection into the heart of the coastal province of Sulaco. The rebellion sparks off local riots and the silver mine itself is under threat. Gould agrees that the most recent shipment of silver should be smuggled out of Sulaco by Nostromo, the leader of the dockworkers, and Martin Decoud who, like Gould, is a returned exile. They take the silver out by small boat but, running in the dark, they collide with Sotillo's troop ship; escaping unharmed, they bury the silver on a nearby island. Nostromo returns to the mainland and undertakes a daring ride across the mountains to alert loyal Ribierist troops to the plight of Sulaco and, thanks to his heroic intervention, they arrive in time to save the city and its leaders from Sotillo. Decoud, alone and despairing amidst the solitude of the island, knows nothing of this and kills himself, fearing that the rebels have overrun Sulaco. The novel draws to its close with the province enjoying renewed prosperity, but Nostromo has now become embittered with his short-lived fame and has kept the secret of the buried silver to himself, gradually stealing from it. He arranges for old Giorgio Viola to be made keeper of the island's lighthouse since, as the fiancé to one of Viola's daughters, this provides him with a cover story for his frequent visits. Nostromo is, however, deceiving his fiancé and secretly meeting with her younger sister, and on one of his visits to take more silver he is shot by Viola who believes him to be a thief. The novel ends with his fiancé declaring her undying fidelity to his memory.

The novel opens with an omniscient narrator setting the scene for the drama to come with an evocation of the Golfo Placido and its legend of lost treasure. Drawing on the perspective of Englishman Captain Mitchell, the local representative of the Oceanic Steam Navigation Company, who alludes to his involvement in the events of some four years past, we are then given an account of the Monterist revolt's impact on Sulaco and its environs. Part 1, Chapters 2–4, all of Part 2 and most of Part 3, save the final three chapters, are taken up with the revolt and its aftermath. The following table offers a chronology of its central events. This table is based on Hartley S. Spatt's chronology presented in his essay 'Nostromo's Chronology: The Shaping of History' (1976) and is supplemented by that given in Keith Carabine's 'Introduction' to the World's Classics edition of the novel (1984:

xxvi–xxx). Page references to key events in the novel are given in parentheses:

Date	Events
21 April	Battle of Socorro, Ribiera Defeated (212).
28 April	Barrios sent by sea to Cayta (212) in an attempt to 'outflank the Monsterist forces in southern Costaguana' (Carabine 1984: xxvi).
29 April	The silver arrives in Sulaco at 5 a.m.
1 May	Riots break out and the Sulaco leaders accept the aid of the bandit leader Hernández.
2 May	Nostromo and Decoud meet in the offices of the *Porvenir* (4 a.m.) (224).
	Ribiera arrives on a lame mule and is aided by Nostromo (225) to escape by boat. Decoud joins the fight at the Amarilla Club (6 a.m.–noon).
	The Monterist committee is formed (8 p.m.) (228).
	Barrios reaches Cayta (233) and Decoud reveals his plans to remove the silver.
3 May	With Sotillo closing in by sea (244) and Pedrito having seized the rail head (243), the Blancos leave for Los Hatos woods and Hernández's aid (351–62). That evening, Decoud writes a letter to his sister (223–49) before setting of with Nostromo and the silver. Their lighter is struck by Sotillo's ship (291). Sotillo arrives in Sulaco 'just before midnight' (Carabine 1984: xxvii).
4 May	During the night, Sotillo questions Dr Monygham and Captain Mitchell. Nostromo and Decoud bury the silver on the Great Isabel. At dawn, Nostromo swims back to shore leaving Decoud on the island. In Sulaco, Pedrito's army arrives (384–94). Later that day, Nostromo awakens after fourteen hours of sleep (411–12), returning to Sulaco where he meets Monygham in the Custom House (425).
5 May	Nostromo rides to Cayta to alert Barrios, arriving on 12 May (456).
16 May	Decoud commits suicide at Dawn (500–1).
17 May	Nostromo jumps from Barrios' ship and swims to the Great Isabel (evening). Barrios attacks by sea (483) and Pepe leads the miners to attack by land, destroying Sotillo and Pedrito's forces.

Readers can steer their way through the novel's disrupted chronology once they realise that 'the 24-hour stretch from the departure of Nostromo and Decoud with the silver to Monygham's confrontation with Nostromo occupies nearly a third of the novel [244–472] and is told more or less sequentially' (Carabine 1984: xxviii).

Nostromo has an experimental approach to narrative organisation, with complex patterns of repetition and shifts in point of view that frustrate the reader's attempts to grasp the events of a three-week period in the turbulent history of the imaginary republic of Costaguana. Whilst the novel uses an author-ial omniscient narrator, much use is made of focalisation and indirect discourse so that, at times, the narrative point of view is close to that of individual characters. One of the main narrative viewpoints is provided by Captain Mitchell, whose lopsided perspective on events seldom coincides with the 'profound knowledge of men and things in the country' (11) that he takes such pride in possessing. As Carabine suggests, on a first reading we are placed in the position of one of Mitchell's listeners '[s]tunned and as it were annihilated mentally by a sudden surfeit of sights, sounds, names, facts, and complicated information imperfectly apprehended' (486–7). Mitchell carries the narrative perspective at the beginning and end of the novel (Part 1 Chapter 2 and Part 3 Chapters 2 and 10), whilst at other points the narration is close to the perspective of journalist and reluctant revolutionist Martin Decoud (Part 2, Chapter 7, also Part 3 Chapter 10, 496–501), Nostromo himself, Mrs Gould, and Holroyd, who all act as focalisers). As Jakob Lothe has argued, whilst Conrad is at pains to establish the 'marked distance in insight and understanding between the narrator and the different characters . . . the distance is certainly much less between the narrator and Decoud' (1989: 185).

Decoud's letter to his sister, which forms the basis of much of Part 2 Chapter 7, provides a useful synopsis of the action to date and also establishes 'Decoud's pivotal position as a main character associated with most of the various cross currents of action in the novel' (Lothe 1989: 193). The other notable feature of Conrad's narrative method in *Nostromo* is the use of time shifts, which, in a novel about the making of history, tend to work for relativism, undermining the signifi-cance of individual acts. The novel opens with an audacious move back in time that spans Part 1 Chapters 2–8 – tracing the circumstances that lead up to deposed dictator Ribiera's flight from the capital to Sulaco so that the man we witness arriving on a lame mule (11) is met again in his full pomp at the opening of the railway (Part 1 Chapter 5) as the narrative runs back through events which are separated in time by a year. Indeed, the text as a whole is framed by the Mitchell focalised narration in Part 1 Chapter 2 and that of Part 3 Chapter 10, which occurs some four years after the main events of the novel have taken place. Within these time shifts, Conrad frequently repeats a scene from a new viewpoint – for example, the riot of Part 1 Chapter 3 is retold from Decoud's perspective in Part 2 Chapter 7.

As befits a panoramic historical novel, there is no single character around whom theme and action are centrally organised – at times one is hard pressed to group the novel's many characters into minor and major figures since all are shown to have some part in the unfolding of the action. Since this is not simply a political novel of revolution but also a work about the psychology of nation-building and, more fundamentally, the human consequences of the pursuit of power, the central characters might be defined as those whom we are given access to in both their public and private spheres. Centrality in this novel is understood not so much in terms of impact on plot but more in relation to the narrative space afforded to a character's activities or to reflections upon them. Thus, the American Banker Holroyd or the old Garabaldino Giorgio Viola, whilst import-ant minor figures, do not hold our attention in the way that Decoud, Charles and

Emilia Gould, Dr Monygham or Nostromo do. These characters are often presented via the narrator's citing of their publicly known roles and personas
and, as more is learnt of their private motivations and beliefs, these strike the
reader as increasingly partial and inadequate. In Costaguana, according to
Monygham, a 'nickname may be the best record of a success' (316) but Nostromo, it could be said, comes to believe his own publicity and so deludes himself
into imagining that given the huge public esteem in which he is held he will be able
to live off the buried treasure and juggle the love of two women with minimal
consequences. Decoud, who begins by cynically spouting the clichés of revolution, also succumbs to the allure of his public persona, taking up arms out of
desire for Antonia, but when he finds himself removed from the sustaining buzz
of his public role, he cannot bear to remain alive. Gould discards his wife's love
as he adopts in his private domain the public role of Master of the San Tome
mine. For all three men, their public persona is shown to dominate them; for all
three it is a case of juggling the competing demands of 'treasure and love'
(566). Given this, one might want to argue, with Conrad, that in the end it is
the silver mine that is the central organising figure of the novel: 'Feared, hated,
wealthy; more soulless than any tyrant, more pitiless and autocratic than the
worst Government; ready to crush innumerable lives in the expansion of its
greatness' (521). The power of the 'material interests' to shape lives is indeed
central to the novel – it galvanises the political scene in Costaguana, destroys
the love in Emilia Gould's marriage, leads Decoud to his death and corrupts
the faithful Nostromo: it is 'the pivot of the moral and material events' (Aubry
1927: II, 296).

Early reviews

Conrad showed no interest in the serial text, allowing the editors at *T.P.'s Weekly*
to organise it as they saw fit (CL3: 91). The serial's ending was abrupt and
Conrad made substantial revision for the first edition – adding over 14,000 words
that enabled him to reflect on Nostromo's changing relationship with the hidden
silver and its impact on his public role (Carabine 1984: xx–xxv). This text
reprints the serial ending as an appendix. Despite his alterations, the book met
with mixed reviews. The *Times Literary Supplement* complained that 'the drama
is overwhelmed by the machinery' and declared that the publication of the novel
'as it stands is an artistic mistake' (Sherry 1973: 164), dismissing the book as
'shapeless' (165). *Black and White* suggested that Conrad had 'hidden what grain
of romance or of realism was in him under a multitude of words and lowering
paragraphs' (Sherry 1973: 166) and the *Daily Telegraph* criticised 'the lack of
artistic instinct which always mars his work as a whole' and went on to lament
the 'wearisome nature' of the novel's 'characteristic digressions' (Sherry 1973:
167). It took Edward Garnett, writing his first signed review of his friend's work,
to set the record straight (see Life and Contexts, pp. 11–12). He argued that the
'author's pre-eminence does not lie specifically in his psychological analysis of
character, but in the delicate relation of his characters to the whole environment'
(Sherry 1973: 175) and praised Conrad's evocation of 'this wonderful mirage of
S. American life' (175). Even Garnett's review, however, argued that the opening

account of Costaguana's history was 'somewhat lengthy' and he declared the ending 'abrupt and hurried' (Sherry 1973: 174).

Later critical response

The novel has been studied as a critique of capitalism, as a modernist *tour de force*, as a shrewd deflation of revolutionary and imperialist ambitions and as a postmodernist critique of the grand narratives of progress. Given the vast range of critical response to the novel, the first-time reader is best served by commencing their engagement with the secondary literature via an introductory guide such as Cedric Watts's *Joseph Conrad: Nostromo* (1990), Ian Watt's *Joseph Conrad: Nostromo* (1988), or Juliet McLauchlan's *Conrad Nostromo* (1977). There are some valuable essays on the novel from the late 1960s and early 1970s collected in C.B. Cox (ed.) *Conrad: Heart of Darkness, Nostromo and Under Western Eyes: A Casebook* (1981), and Keith Carabine's *Joseph Conrad: Critical Assessments* (1992) provides a judicious selection of material. Harold Bloom, ed., *Joseph Conrad's Nostromo* (1987a) offers extracts and full text reprints from selected critical work published since the 1950s.

There is useful material on the novel's narrative organisation in Jakob Lothe's *Conrad's Narrative Method* (1989), which provides a detailed study of Conrad's handing of time shifts, focalisation and the role of 'authorial narrative' (1989: 205). Jeremy Hawthorn's *Joseph Conrad: Narrative Technique and Ideological Commitment* (1990) offers a useful supplement to Lothe in its careful account of the use of the represented speech and thought of key characters. Bruce Henricksen's complex but rewarding Bahktinian study, *Nomadic Voices: Conrad and the Subject of Narrative* (1992), provides a sophisticated reading of the novel's handling of chronology. Eloise Knapp Hay's essay on the novel (1996) offers an excellent introduction to the political reading of the text, and her earlier work on it in *The Political Novels of Joseph Conrad* (1963) contains an account of the ways in which the novel worked for a critique of American imperialism. There is useful discussion of the novel's political concerns in both Irving Howe's *Politics and the Novel* (1957) and Avron Fleishman's *Conrad's Politics* (1967) (see Criticism, p. **164**). Fredric Jameson's *The Political Unconscious: Narrative as a Socially Symbolic Act* (1981) comments on the ways in which the novel is organised around 'auditory perceptions' (1981: 241) and criticises its depiction of Latin American peoples as based on Anglo stereotypes. Jameson concludes that *Nostromo* is not a political novel because Conrad makes it all too plain on whose side he sits. Daphna Erdinast Vulcan's *Joseph Conrad and the Modern Temper* (1991) examined the novel's use of mythic and historical narrative modes. Casting the book as one whose narration makes frequent 'violations of the borderline between history and fiction' (Vulcan 1991: 68) Vulcan argues that its narrative organisation works to challenge idealist framings of national development with the random and diverse mess that is history. As with many other critics, she is unconvinced by the novel's closure, seeing in Emilia Gould's complicit preservation of the public myth of Nostromo a return to the atemporal perspective on community and character which is figured in the novel's opening tale of the two gringos of Azuera. Jim Reilly's *Shadowtime: History and Representation* *in Hardy, Conrad and George Eliot* (1993) explores similar material, examining the ways in which the notion of history is problematised within the novel. Seeing *Nostromo* as 'not merely a self-conscious, but actually a self-critical text' (Reilly 1993: 143), Reilly argues that the novel's 'central and brilliant insight' (1993: 163) is to show that under capitalism 'two apparently distinct categories of experience – the value of commodities and the fact of history – are actually perversely interrelated and share a common fate in dissolution and abstraction' (163).

The Secret Agent (1907)

The novel is one of Conrad's great city novels (the other being *Under Western Eyes*; see Works, **pp. 82–7**) and it offers an unrelentingly ironic treatment of anarchist activity in London of the 1890s. The novel has been celebrated for its portrayal of the double agent Verloc, his wife Winnie and her simple-minded brother Stevie. Its presentation of the city and police owed a debt to Charles Dickens, especially his novel *Bleak House* – in *A Personal Record*, Conrad declared this novel to be 'a work of the master for which I have such an admiration, or rather such an intense and unreasoning affection, dating from the days of my childhood, that its very weaknesses are more precious to me than the strengths of other men's works' (*A Personal Record*, 124).

Early in February 1906, after a year of false starts on what was to become *Chance* (see Works, **pp. 98–103**) and ongoing but fruitless tinkering with the long-delayed novel *The Rescue* (see Works, **pp. 121–5**), Conrad began what he thought of as a short story entitled 'Verloc' (CL3: 316). In late 1905 he had already written two short stories dealing with anarchists – 'An Anarchist' and 'The Informer' – and there are many connections to be made between these tales and the novel (see Works, **pp. 74–9**). By March, Conrad noted that 'Verloc is extending' (CL3: 318), but he took until November to complete the story for its serial publication in the American journal *Ridgways: A Militant Weekly for God and Country*. Conrad saw the serial as 'an *extended, uncorrected* copy' (CL3: 364), which was just as well since the editors cut freely to suit their needs – provoking Conrad's wry comment, 'I see they are "editing" the stuff pretty severely' (CL3: 369). In May 1907, Conrad began revising the text for book publication, adding Chapter 10 and substantially reworking the ending to develop Winnie's story – 'the end is rounded properly – the theme is developed and concluded decently' (CL3: 445). The novel was published in September by Methuen in England and by Harpers in the USA.

Despite its subject matter, Conrad was cautious about emphasising the novel's political content: he told his publisher that it was 'purely a work of imagination' and that it had 'no social or philosophic intention' (CL3: 371). He believed that it was 'a distinctly new departure in my work' (CL3: 434) and suggested that it 'had some importance for me as a new departure in *genre* and as a sustained effort in ironical treatment of a melodramatic subject – which was my technical intention' (CL3: 491). The novel is set in 1886 and, whilst the 1880s did see a number of bombings in London carried out by Irish nationalists, Conrad makes no attempt to cite any of these in his work. Whilst the novel's ostensible source was the failed attempt to bomb Greenwich Observatory in 1894, allegedly supplemented by information from Ford Madox Ford (see Life and Contexts, **pp. 12–13**) about anarchist activity in the 1890s, Conrad would later suggest that he had no personal knowledge of the Observatory incident and that the novel's real 'intention' was to offer 'the history of Winnie Verloc' (Aubry 1927: II, 322). Against this might be set his comment to his publisher that the novel is 'based on the inside knowledge of a certain event in the history of active anarchism' (CL3: 371). Yet as the book's publication approached, Conrad declared that his revised subtitle – 'A Simple Tale' – was expressly chosen to avoid the story being 'misunderstood' as having 'any sort of social or polemical intention' (CL3: 446).

Commentary

Verloc, a double agent whose cover is operating a pornography shop in London's Soho, is told by his ostensibly Russian masters to plant a bomb that will be 'sufficiently startling' (30) so as to outrage the British establishment into taking measures against the revolutionary exiles from eastern Europe who are using liberal England as a base. Verloc's livelihood is under threat unless he acts swiftly, but he cannot use one of his regular associates – since this might blow his cover. He therefore decides to use his simple-minded brother-in-law Stevie as his accomplice in his attempt to blow up the Greenwich Observatory but, en route to the target, Stevie stumbles and is killed by the premature blast. When Winnie, Verloc's wife, discovers his involvement in her brother's death, she murders him and is then persuaded to flee to France by Ossipon – one of Verloc's revolutionary associates. Ossipon abandons her on the boat train and she commits suicide by jumping from the cross-channel ferry.

The novel is interested in both secrecy and agency and it explores hidden motivations and complicated intersections of circumstance and environment via what is often a bleakly comic account of familial and societal complicity and duplicity. As was the case in *Nostromo*, the reader is given access to the tensions arising from the mismatch between characters' public and private personas through a third-person omniscient narrative that makes use of focalised perspectives from central characters. There is some reliance upon disrupted chronology to create effects – thus Chapters 1–3 set the scene and Chapter 4 jumps one month forward to the day of the failed bombing. Chapters 5–7 recount the events of the day, but the narrative breaks off in Chapter 8 to recount Winnie's mother's departure to an almshouse some days prior to the bomb attempt. Chapter 9 presents Winnie overhearing Verloc's confession of complicity in Stevie's death to Inspector Heat, but the chronology is broken again by Chapter 10 which deals with the Assistant Commissioner's report on the case to Sir Ethelred. In Chapter 11 we return to the Verloc house and witness Winnie's murder of her insensitive husband. Chapter 12 deals with her flight with and eventual abandonment by Ossipon. Chapter 13, some ten days after the events of Chapters 11 and 12, reflects on Ossipon's feelings on learning that Winnie has committed suicide.

For all its focus on anarchist activity, the novel is, as Conrad suggested, essentially a domestic drama – Verloc is driven to act because 'he had a woman to provide for' (54) and the police are able to trace him because Winnie 'had the unlucky notion of sewing on the address inside Stevie's overcoat' (235). At the centre of the novel is Verloc's failure to understand Winnie, something that is evident from the very start, and his inability to grasp her true feelings in either their 'nature or . . . whole extent' (233) leads inexorably to his death. Winnie's whole life has been built around providing for Stevie, and Verloc's actions have revealed that all her investment in their dull marriage of convenience has been based upon a 'supreme illusion' (244). Her state of mind is summed up as 'astonishment and despair' (244) and since '[s]he did not see any alternative between screaming and silence' she 'instinctively . . . chose silence' (246), which Verloc misreads as acceptance of his plans for the future on the grounds that 'Winnie was always undemonstrative and silent' (252). Winnie, however, has decided that she is now 'a free woman' but 'she did not exactly know what use to make of her freedom' (254). She prepares to leave the house, but Verloc prevents her and, becoming irritated by her silence, he argues that 'you've killed him as much as I' (258). He takes to the sofa in a sulk but again misinterprets Winnie's silence as tacit acceptance of his argument and seizes what he mistakenly believes to be an opportunity to make things up. The outraged Winnie stabs him with a carving knife, gripped by 'the simple ferocity of the age of caverns and the unbalanced nervous fury of the age of bar-rooms' (263).

Whilst Verloc and Winnie engage much of our attention, Conrad's representation of the official world of police and embassies is also of interest. Chief Inspector Heat, the Assistant Commissioner, Sir Ethelred and his secretary Toodles are splendidly drawn Dickensian figures. Much of the novel's comedy derives from these characters; the stolidly procedural report to Inspector Heat on the aftermath of Stevie's death (84) being a celebrated example The anarchists themselves are largely two-dimensional characters whom Conrad himself dismissed as 'shams' (CL3: 491), although the Professor, English literature's first suicide bomber, seems to be a more dangerous figure – 'unsuspected and deadly' (311) – Conrad describes him as 'a megalomaniac of an extreme type' (311).

Winnie's role in the serial version was not pronounced – indeed she was called Minnie in that text – since it was more engaged with depicting the public world of 'the Anarchists of London' (the serial's subtitle). The novel, some 31,000 words longer, was more firmly anchored in the Verlocs' domestic life, since the bulk of the text that Conrad added to the serial came in the original last four chapters. In unravelling the interconnection between Verloc's private and public life, the novel, whilst remaining a satire of political fictions, becomes also a book about the role of women in 'the age of bar rooms' (263) – a book which chimed with growing public debate about the apparent dissolution of what, in the nineteenth century, had been generally accepted as a divinely ordained separation of life into gendered spheres. By the mid-1900s, the presence of women in political and public life of the nation was such that there were concerns that Britain's military strength could be under threat by what reactionary commentators saw as the feminisation of the public sphere (Harris 1993: 27–9). By expanding the material on Winnie, Conrad was developing that part of the novel which could speak directly to readers of the day – perhaps this was partly in his mind when, as he began the revision of the serial, he told Pinker that 'my mind runs very much on popularity just now' (CL3: 439).

In the character of Stevie, Conrad touched upon period concerns regarding what was held to be the hereditary degeneracy of the lower orders. This 'delicate' boy, with 'a vacant droop of his lower lip' (8) is a classic representation of the feeble-minded – a social type whose emergence as a public concern in the 1900s was an unforeseen consequence of the expansion of compulsory education which provided the occasion for their identification. The characteristics of this social type include some traits which are attributed to Stevie, including dumbness and aphasia (Harris 1993: 245). During the writing of the novel, Conrad would have seen press coverage of the findings of the Royal Commission on the Feeble Minded which had sat between 1904 and 1908. Conrad rather playfully subverted this type, and although Ossipon is quick to label him a degenerate, Stevie is established as an alternative moral centre to the anarchists, with none of the 'moral defectiveness' popularly associated with the feeble-minded (Harris 1993: 245). Whilst the anarchists' talk is filled with hatred, Stevie is filled with overwhelming compassion and empathy as witnessed in his concern for the plight of the grotesque cab-driver and his suffering horse (166–72). Stevie's habitual occupation is drawing circles: 'Innumerable circles, concentric, eccentric; a coruscating whirl of circles that by their tangled multitude of repeated curves, uniformity of form, and confusion of intersecting lines suggested a rendering of cosmic chaos, the symbolism of a mad art attempting the inconceivable' (45).

This response to the world is not a mad one; indeed, its emphasis on interconnection is borne out in the novel's narrative, which works to reveal the intersecting nature of public and private lives. His stumbling declaration that it is a 'Bad world for poor people' (171) has far more eloquence than the weary clichés of the anarchists. It is tempting to see in Stevie's art another evocation of period concerns as the proto-cubist painter Cézanne's work was beginning to be more widely known from 1906 and Stevie's art – all 'uniformity of form' seems comparable with Cézanne's predilection for spheres and cylindrical shapes and his notion that these abstract forms were a means to capture 'a record of personal experience and emotion' (Macleod 1999: 195, Biddiss 1977: 167).

Early reviews

The novel was met by a characteristically mixed reception – the *Manchester Guardian* complained that 'his revolutionaries and their opponents are not engaging' but noted that 'Mr. Conrad approaches them with a nimble, even whimsical humour' (Sherry 1973: 182). The *Times Literary Supplement* noted the 'fine humour' (Sherry 1973: 184) and praised the creation of the Professor and Inspector Heat. *Country Life*'s review stung Conrad since it completely misconstrued his narrative method, lamenting as an 'excrescence' the 'enormously drawn out tale' of Mrs Verloc's departure to the almshouse and declaring 'the whole thing is indecent' (Sherry 1973: 188, CL3: 48). Writing in *The Nation*, Edward Garnett was generous in his criticism but did suggest that the Verloc's were 'at certain moments ... automata' (Sherry 1973: 193). He also suggested that 'the real heroine of the story is concealed in the trivial figure of Mrs Verloc's mother in law' (193) – a suggestion to which Conrad assented (CL3: 487). Garnett's review concluded with an emphasis on Conrad's

Slavonic origins and this note was picked up in the *Glasgow News* review which declared that the novel 'does not feel . . . British at all: its is Slavonic' (Sherry 1973: 195).

Later critical response

Modern appreciation for the novel stems from F. R. Leavis's account of it in *The Great Tradition* (1948) where he argues that the work is perfect in its structure (1948: 243) and citing the final scene between Winnie and her husband as 'one of the most astonishing triumphs of genius in fiction' (1948: 245). He concludes that the work is 'one of the two unquestionable classics of the first order' that Conrad 'added to the English novel' (Leavis 1948: 251) – the other being *Nostromo* (see Works, pp. 63–8). Ian Watt's *Conrad: The Secret Agent: A Casebook* (1973a) covered the early critical response, with longer studies from the late 1940s through to the late 1960s, including important work from Leavis, Irving Howe, Albert Guerard and Avrom Fleishman. A study missing from Watt's collection is Eloise Knapp Hay's *The Political Novels of Joseph Conrad* (1963) which sees the book as 'frolicsome as any melodrama' but also 'profoundly disturbing' for its depiction of the fate of Winnie Verloc (1963: 239). Claire Rosenfield's chapter on the novel in *Paradise of Snakes* (1967) offers detailed coverage of the representation of London. Barbara Melchiori, *Terrorism in the Late Victorian Novel* (1985) places the book in the broader literary context of dynamite novels and other fictions of revolution. Illuminating introductory readings are provided by Ian Watt's essay, written for his *Casebook* (1973c) and Jacques Berthoud's chapters on the novel in his *Joseph Conrad: The Major Phase* (1978) and *The Cambridge Companion to Joseph Conrad* (1996).

Daniel Schwarz's *Conrad: Almayer's Folly to Under Western Eyes* (1980) examines 'the narrator's disciplined use of ironic language' in terms of its ability to manipulate 'his audience to accept his satiric indictment of contemporary London' (1980: 163). Sue Tyley's 'Time and Space in *The Secret Agent*' (1983) examines the city as an 'aqueous abyss' (1983: 35). Robert Hampson's *Joseph Conrad: Betrayal and Identity* (1992) comments on Conrad's use of period criminal anthropology in his characterisation and examines the novel's critical representation of urban society. There are several important essays on the novel's depiction of the city in Gene Moore (ed.) *Conrad's Cities* (1992), including Hugh Epstein's account of Conrad's debts to Dickens's London, 'A Pier Glass in the Cavern: London in *The Secret Agent*'. Rebecca Stott's 'The Woman in Black: Race and Gender in *The Secret Agent*' (1993) provides a theorised account of the interweaving of 'imperial, racial, and sexual discourses' (1993: 47) in the construction of the text. Carola Kaplan's 'No Refuge: The Duplicity of Domestic Safety in Conrad's Fiction' (1997) examines the novel's representation of the 'extreme failure of the domestic sphere to provide refuge from the larger world' (1997: 139). Andrew Michael Roberts has also studied the text in terms of gendered identity, showing 'how the status and ultimate fate of Stevie's ambivalently masculine body and identity is interwoven with Conrad's moral and political critique of urban Western society' (2000: 82). Con Coroneos's *Space, Conrad and Modernity* (2002) examines the novel in terms of spatial theory and Lissa Schneider's

Conrad's Narratives of Difference (2003) develops a reading of the role of the domestic and the 'fugitive' presentation of women in the text (2003: 104).

A Set of Six (1908)

The collection was mooted in a letter to Conrad's agent in October 1907 (CL3: 484), and its stories had been written in the period 1904–7. They were all works written as a means of dealing with mounting financial pressures, but it would be wrong, however, to write them off as mere potboilers. Indeed, nearly all of Conrad's work might be said, from his perspective at least, to have been written under mounting financial pressure. The collection can thus be viewed as a not-untypical example of how Conrad's art reacted to the pressures and opportunities of a burgeoning literary scene. The marketplace was, of course, a defining factor in much Edwardian writing and, like most writers of the period, Conrad experienced the pressures to be popular 'as both a goal and a trap' (Wexler 1997: 3). Forced to gloss the collection for his publisher, Conrad suggested that it consisted of 'stories of incident – action – not of analysis' and that all but two 'draw their significance from the love interest – though of course they are not conventional love stories' (CL4: 29–30). As recent critics have argued, Conrad's textual practice in these stories is shorn of dramatic incidents and many of the tales rely for their effect on subtle and often complex narrative strategies that undermine the authority of their tellers. Keith Carabine has written persuasively on this subject in the 'Introduction' to his edition of Conrad's *Selected Short Stories* (1997, xv–xx), and it is central to Daphna Erdinast-Vulcan's account of Conrad's 'abdication . . . of the authorial position' (1999: 2). Although the collection appeared in the UK in 1908, a US edition would not appear until 1915.

Commentary

'Gaspar Ruiz – A Romantic Tale'

'Gaspar Ruiz' had its origins in Conrad's reading of the piratical exploits of one Vicente Benavides in Basil Hall's *Extracts from a Journal Written on the Coasts of Chili, Peru, and Mexico in the Years 1820, 1821, 1822* (CL3: 171, note 1). In its earliest conception, the story was called 'Benavides' (CL3: 171), and Conrad planned two more tales on this subject but would eventually incorporate all of the material into 'Gaspar Ruiz'. He began writing the story in October 1904 and was still working on 'Benavides' stories in October 1905 (CL3: 286), but by January 1906 Conrad was referring to the work as 'Gaspar Ruiz' (CL3: 305) and in March he was correcting proofs (CL3: 318). The story ran in *Pall Mall* between July and October 1906. It is a rather overblown tale of revenge set in Chile and very much populist magazine fodder.

Ruiz, accused of desertion, survives death by firing squad and is nursed back to health by Erminia, daughter of a 'mad Royalist' (31). She goads him into seeking revenge for himself and for her family. The Republican forces realise Ruiz is hiding with the royalist family and come to capture him, only to be thwarted by a timely earthquake during which Ruiz saves Erminia's life and that of the republican General Robles. Officially pardoned, Ruiz is made a captain in the republican army but, with the prompting of the 'insatiable' (48) Erminia, now his wife, he leads a failed uprising and then mounts a guerrilla war in which he is killed whilst attacking a republican fortress where his wife and daughter are held captive. Following his death, his wife commits suicide. The story has little of interest in it when compared to Conrad's major works. The manipulation of Ruiz by his wife is cast in a gothic light with the suggestion that she is a witch (48) who has used him to further her own ambitions but this is no Chilean *Macbeth*. The unbalanced nature of their relationship makes ironic the subtitle 'A Romantic Tale'.

'The Informer – An Ironic Tale'

'The Informer' is one of Conrad's anarchist tales, written between December 1905 and January 1906 immediately after 'An Anarchist' and shortly before work commenced on the story that would become *The Secret Agent* (see Works, pp. 69–73). Even in June 1906 Conrad thought that the three tales would make a 'special volume' on anarchists (CL3: 338). Conrad was not happy with the story's title, suggesting 'Gestures', which he felt emphasised the 'moral satirical idea' (CL3: 305). The story was published in *Harper's Magazine* in December 1906.

The narrator retells the experience of Mr X, a collector of Chinese bronzes and porcelain and a 'revolutionary writer whose savage irony has laid bare the rottenness of the most respectable institutions' (74). Early on, the narrator proclaims his inability to 'understand anarchists' (75) and is appalled that Mr X can present himself to the world in so conventionally polished a fashion – 'he had the manner of good society' (76) – whilst believing that '[t]here's no amendment to be got out of mankind expect by terror and violence' (77). The narrator's delicate sensibilities and his 'impressionable and imaginative' (77) nature make him singularly unsuited to tell Mr X's story.

Mr X is a bestselling writer – author of pamphlets printed in 'millions' (77) and books distributed in 'hundreds of thousands' (77–8) – and, by way of illustrating his claims that the bourgeoisie naïvely support anarchism, he tells the narrator the story of a middle-class girl who takes up anarchism 'to assert her individuality' (81). She offers a property in London's Hermione Street as a base for an anarchist cell that is thus 'in a position to pursue its work of propaganda, and the other kind of work too, under very advantageous conditions' (83). The group, however, has a double agent in its midst since 'plans prepared in Hermione Street almost invariable failed' (84), and Mr X is sent over from Brussels to investigate. He sets up a fake police raid in the hope of flushing out the informer. During the raid, the middle-class girl is found to be on the premises and this prompts her anarchist lover, Sevrin, to reveal himself as the informer in order to save her from what he believes to be imminent arrest. On learning of his duplicity, she rejects him and he commits suicide and then, in an act that Mr X dismisses as a mere melodramatic gesture, the young woman retires to a convent. The tale ends with the narrator complaining that X's 'cynicism was simply abominable' (101) and his friend, who arranged for X to meet him, comments that X 'likes to have his little joke' (102) – to which the narrator observes that he has been 'utterly unable to discover where in all this the joke comes in' (102).

This pointer to the reader has been interpreted in a variety of ways. The tale works to establish links between anarchism and the bourgeois world – connoisseurs such as Mr X and the lady anarchist are established as exemplars of a wider trend of dilettantish involvement which stems from a fin-de-siècle ennui, and their action provides evidence for the notion that 'an idle and a selfish class loves to see mischief being made, even if it is made at it own expense' (78). With the exception of real anarchists such as the Professor, who shows no interest in anything but his explosives (88), all the others lead double lives and are adept at presenting faked identities to the wider world; in establishing this pervasive duplicity, the tale undermines not only the narrator but also Mr X (Vulcan 1999: 126). The story may also be read as an example of a Conradian mistrust of eloquence – Mr X and the fanatical Horne are both demagogues who carry the 'amateurs of emotion' (78) with them – and of its power to corrupt the weak (on this see Billy 1997: 108–21). Conrad's playful destabilising of both narrators might be read as part of an ongoing commitment to making his readers see things for which they have forgotten to ask – a strategy designed, he may have hoped, to enable the 'good and otherwise harmless' (78) readers of Pall Mall Magazine to express 'ecstasies over your collection without having the slightest notion in what its marvellousness really consists' (78).

'The Brute – An Indignant Tale'

'The Brute' was written with uncharacteristic rapidity in January 1906 and, having been rejected by Blackwood's, was eventually published in the Daily Chronicle in December 1906 with the subtitle 'tale of a bloodthirsty brig'. It was published in the USA by McClure's Magazine in November 1907 with the new subtitle 'A Piece of Invective'. The first-person frame narrator recounts the tale he hears in a pub from an ex-crewman on the Apse Family, the rogue ship of the title. The ship – 'the clumsiest, heaviest ship of her size' (111) – seems to have a cursed history since it kills someone on every voyage it makes and this means it is regarded by its crew as being 'mad in a ship-like way' (112). The central event of the tale is the killing of Maggie Colchester who is dragged overboard by the ship's anchor. This prompts her uncle, Captain Colchester, to resign his command and a new captain takes over. On the ship's next voyage, the officer on watch, Wilmot, is distracted from his duties by a flirtatious passenger and the ship runs aground and is then broken up. This is seen as 'poetical justice' (130) by the narrator since the ship is destroyed because of a burgeoning romance not long after it had ended the developing love between Chief Mate Charley and Maggie Colchester.

'An Anarchist – A Desperate Tale'

'An Anarchist' was written in December 1905 and first published in Harper's Magazine in August 1906. The story is told by a butterfly collector who has spent a summer on the island estate of a South American meat-processing company. It opens with a sarcastic account of the 'atrocious . . . allegory' (135) of the company's logo, and this vein of criticism of the facile rhetoric of capitalism runs throughout the tale. The story concerns the engineer on one of the company's steam launches which services the island. Nicknamed 'Crocodile', this man is presented to the narrator as a 'citizen anarchist of Barcelona' (139) and an escaped convict whom the local company manager has employed because he knows he will not throw up the job. We learn that the company manager has, in the absence of any particular information, simply labelled this man an anarchist – in part because it will make sure that he cannot leave the island since the people of the nearby town 'had been reading of the anarchists in Europe' and would be 'afraid of having anything to do with him' (143). The narrator discovers that the engineer is called Paul and 'was of Paris, not of Barcelona at all' (145). On his twenty-fifth birthday he got very drunk and was overwhelmed by the '[g]loomy ideas' (146) he heard from some strangers in the bar. Egged on by these strangers he bursts out shouting 'Death to the Capitalists!' (147) and then struggles with the police called by the bar owner. He awakes the next day to find himself 'in a police cell, locked up on a charge of assault, seditious cries, and anarchist propaganda' (147). Defended by an idealistic and ineffectual young lawyer who argues for him being viewed as 'the victim of society' (147) he is sent to prison and when released finds that he is treated as if he was a notorious anarchist and so drifts into the company of revolutionaries. He assists in a botched bank raid and is arrested and deported to Cayenne in French Guyana. Here he witnesses a prisoners' revolt, escapes in a rowing boat, meets two other prisoners whom he makes row the boat for him before he shoots them and is finally picked up by a ship which puts him ashore on the island owned by the meat-processing company. The narrator concludes that the engineer is in fact 'much more of an anarchist than he confessed to me or himself' (160) on account of his 'warm heart and weak head' (161).

'The Duel – A Military Tale'

'The Duel' was begun in late 1906 and completed in April 1907. An early title for it was 'The Masters of Europe: A Military Tale' (CL4: 60), and the story of D'Hubert and Feraud spans the era of the Napoleonic wars from 1801 to 1815. Conrad felt that the story would be easy to place in a magazine (CL3: 431) but in fact periodicals were reluctant to take it, and it was not published until 1908 by *Pall Mall Magazine* (January–May). It was published in the USA as 'A Point of Honour' in *Forum* magazine between July and October 1908. The tale is told by an omniscient narrator and relates the obsessive relationship between two obstinate men whose professional lives as military officers are closely entwined. D'Hubert is injured in battle and Feraud is promoted to General in his stead. The injury means that D'Hubert is unfit for duty and so does not suffer when the empire fails and the royalists are in the ascendancy. Taking service with the King, D'Hubert discovers that Feraud is due to be tried for his services to the failed Emperor and he successfully arranges for him to be spared. D'Hubert retires from public life and becomes engaged but Feraud tracks him down to fight one last duel, which is to be 'war to the death' (250). In fact Feraud misses with both his pistols and D'Hubert claims his life but refuses to 'take it now' (257). This means that Feraud is powerless and unable to pursue the matter. D'Hubert returns home to discover that his fiancé, whose motivation for marrying him he has had some doubts about, has learnt of the duel and run 2 miles barefoot to discover his fate – thus 'proving' her devotion. For prompting this revelation, D'Hubert feels indebted and secretly arranges a pension for the penniless Feraud. Conrad described the story as 'all duel and nothing but a duel. [. . .] Whatever sentiments come into it they all flow out from duelling pure and simple – in all its naked absurdity' (CL3: 506).

'Il Conde – A Pathetic Tale'

'Il Conde', the final story in *A Set of Six*, works to undermine its narrator's authority by encouraging the reader to question the veracity of his account. Conrad noted in the 1920 'Author's Note' that the title was a misspelling – the correct Italian being 'Conte'. This 'Note' also offered a steer to the reader since it emphasised the constructed nature of the tale – 'it is something more than a verbatim report' (vii) – and characterised the narrator as 'extremely suggestive' (vii). The story was written in ten days during December 1906, after Conrad had completed work on *The Secret Agent* (CL4: 104). According to the 'Author's Note', the story is based on 'the tale told me by a very charming old gentleman whom I met in Italy': the editors of Conrad's *Collected Letters* suggest that this man was Count Zygmunt Szembek, a Polish aristocrat whom the Conrads met whilst on Capri (CL3: xxxix). The story was published in *Cassell's Magazine* in August 1908 and in *Hampton's Magazine* in the USA in February 1909.

The tale is narrated by an unnamed tourist who is visiting Naples and encounters the Count, whom he has known 'by sight for some few days' (269) on account of them staying at the same hotel and visiting the same sights. The Count 'made a restful, easy, pleasant companion for the hours between dinner and bedtime' (273). The narrator then has to leave Naples to visit a sick friend and in the intervening ten days the Count has an 'abominable adventure' (274) in which he is mugged at knifepoint. Returning to his hotel after the incident, the Count, having discovered a forgotten sovereign in his pocket, stops to eat at a restaurant where he sees a man whom he believe to be his mugger being treated with some respect. On inquiring, he learns that the youth is a student from 'a very good family' (287) and leader of 'an association of young men – of very nice young men' (287), a 'Camorra' or secret society which is so powerful that even the professors fear it. The young man tells the Count that 'you are not done with me yet' (288) and he feels that he is now a 'marked man' who must leave his beloved Naples for ever – a departure which, due to his delicate health, is effectively a suicide in the narrator's eyes (288). Keith Carabine has convincingly argued that the narrative is replete with pointers that encourage 'the discriminating reader to construct an alternative explanation against the grain of both the . . . [Count's] telling and the . . . [narrator's] empathetic commentary: the fastidious Count is unable to admit his homosexual inclinations and the gullible, sympathetic frame narrator is unable to detect them' (1997: xix).

Early reviews

A Set of Six received mixed reviews, one of which infuriated Conrad. Robert Lynd's review in the *Daily News* (10 August 1908) criticised him for writing in English, suggesting that he ought to have stuck to his native Polish, as his translated work would be 'a more precious possession on English shelves'

(Sherry 1973: 211). Lynd singled out 'The Duel' and 'The Brute' for praise but suggested that 'Gapsar Ruiz' 'is worth all the rest of the book' (Sherry 1973: 212). Writing in the *Daily Telegraph*, W. L. Courtney noted that 'Mr Conrad tell us his story not as though he were particularly enlisted on the side of his hero, not even wishing us to be very interested but merely as one who draws up the veil of an unknown corner of life, and bids us watch the blind happenings of destiny' (Sherry 1973: 215). Again 'Gaspar Ruiz' and 'The Brute' were praised, along with 'An Anarchist', as 'fine achievements' (Sherry 1973: 217). *Country Life* was dismissive, suggesting that there was little coherence in the collection and criticising the tales' subtitles as 'superfluous' and 'no more than an essay in the art of literary window dressing' (Sherry 1973: 217). Despite these misgivings, the reviewer felt able to identify 'The Duel' as 'as fine as anything he has done recently' (Sherry 1973: 218) whilst 'Gaspar Ruiz' was criticised for its 'brutal realism' which 'is not very great art' being too akin to that of a 'sensational reporter' (279). Writing in *The Nation*, Edward Garnett also addressed issuses of nationality, arguing that 'Mr Conrad's rare gifts may, indeed have been fertilised by his cosmopolitan life, but anything less English than his ironic, tender, and sombre vision of life it would be hard to find' (Sherry 1973: 221). Garnett also returned to his notion that Conrad's writing was distinctively Slavonic 'in its ironic acceptance of the pathetic futility of human nature, and quite un-English in its refinement of tender, critical malice' (Sherry 1973: 223). Garnett went on to argue that whilst Conrad 'has a special affection for the Englishman's bluff code, practical creed, and simplicity of outlook', readers should 'not presume on this, or conclude on such slender evidence that his stories are "characteristically English"' (Sherry 1973: 222). Garnett welcomed 'The Anarchist' [*sic*] for its 'ironical and picturesque observation of men', and 'The Brute' and 'The Duel' were also praised – the latter being seen as 'a masterpiece of style . . . a perfect whole' (Sherry 1973: 223). 'The Informer' was criticised for the implausibility of its central characters and 'Gaspar Ruiz' was politely described as 'lacking in subtlety of atmosphere' (Sherry 1973: 223). Conrad wrote to Garnett to thank him for the review, which he declared 'eminently satisfactory' (CL4: 106). In this letter, Conrad lamented that no reviewers had spotted the 'Napoleonic feeling' (CL4: 107) he had put in to 'The Duel' and dismissed 'Gaspar Ruiz' as an 'infernal magazine fake' (CL4: 108). He also criticised Lynd's review as beyond 'common decency' (CL4: 109).

Later critical response

'Gaspar Ruiz'

The first major study was Paul Kirschner's 'Conrad's Strong Man' (1964), which examines the origins of the tale in Captain Basil Hall's *Extracts from a Journal Written on the Coasts of Chile, Peru and Mexico in the Years 1820, 21, 22*, and suggests parallels between the story and *The Arrow of Gold* (see Works, pp. 117–20). Lawrence Graver's *Conrad's Short Fiction* (1969) regards it as 'over-extended' and reads it as an example of 'the deterioration in Conrad's method' (1969: 126). W. R. Martin 'Gaspar Ruiz: A Conradian Hero' (1971–2) suggests parallels between Ruiz and Singleton in *The Nigger of the 'Narcissus'*, MacWhirr in 'Typhoon' and Peyrol in *The Rover* (see Works, pp. 31–5, 57–61, 127–9).

Gilbert M. Cuthbertson examines the absurdist aspects of the tale in his 'Free-dom, Absurdity, and Destruction: The Political Theory of Conrad's *A Set of Six*' (1974). In his '*A Set of Six*: Variations on a Theme' (1975), Addison Bross suggests that the story figures idealism as noble but ultimately futile. Daniel R. Schwarz's *Conrad: Almayer's Folly to Under Western Eyes* (1980) notes some echoes of *Nostromo*, and comments on the role of General Santierra as a narrator whose 'wordiness . . . implies a solipsism which is part of character' (1980: 181). Gene Moore has written on Conrad's adaptation of the story as a silent film script in 'Conrad's "Film–Play": *Gaspar the Strong Man*' (Moore 1997: 31–47). More recently, Sema Postacioglu–Banon's ' "Gaspar Ruiz": A Vitagraph of Desire' (2003), has presented the screenplay as the more successful text for its articulation of Gaspar's emotions.

'The Informer'

John V. Hagopian's 'The Informer' (1964) provides a student-oriented introduc-tion which seeks to explain the complexity of the tale's narration. Lawrence Graver suggests that Conrad's 'evocation of the duplicity that surrounds anarch-ist activities has an impressive credibility' but claims that the story is ultimately a failure because its central characters are two-dimensional, and he sums it up as 'a piece of invective' (1969: 141). Diana Cuthbertson, ' "The Informer": Conrad's Little Joke' (1974) also examines the narrative, suggesting that Conrad was parodying himself in the figure of Mr X and mocking the reader. Gilbert Cuthbertson, 'Freedom, Absurdity, and Destruction: The Political Theory of Conrad's *A Set of Six*' (1974) examines the absurdist elements of this tale of anarchists undone by an anarchist. Daniel R. Schwarz, points up the narrator's lack of understanding of the story he recounts and Mr X's unwitting revelation of himself as 'a malicious, petty aristocrat' (1980: 188). Ted Billy's *A Wilderness of Words* suggests that the depiction of the narrator might be read as a satire of the dandies of the late nineteenth-century aesthetic movement and considers the ways in which the tale could be seen to present anarchism as 'a metaphor for the bohemian life of the [. . .] aesthete manqué' (1997: 109, 111). Daphna Erdinast Vulcan (1999) focuses on the role of Mr X, whom she presents as an authorial figure, in straddling the bourgeois world of the collector frame narrator and that of the anarchists. Keith Carabine's ' "Gestures" and "The Moral Satirical Idea" in Conrad's "The Informer" ' (1999) identifies within Mr X's narrative 'a tale of thwarted love and human misery, that reveals the imbecility of his ideas and the baseness of his judgements' (1999: 38). P. A. Russell-March, 'The Anarchy of Love: "The Informer" ' (2003: 45–59), builds on Carabine's work to offer a study of the ways in which the tale articulated a postmodern ethics.

'The Brute'

The story has received little critical attention, with many scholars regarding it as one of Conrad's weakest works. Lawrence Graver complains that the story 'never rises above the anecdotal' (1969: 131), citing Conrad's use of a direct address to the reader as evidence of its failure. Daniel Schwarz sees the tale as 'an instance of Conrad's own bad taste in dealing with sexual materials' (1980: 182). Michael

Lucas has recently made a brave attempt at 'Rehabilitating "The Brute"' (2003), suggesting that the story shows 'mastery of narrative technique' (2003: 69).

'An Anarchist'

Lawrence Graver laments that the story is 'purely circumstantial; no coherent view of conspiracy and sedition can be sifted from its pages' (1969: 134). Daniel Schwarz's 'The Lepidopterist's Revenge: Theme and Structure in Conrad's "An Anarchist"' (1971a) sees the narrator as working out his own revenge fantasies via Paul's story. Jennifer Shaddock 'Hanging a Dog: The Politics of Naming in "An Anarchist"' (1994) examines the narrator's 'gross inability to understand Paul' and his failure to control 'the language he uses to describe' (66). Daphna Erdinast Vulcan's *The Strange Short Fiction of Joseph Conrad* (1999) also focuses on the narrator, seeing him as someone who, through his narration, brought about 'the conversion of cant into satire' (1999: 116). Stephen Donovan's engaging account of 'Magic Letters and Mental Degradation: Advertising in "An Anarchist" and "The Partner"' (2003) reads the text as a deliberate subversion of the conventions of magazine fiction.

'The Duel'

Lawrence Graver suggests that the story was 'fragile' and hampered by Conrad's interest in 'the spirit of the Napoleonic age' (1969: 145). For Graver, Conrad failed to analyse 'the obsessive psychology of the two officers', falling back on 'the absurd fatality of their predicament and its relation to the spectacular passions of the age' (1969: 146). Addison Bross suggests that the story depicts an innocent man pushed to act by the simplistic beliefs of his foe (1975). Daniel Schwarz sees the tale as an examination of 'the military sensibility' and a 'parody of military struggle' (1980: 192). Schwarz, like Graver, also sees thematic links with 'The Secret Sharer', the story that Conrad would write after completing 'The Duel' (see Works, **pp.** 94–5). John Stape, in 'Conrad's "The Duel": A Reconsideration' (1992), argues that the tale moves purposefully from 'wooden allegory to psychological realism' (1992: 124) in its depiction of D'Hubert. Stape's cogent reading concludes that the story is 'one of Conrad's clearest statements about the complicity of "legitimate" and "outlawed" impulses both in the individual and in society at large' (1992: 125). Allan Simmons has studied the text in relation to the film adaptation *The Duellists* (1977) in his 'Cinematic Fidelities in *The Rover* and *The Duellists*' (1997b).

'Il Conde'

John Howard Willis's 'Adam, Axel, and "Il Conde"' (1955) reads the tale as an allegory of the expulsion from Eden. John Hagopian, 'The Pathos of "Il Conde"' (1965) rejects this reading and sees the tale as a study of a pathetic victim. Graver reads this story as 'free from the obvious faults that mar the other works in *A Set of Six*' (1969: 141). He argues that through 'the careful juxtaposition of ironic detail', Conrad 'creates sympathy for the old man and yet leaves no doubt that he is an accessory in the unsettling crisis of his old age' (1969: 142). Douglas Hughes, 'Conrad's "Il Conde": "Deucedly Queer Story"' (1975) reads the story in terms of its unreliable narrator's failure to identify the Count's homosexuality. Daniel Schwarz reads the narrator as 'another of Conrad's imperceptive speakers' (1980: 188) and Ted Billy examines 'the derelict sensibility of the Count' (1997: 203) via a close reading of the story's beginning and ending.

Under Western Eyes (1911)

In many critical estimations, this is both Conrad's most profound novel and also the last of his works with any lasting literary historical significance. Conrad's struggles with *Chance* (see Works, **pp. 98–103**) were set aside in December 1907, and by mid-December he had completed ten pages of a short story with the title 'Razumov' (CL3: 515) in which he hoped 'to capture the very soul of things Russian' (CL4: 8). At this stage, Razumov was to marry Natalia Haldin and would eventually confess his complicity in her brother's death owning to their child's uncanny resemblance to the dead Haldin (CL4: 9). Conrad stressed that the 'psychological developments' of Razumov's feelings of guilt 'form the real subject of the story' (CL4: 9). By March, the story had grown in Conrad's mind (if not in the actual manuscript) to something of novella length (CL4: 55) which would 'be Russian, very Russian in fact. Absolutism and Revolution – and the moral pangs of . . . Razumov – quiet student – who dies of them. . . . the "grand passion" shows itself only at the end. For the rest, analysis – but movement enough all the same – that's the *tone* of the novel' (CL4: 59).

During the writing of the novel, Conrad's financial problems began to worsen and his mental health was further exacerbated by his agent's growing reluctance to agree to his seemingly unstoppable demands for more money. In order to earn additional cash, Conrad broke off from work on the novel to write the series of articles for the *English Review* that would become *A Personal Record* (see Works, **pp. 88–92**). Writer's block with the novel and work on his reminiscences, coupled with periods of illness and domestic upsets, meant that between autumn 1908 and 1909 little progress was made. He returned to work on the novel in earnest in September 1909 and 'worked steadily' until its completion in January 1910, pausing in December 1909 to write 'The Secret Sharer' in a ten-day burst of inspiration (Carabine 1996a: 50, CL4: 296) (see Works, **pp. 94–5**). Shortly after completing the manuscript, Conrad had a major argument with his agent and on 30 January 1910 he suffered a complete nervous breakdown, doubtless brought on by the strains of finishing the novel, anxiety at his mounting debts and fear that in the future he would no longer be able to rely on his agent's generous support. Conrad was ill for six weeks but began work to prepare the manuscript for serial publication in spring 1910, cutting nearly 18,000 words from the typescript (Carabine 1996a: 62). Carabine has argued that the manuscript of *Razumov* and the typescript of *Under Western Eyes* are of great importance in understanding Conrad's aims, and the Cambridge edition of *Under Western Eyes*, which he is co-editing, will offer detailed coverage of these variants and may provide a complete text of *Razumov* to read alongside the finished novel.

Commentary

Under Western Eyes is an intimate study of the politics of nationalism which, like *Nostromo*, deploys a modernist poetics to offer a powerful study of guilt and the psychology of betrayal. At the start of the novel, the narrator of this tale of Russian revolutionaries disconcertingly informs the reader that he has 'no comprehension of the Russian character' (4) and he styles himself 'a mute witness of things Russian, unrolling their Eastern logic under my Western eyes' (381). He has based his narration on a document which belonged to Razumov, 'something in the nature of a journal, a diary, yet not exactly that in its actual form' (4). The old teacher of languages who tells Razumov's story supplements this source with his own asides and perspectives, rooted in his Western prejudices and leavened by his own observations of the revolutionaries in Geneva which he acquires in part whilst working as tutor to Natalia Haldin. His baffled engagement with the subject matter of his own narration is one of Conrad's great achievements; it is through the narrator's own misreading that the reader comes to see the limitation and implication of reading Russia with Western eyes. As with the Marlow-narrated novels, or the various narrative viewpoints in *Nostromo*, the old language teacher provides Conrad with a persona that can mask even as it provides a helpfully displaced outlet for authorial perspectives – and in this novel of things Russian written by a man whose parents' death can be laid at the door of the Russian State, such displacement was essential (see Life and Contexts, p. 91). Within the frame of the text, the old language teacher's narration also works as a mask for Razumov, since it is the narrator who translates his journal into English. One of the narrator's recurrent topics is his problem with language, and the apparently simple irony of a language teacher who doubts the capacity of words to describe experience provides Conrad with a means of reflecting on the problems of writing fiction at the same time as it opens up the whole question of the relationship between word and deed which are central to Razumov's story.

Razumov has no family and relies on the patronage of 'a distinguished nobleman' (6) and believes that his social standing is the key to his future: he is also arrogantly confident in his sense of 'intellectual superiority' (89). It is this mix of conformist disdain that makes revolutionaries such as Haldin so distasteful to his 'conservative convictions' (67) and underpins his epigrammatic credo:

> History not Theory.
> Patriotism not Internationalism.
> Evolution not Revolution.
> Direction not Destruction.
> Unity not Disruption.
>
> (66)

This yoking together of opposites prefigures the doubling that is so pervasive a feature of this novel's organisation in which, for example, one may read Razumov as an antithetical Haldin or view the language teacher as a prolix and pedestrian Razumov. This doubling is something that only narrator and reader are aware of since, for most of the text, Razumov's position is founded upon people misreading him – 'he had been made a personage without knowing anything about it'

(82–3) – but the fact that this misreading might also be extended to the narrator's account (which is, of course, partly derived from Razumov's own journal) is only apparent on subsequent readings of the novel. As Bruce Henricksen argues, 'We often cannot be entirely sure *whose* discourse or story we are hearing. The dialogic sharing of language makes such clear oppositions as story versus discourse and narrator's word versus Razumov's impossible to sustain as one addresses specific utterances in the novel' (1992: 141). In other words, the text resists the binary logic inherent in Razumov's credo and its dialogic organisation works to subvert the narrator's attempts to bring Razumov's Eastern words into Western language.

The shift from the St Petersburg scenes of Part 1 to Geneva in Part 2 also marks a shift in the narrative's focus away from Razumov and onto Haldin's mother and sister. A further complicating factor affecting the narrator's reliability soon emerges as it becomes obvious that he is attracted to Natalia even though he accepts that this feeling will never be returned (102). With the narrator, we witness the gradual emergence of the news of de P—'s assassination amongst the Russian exiles in Geneva; the Haldin's growing concerns over Victor's long silence and the impact of the news of his execution. Peter Ivanovitch, the advocate of women's 'spiritual superiority' (121), is introduced in disparaging terms, primarily because the narrator sees him as a threat to his cosy relations with the Haldins. Ivanovitch has come to tell them of the recent arrival of Razumov and to encourage Natalia to seek the support of the Russian community of radicals in Geneva by attending the regular salons of his patroness, Madame de S—. Razumov enters the narrative via one of Haldin's letters, where he is described as 'a man of "unstained, lofty, and solitary existence"' (135), someone whom Natalia assumes to have been her brother's 'intimate friend' (135). On a first reading, there is some irony here since the reader knows the true nature of Haldin's relations with Razumov, but on a second reading, when we known that Razumov's arrival in Geneva has been carefully managed by Councillor Mikulin, the irony intensifies, creating additional sympathy for the innocent Natalia. Throughout her narration, the narrator interrupts to ask questions and before Natalia's meeting with Razumov gets narrated he breaks off completely from his recollection of her account of her visit to explain to the reader how he personally comes to 'know so much about' (162) Madame de S—: a break which is very much about asserting his control over events in the interests of making the story 'a little more credible . . . for Western ears' (163). He then continues his metanarrative with some reflections on his feelings for Natalia and his contemporary thoughts about Razumov – all of which further delay the account of the meeting between her and Razumov that we are anticipating. Even when she begins to recount this event, her narration is further disrupted by the narrator's questions and by her meditations on the event. Thus, as part of Conrad's artful narrative strategy, we are distanced from a direct engagement with this scene. Having no direct access to Razumov's thoughts, we see his responses through Natalia's eyes but read them with our knowledge of his duplicity. Thus, statements like '[t]heir friendship must have been the very brotherhood of souls' (172) are read as bitterly ironic. Their second meeting is another brief one as Natalia has to return to her sick mother and this leaves Razumov with the narrator for what is their first encounter (Part 2 Chapter 5). Here the irony is intense since the narrator's line of questions repeatedly but unwittingly touches Razumov's feelings of guilt as he seeks to explain why Natalia is so anxious to speak with him about her brother. The narrator interprets Razumov's 'weary indifference' (192) and apparent lack of emotion as a true revolutionist's detachment when the reader knows it is in fact just a pose.

After the intensity of Part 1, the drawing-room scenes, political debating and general adumbrations of plot and character offered in Part 2 tend to drag on a first reading. They provide the narrator with further opportunity to express his conservative anti-Russian views and so enable the reader to see his inability to comprehend the motivation of the characters whose lives he is recounting. Throughout this section, the narrator refuses to draw on information he possesses to illuminate scenes – thus his encounter with Razumov shows none of the knowledge of the inner feelings that 'are recorded' (192) in his journal: the reader is left with the simple irony of the Geneva Russians welcoming as a comrade the betrayer of Haldin. Part 3 shifts to Razumov's perspective and picks up where Part 2 ends. The opening of this section of the novel relies upon a third-person narrative but it is a perspective that remains coy about Razumov's role as spy and about his inner thoughts and motivation. Razumov's reflections upon the old teacher of languages, whom he dismisses as 'blundering' (199), further undermines the latter's credibility – although Razumov is merely pointing up what the reader will already have seen as the narrator's inability to read him. The narrative point of view shifts back to the language teacher for a brief section (200–3) in which he recounts a conversation with Natalia before it shifts back to third person to narrate Razumov's conversation with Ivanovitch (203–4) during which his interlocutor repeatedly and unwittingly touches upon Razumov's guilt. For his part, Razumov has no desire to have this conversation and indulges himself by working up his persona as bitter and taciturn revolutionary and flirting with discovery by teasingly addressing Ivanovitch: 'if only you knew the force which . . . drove me towards you . . . I have been impelled, compelled, or rather sent . . . towards you' (228).

This sequence also draws upon a Gothic vein in which Chateau Borel is viewed as 'damp, gloomy and deserted' (210–11), fit only to be 'haunted in traditional style by some doleful, groaning, futile ghost of a middle class order' (211) and which casts Madame de S—as a 'witch in Parisian clothes' (215), a 'grinning skull', a 'galvanized corpse out of some Hoffman's Tale' and an 'ancient, painted mummy' (215). Conrad's narrator savagely lampoons Ivanovitch's patroness and Razumov is shown to be alert to the 'fantastic absurdity' (220) of his own situation. Before he leaves the Chateau, Razumov encounters Tekla, another person willing to put their trust in what he appears to be, and the perceptive Sophia Antonovna, whose criticism of his masculine cynicism centres upon the idea that 'perhaps . . . you are only playing a part' (251) and whose penetrating questions make her by far the most 'dangerous adversary' (255) he has yet had to face: 'It gave him a feeling of triumphant pleasure to deceive her out of her own mouth. The epigrammatic saying that speech has been given to us for the purpose of concealing our thoughts came into his mind' (261).

Yet by the end of their conversation, Razumov feels choked by the 'fumes of falsehood' (269). Sophia has information about the peasant Ziemianitch who was to help Haldin escape and also knows that the peasant was beaten by a 'swarthy young man in a student's cloak' (281) whilst we know that Razumov beat this man unconscious in a rage. Sophia is deceived out of her own mouth when Razumov's hesitating replies lead her to conclude that the peasant hung himself out of guilt at his involvement in Haldin's capture. Having endured a day of difficult conversations, Razumov is gripped with the desire to write his first report for Mikulin (289) and settles down beneath the statue of Rousseau on the shore of Lake Geneva to begin writing. At this point the narrative breaks off for Part 4 which jumps back to the end of Part 1 with a repetition of Mikulin's question 'Where to?' and tracks the phases leading up to Razumov's acceptance of the role of spy and his departure from St Petersburg. The narrative returns to Geneva in Part 4 Chapter 2 with Razumov still amazed at the predicament in which he has found himself. The narrative perspective shifts to Natalia, who asks the language teacher to help her find Razumov so that her mother can hear from him at first hand any reminiscences of her brother. They seek the advice of Ivanovitch whom they find in his hotel with a group of revolutionaries: Sophia tells Natalia that the betrayer of Haldin has been identified as the peasant. Natalia and the narrator go to Razumov's lodgings only to find him out but on returning to her home discover that he is there, increasingly showing the strain of maintaining his pose as Haldin's friend. The narrator, who is a largely silent witness to this meeting, even thinks him 'deranged' (350). Razumov suggests another candidate for betrayer of Haldin – 'a young man, educated, an intellectual worker thoughtful, a man your brother might have trusted lightly' (353). At this point, the watching narrator realises that Razumov is trying to confess his role but suggests that Natalia is 'unable to see the truth struggling on his lips' (354). Finally, when Razumov has 'pressed a denunciatory finger to his breast' (354), Natalia realises his guilt. Razumov returns to his lodgings to write his journal, 'trying to express in broken sentences' (358) his feelings for Natalia whom he believes has undone 'the evil' of his betrayal by forcing him to confess – 'to betray myself back into truth and peace' (358). What the journal entry also reveals is that Razumov, unbeknownst to the unperceptive narrator, has slowly fallen in love with Natalia. Caught between her confidence in him and his self-loathing, he is forced to make the confession that will destroy any chance of his love for her being returned. His sequence of actions seem horribly clear – 'Confess, go out, – and perish' (361). Razumov goes to where the revolutionaries are gathered and confesses his guilt. They turn on him and he is held down – even though he 'did not struggle' (368) – whilst his eardrums are burst. He runs out into the night and is knocked over by a tram that he does not hear coming since he is now deaf. He lives, nursed by Tekla and eventually leaves Geneva with her to return to Russia where he lives 'crippled' (379) in an out-of-the-way town but, surprisingly, is visited by revolutionaries.

Early reviews

Under Western Eyes was praised by contemporary reviewers for its psychological insight. The *Pall Mall Gazette* called it a 'psychological study of remarkable penetration' (Sherry 1973: 226). The *Morning Post* called it an 'able and convincing study of soul in the cruel, remorseless grip of fate' (Sherry 1973: 233).

Many reviewers commented on Conrad's depiction of Russia, and several drew out the links between this novel and Dostoevsky's *Crime and Punishment* (1866). *The Athenaeum* detected a Russian influence in the novel but admonished Conrad for being 'reckless in the form of his narrative' to the point of being 'tiresome' (Carabine 1992: III, 340). The *Westminster Gazette* argued that the novel could be read as 'an explanation of the works of Russian novelists; it helps us to understand Turgenev and Dostoevsky' (Sherry 1973: 234). Edward Garnett, writing in *The Nation*, argued that Conrad's novel 'bears affinities and owes a debt' to the work of Dostoevsky and Turgenev (Sherry 1973: 239). Conrad expressed repugnance at Dostoevsky's fiction but, as many critics from the 1910s to the present have argued, the relationship between Conrad and the author of 'fierce mouthings from prehistoric ages' (CL5: 70) is a complex one, and interested readers may like to consult the special issue of *Conradiana* (12, 1, 1980), David R. Smith's essay 'Dostoevsky and Conrad' (1991) or Carabine's chapter on 'Conrad, Apollo Korzeniowski and Dostoevsky', in *The Life and the Art: A Study of Conrad's 'Under Western Eyes'* (1996a) for further information.

Later critical response

For readers coming to the work for the first time, there are a number of introductory accounts that can be recommended, including Jacques Berthoud's essay on the novel in *Joseph Conrad: The Major Phase* (1978) and Keith Carabine's more recent account in *The Cambridge Companion to Joseph Conrad* (1996b). Of the editions aimed at a student readership, Jeremy Hawthorn's 'Introduction' to his World's Classics edition (2003b) and Paul Kirschner's for his Penguin edition (1996) also provide good starting points.

The criticism generated by the novel is wide-ranging but has tended to focus either on Conrad's representation of Russia and revolutionary activity or on the book's complex narrative organisation. C. B. Cox, in *Conrad: Heart of Darkness, Nostromo and Under Western Eyes: A Casebook* (1981) provides a selection of early reviews and critical essays from the 1950s to 1970s, including important essays by Thomas Moser and Tony Tanner. This selection is supplemented by the material reprinted in Carabine, *Joseph Conrad: Critical Assessments*, Volume III (1992), which also reprints Tanner's 1962 essay and offers a selection of essays from the late 1960s to the early 1990s. Neither Cox nor Carabine reprint Eloise Knapp Hay's early study of the work in her *The Political Novels of Joseph Conrad* (1963). David R. Smith's *Joseph Conrad's Under Western Eyes: Beginnings, Revisions, Final Forms: Five Essays* (1991b) offers work from the late 1980s that place particular emphasis on manuscript and typescript versions of the novel. There are useful studies of the novel's narrative organisation in Jakob Lothe's *Conrad's Narrative Method* (1989) and Bruce Henricksen's *Nomadic Voices* (1992). Lothe focuses on the 'diverse narrative functions' of the English teacher of languages' (1989: 264) whilst Henricksen's Bahktinian reading emphasises the 'relationships between inferred author, narrator, and the myriad metastories that constitute their discursive material' (1992: 140), arguing that the novel's narration 'draws attention to the always open, supplemental, and unfinished nature of the social discourse of which . . . the genre of the novel is an image' (60). Daphna

Erdinast Vulcan's *Joseph Conrad and the Modern Temper* (1991) studies the narrator as 'thoroughly modern and Westernized in his renunciation of knowledge and authority' (1991: 126), whilst Christopher GoGwilt's *The Invention of the West* (1995) examined 'the problematic limitations of the novel's "Western Eyes"' (1995: 170) in his account of the role of the narrator. The most detailed study of the novel's composition and concerns to date is Keith Carabine's *The Life and the Art: A Study of Conrad's 'Under Western Eyes'* (1996a).

A Personal Record (1912)

First published in the *English Review*, December 1908–June 1909, as 'Some Reminiscences', the collection was published as a small circulation pamphlet in the USA in 1908 'to secure American copyright' (Knowles and Moore 2000: 277). In 1912, *Some Reminiscences* was published in England by Everleigh Nash with the addition of 'A Familiar Preface'. The US edition was published under the title of *A Personal Record* and this title was then used for the second English edition published in 1916. For simplicity's sake, I will refer to the work by its more familiar second title.

The history of the text is informed by Conrad's changing relationship with his friend and literary collaborator Ford Madox Ford (see Life and Contexts, **pp. 12–13**) and his increasingly antagonistic relationship with his agent J. B. Pinker (see Life and Contexts, **pp. 13–14**). Aesthetically and emotionally, the work seems to have been a means of working out issues of nation and belonging related to his concerns in *Under Western Eyes* (see Works, **pp. 82–7**). Fellow novelist Arnold Bennett spotted the links between the two books and referred to them in a letter:

> What I chiefly like in your book of *Reminiscences* is the increasingly sardonic quality of them – the rich veins of dark and glittering satire and sarcasm. We want a lot more of that in English literature. There was a lot of it, too, in the latter half of *Under Western Eyes*.
> (Stape and Knowles 1996: 87–8; for Conrad's reply, see CL5: 135–6)

The narrative structure of *A Personal Record*, like that of the novel, works to draw out connections between past and present, and the two books also reflect on the act of writing. For Conrad, *A Personal Record* dealt with the double call of the sea and of writing (CL4: 441) and was intended as a 'disclosure of personality' (CL4: 441). It is striking that in both cases, that call is from England (the English Merchant Marine and English Literature) and that the personality evoked in its pages might be described as English (Bennett's identification of sarcasm as a virtue might be seen as peculiarly English). The book is central to any understanding of Conrad's sense of the relationship between his life and his art.

Commentary

The opening chapter works to connect Conrad's Polish childhood with his mature worldview. This is done by acknowledging 'the still voice from that inexorable past from which his work[s] of fiction are remotely derived' (25). Poland offers a legacy of imagination, that capacity to evoke what might be despite all that makes it not so, which is a key factor in the idealistic patriotism of his family. Conrad's reminiscences are a mechanism whereby he puts into dialogue competing aspects of himself; the text works through association, condensation and juxtaposition and so serves as an evocation of the processes of reminiscing even as it recuperates reminiscence as the basis of something larger. His reminiscences are about translating into words his three lives and their associated cultures and memories. They disclose a self whose origins are traced from Polish outsider to English writer via a sustained act of imaginative reconstruction:

> Only in men's imagination does every truth find an effective and undeniable existence. Imagination, not invention, is the supreme master of art as of life. An imaginative and exact rendering of authentic memories may serve worthily that spirit of piety towards all things human which sanctions the conceptions of writer of tales, and the emotions of the man reviewing his own experience.
>
> (25)

Imagination alone is a dangerous tool, countered here by the demand for precision and accuracy – restraining elements which ensure that the artist can achieve a high moral purpose. Conrad the artist seeks to steer with care in order to get beyond the Marlovian 'surface truth' ('Heart of Darkness', 97) whilst avoiding the pitfalls of imaginative beggardom that so paralyse Jim (*Lord Jim*, 224). In retelling the experiences of his Great Uncle Nicholas – the Polish patriot whose extreme fidelity to his nation meant that he once ate a dog so that he could keep the strength to carry on fighting – Conrad contrasts romantic and imaginative patriotism. Conrad's sardonic perspective on his uncle's extravagant act was cogently summarised by Jacques Berthoud: 'By devoting himself to his country he gradually made himself incapable of serving it. Nicholas chose Poland; Conrad did not. From the patriotic point of view the uncle's choice condemns the nephew. But if one remembers his fate, it also vindicates it' (Berthoud 1978: 19).

Conrad anticipates and counters claims of desertion of his native country with the argument that 'fidelity to a special tradition may last through the events of an unrelated existence' (36), and he further argues that citizenship (and so allegiance to national codes of conduct) cannot be expected of the Quixotic or the imaginative (37). Conrad seems to be arguing that temperamentally he was always already an exile, unsuited to the role of a citizen. Conrad looks to his past not to identify where the buried truth of his existence lies but rather to trace the forces that impelled him upon a course of action that took him away from the scenes of his early life and that kept on impelling him, through his sea career and, finally, into writing; as he puts it, 'I dare say I am compelled, unconsciously compelled, now to write volume after volume, as in past years I was compelled to go to sea, voyage after voyage' (18). Conrad sees this compulsion as a seeking after Truth (18), a search that forces him to dispense with existing ideologies and speak:

> to our capacity for delight and wonder, to the sense of mystery surrounding our lives; to our sense of pity, and beauty, and pain; to the

latent feeling of fellowship with all creation – and to the subtle but invincible conviction of solidarity that knits together the loneliness of innumerable hearts, to the solidarity in dreams, in joy, in sorrow, in aspirations, in illusions, in hope, in fear, which binds men to each other, which binds together all humanity – the dead to the living and the living to the unborn

('Preface' to *The Nigger of the 'Narcissus'*, viii)

An art that transcends locales is evoked here but, as the reminiscences suggest, it is often the intersection of place and person that sets in train outcomes that cannot be anticipated. The notion of art transcending region is returned to in the fourth section of *A Personal Record* when Conrad discusses his reading of English authors in translation. The ease with which Dickens or Shakespeare could be rendered into Polish is part of his wider point about art's capacity to speak to a common humanity. In the fifth section, this issue is examined in more detail when Conrad talks about the constraints that operate on the novelist who, if they are to be regarded as successful, must demonstrate an 'exact understanding of the limits traced by the reality of his time to the play of his invention' (95). As Conrad goes on to explain: 'Inspiration comes from the earth, which has a past, a history, a future, not from the cold and immutable heaven. A writer of imaginative prose . . . stands confessed in his works. His conscience, his deeper sense of things, lawful and unlawful, gives him his attitude before the world' (95).

Conrad has a wide vision of what the novelist can achieve, declaring that 'all ambitions are lawful expect those which climb upward on the miseries or credulities of mankind' (*A Personal Record*, xviii). This does not, then, permit the writer to draw of a veil over 'proceedings too terrible to relate' but rather envisages a bold encounter with difficult truths:

An historian of hearts is not an historian of emotions, yet he penetrates further, restrained as he may be, since his aim is to reach the very fount of laughter and tears. . . . Resignation, not mystic, not detached, but resignation open-eyed, conscious, and informed by love, is the only one of our feelings for which it is impossible to become a sham.

Not that I think resignation the last word of wisdom. I am too much a creature of my time for that.

(*A Personal Record*, xix)

In *A Personal Record*, Conrad describes his own time as one of revolution in which:

Rules, principles and standards die and vanish everyday. Perhaps they are all dead and vanished by this time. These, if ever, are the brave free days of destroyed landmarks, while the ingenious minds are busy inventing the forms of the new beacons which, it is consoling to think, will be set up presently in the old places.

(96)

Set against this is a commitment to long-held beliefs and values:

Those who read me know my conviction that the world, the temporal world, rests on a few very simple ideas; so simple that they must be as old as the hills. It rests notably, among others, on the idea of Fidelity. At a time when nothing which is not revolutionary in someway or other can expect to attract much attention I have not been revolutionary in my writings. The revolutionary spirit is mighty convenient in this, that it frees one from all scruples as regards ideas. Its hard, absolute optimism is repulsive to my mind by the menace of fanaticism and intolerance it contains.

(*A Personal Record*, xix–xx)

For an English readership who, in 1909, felt menaced by the perceived threat of domestic outbreaks of Bolshevik fanaticism, this was well pitched. Conrad began his writing career at a time when the centre of gravity in English life was moving, with apparently unstoppable momentum, away from the regional to the metropolitan and national (Giles and Middleton 1995). Indeed, part of the vigour of English cultural life in the late nineteenth and early twentieth centuries depended upon the influx of non-nationals such as he was, but for his purposes here, Conrad needs to tell a tale of his shedding of foreign characteristics and the acquisition of English sensibilities. By offering personal experience as an alternative to public history, his collection of reminiscences was deliberately pitched for a culture increasingly anxious about the loss of a sense of continuity and tradition. *A Personal Record* is all about Conrad's attempt to position himself as 'a not altogether contemptible personality' (CL4: 225) by demonstrating the inevitability of his becoming an English writer. Chapter 6 of *A Personal Record* continued in this vein when it describes aspects of the interviews which Conrad had to undergo at various stages of his career in the merchant marine. Here he promotes the idea that he had a long-term wish – stemming perhaps from his encounter with an Englishman on the Furca Pass (119) – to be an English sailor and whilst the inaccuracy of his claim has been thoroughly discussed by biographers, its truth matters rather less than the fact that Conrad felt it necessary to make it. The book ends with the young Conrad on board a French pilot ship as it goes to meet an English ship entering Marseilles (134–5). He recalls being addressed in English – 'the speech of my secret choice, of my future' (136) – and concludes with his first sight of the Red Ensign in the half-light – both a 'protecting warm bit of bunting' and 'destined for so many years to be the only roof over my head' (138).

It is worth noting that Conrad playfully signed off the work's 'A Familiar Preface' with the initials 'J. C. K', offering a characteristically Conradian insistence on the duality of identity – the Anglicised 'Joseph Conrad' (rather than 'Jozef Konrad') being yoked to the Polish 'Korzeniowski' (Knowles and Moore 2000: 277). But in 1919 Conrad used his 'Author's Note' to the work to criticise the ongoing labelling of him as a Slavic writer ('[n]othing is more foreign' [vi]); to correct the notion that he was 'the son of a revolutionist' (vii); and to argue against the idea that writing in English was second choice for him, declaring that he was 'adopted by the genius of the language, which . . . made me its own so completely that its very idioms . . . had a direct action on my temperament and fashioned my still plastic character' (v). He signed this text off with the initials J. C., emphasising his English identity.

Early reviews

Most early reviews were polite but often a little baffled by the book's organisation. *The Bookman* saw the collection as evidence of Conrad's individuality
whilst *The Spectator* saw the book as underpinned by a dull heat of irony
arising from the author's fierce objectivity (Carabine 1992: III, 342). The New
York *Nation* noted Conrad's use of the strategies of fiction in what it saw as
the book's fragmentary narrative. The London *Nation* regarded the volume
as 'wild in its disorder' and suggested that behind 'the excellent, though always
foreign, English, we catch glimpses of a strange and alluring personality' (cited in
Carabine 1992: III, 345). The *North American Review* continued in this vein,
noting that the real story of Conrad's art would remain 'shut in his own bosom'
and would only be revealed by 'indirection' (Teets and Gerber 1971: 44). *The
Athenaeum* noted the legacy of the forefather of experimental English fiction,
novelist Laurence Sterne (1712–68) in what it saw as the book's 'indifference
to the claims of mere narrative and the subtlety of its touches' (3 February 1912,
p. 124).

Later critical response

A pioneering study is provided by Edward Said's *Joseph Conrad and the Fiction
of Autobiography* (1966) which briefly discusses the work as an 'evasive masterpiece of truly impersonal intimacy' (1966: 58). A fuller study is provided by J. M.
Kertzer 'Conrad's Personal Record' (1974–5), which considers the book as 'an
extension of Conrad's novel writing' for its 'artful examination' of personal
experience' (1974–5: 253) which turns 'Conrad's life into a moral romance'
(263). David Thorburn's *Conrad's Romanticism* (1974) examines the book's narrative organisation in some detail whilst Jacques Berthoud's *Joseph Conrad: The
Major Phase* (1978) treats Conrad's reminiscences as a work that 'formulates a
view of the relationship between life and art' (1978: 7). Zdislaw Najder's brief but
illuminating account in his 'Introduction' to his World's Classics edition (1988)
argues that '[w]riting about himself was for Conrad a way of dealing not only
with his readers, but first with himself. He wanted to be, not only to be seen like
that' (1988: xx).

'Twixt Land and Sea (1912)

In a long letter to his agent, written in early November 1911, Conrad argued that
the three stories in this collection – 'The Secret Sharer', 'Freya of the Seven Isles'
and 'A Smile of Fortune' – possessed a 'common character' that was 'slightly
different from any short stories I ever wrote. It's my second manner, less forcible,
more popular than the Typhoon set and in another tone than the [Set of] Six'
(CL4: 504).

Commentary

'A Smile of Fortune'

'A Smile of Fortune', the first story in the collection, was written immediately after Conrad's post-*Under Western Eyes* illness and during his break with his agent. Tentatively begun in May 1910 and completed in late August, it was first published in the *London Magazine*, in February 1911. Conrad described it as 'comical in a nautical setting' and as 'a good short serial' work (CL4: 329, 362). Conrad's first title was 'A Deal in Potatoes' (CL5: 134). The story drew upon his experience whilst on Mauritius as Captain of the *Otago* (whose first mate was a Mr Born rather than the story's Mr Burns) in August of 1888 (see Chronology, p. 173). During this visit, he flirted with a young woman from one of the island's old families, proposing marriage only to be rejected. Whilst the captain in this tale resigns his post on return to Australia, in Conrad's case it would be a further three months before he tendered his resignation and, like the narrator of the story, returned to Europe as a passenger. Although one biographer sees 'A Smile of Fortune' as a 'fantasy designed to convert humiliation and defeat into bittersweet success', others caution against accepting the story as anything more than a fiction (Karl 1979: 260 and note). Najder convincingly argues that Conrad's decision to resign the command appears to owe more to the decision of the Russian authorities to free him from the claims of citizenship than it did to failure in romance (1983a: 112).

The narrator is bothered by the need to make a profit for the shipowners, who have left the cargo arrangements to his judgement. The 'horrid thoughts of business' (3) and 'commercial interests' spoil 'the finest life under the sun' (6). Charged with calling on Mr Jacobus, the narrator is astonished to find a Mr Jacobus on board at half past seven in the morning, a feat he is tempted to put down to 'white magic or merely some black trick of trade' (7). At the end of their first meeting, the narrator learns that this is 'the wrong Jacobus' (13) – Alfred, a 'dealer in every description of ship's stores' (12), and not Ernest, the wealthy merchant – and that the two brothers have not spoken to each other for over eighteen years. Once ashore, the narrator picks up conflicting views of Alfred, culminating in the information gleaned by his chief mate, including the notion that 'no respectable person in the whole town would come near' him and the rumour that he is said to 'keep a girl shut up' in his house (21). The Captain soon learns that Ernest is also disliked – 'objectionable to the authorities' – but is also 'a local personage', someone whose weekly parties are 'attended by the best people in the colonies' (25). Ernest has an illegitimate son whom he mistreats, and this so scandalises the Captain that, at their first meeting, he refuses to be polite and leaves without entering into any trade. The Captain also learns that Alfred had achieved notoriety in the past by running off after a circus horserider, leaving Ernest to take care of his brother's abandoned wife and daughter. He also learns that the girl in Alfred's house is the latter's illegitimate child by the circus woman. Conrad is quick to point up the hypocrisy inherent in the island's treatment of the two men – the racism that tolerates the mistreatment of Ernest's mulatto son is criticised and (by implication at least) so is the conventional morality that ostracizes Alfred and his illegitimate daughter.

The narrator is delayed for want of sacks to hold his cargo of sugar, and Alfred suggests he might be able to help him but proposes they discuss terms at his home. Once there he is captivated by the sight of Alice and her 'magnificently cynical' (44) hair which barely disguises the fact that she is virtually naked – the 'wicker arm chair was the most substantial thing about her person' (44). The narrator soon overcomes his embarrassment and talks to her with what he hopes is 'ingratiating softness' (45). Alice is a cliché from magazine fiction – a gauche femme-fatale – and whilst Conrad claimed that he tried to make her 'pathetic', most reviewers saw her as wild and animal-like (CL5: 122). Whilst the narrator waits for news of the sacks, he pays court to Alice under the gaze of Jacobus who looks on 'with a sort of approving anxiety' at his 'efforts to make his daughter smile' (51). The narrator's visits become a source of scandal in the town but he has become obsessed with the girl: 'I loved to watch her slow changes of pose, to look at her long immobilities composed in the graceful lines of her body . . . She was like a spellbound creature with the forehead of a goddess crowned by the dishevelled magnificent hair of a gipsy tramp. Even her indifference was seductive' (58–9).

On the eve of his departure, the narrator succumbs to temptation – 'cool reflection had nothing to do with the circumstance' (69) – and kisses her in a passionate 'storm of haphazard caresses' (69) which are witnessed by Alfred. The narrator cannot read her father's reaction but agrees to buy potatoes from him as a means of forestalling any animosity. The narrator no longer feels any desire for Alice, expressing a 'weary conviction of the emptiness of all things under Heaven' (79) and, realising 'with a sort of terror my complete detachment from that unfortunate creature' (79), he departs. The potatoes he bought turn out to be a shrewd investment, but Jacobus (a homophone for succubus) has latched onto him and the narrator resigns his command rather than face the prospect of a return to the island.

The story touches on the theme of the doppelganger, which is developed more fully in 'The Secret Sharer', and appears to involve the same ship. Here the theme is played for comedy, as the narrator has to deal with scandalous Alfred and his superficially respectable brother Ernest Jacobus. The story is a tale about the relationship between desire and propriety in which both Jacobus brothers have succumbed to desire but since Ernest's is the socially sanctioned route of sleeping with a slave, he escapes the censure that his brother endures for pursuing the circus woman. Alfred brings to his chandlery business the same obessiveness he brought to his failed relationship and in this the story makes a connection between capitalism and sexual relations in terms of their ultimate carelessness of human emotions. In succumbing to his desire for Alice, the narrator eventually pays a high price since he relinquishes the ship he loves because of his indiscretion.

'The Secret Sharer'

'The Secret Sharer' was written during the composition of *Under Western Eyes* (see Works, **pp. 82–7**) and, with its theme of the doppelganger, many critics have seen connections between the two works. The story was begun in December 1909, shortly after Conrad's birthday, and was written for money at the prompting of the literary editor of the *Daily Mail*. Conrad claimed 'it is a very characteristic Conrad' (CL4: 297, 298) in its psychological take on the pressures of first command. He couldn't settle on a title for the story, suggesting 'The Second Self. An Episode from the Sea' (CL4: 299), 'The Secret Self' and 'The Other Self', as well as 'The Secret Sharer but that may be *too* enigmatic' (CL4: 300). The writing of the story prompted a temporary break with his agent who, irritated at this further delay in work on *Under Western Eyes*, threatened to 'slam the door' on him (CL4: 303). On completing the tale, Conrad wrote to Edward Garnett, gloating that 'the Secret Sharer is *it*. Eh? No damned tricks with girls there. Eh? Every word fits and there is not a single uncertain note. Luck my boy. Pure luck' (CL5: 128). The story was first published in the USA in the August and September 1910 issues of *Harper's Magazine*: Conrad felt it a 'Beastly shame' (CL4: 354) that it was split into two instalments. To American novelist Edith Wharton (1862–1937) Conrad suggested that the story was 'particularly English in moral atmosphere, in feeling, in every detail' (CL5: 152). The 'Author's Note' informed the reader that the germ of the tale came from a real incident that occurred on board the *Cutty Sark* in which a black sailor was killed by the Chief Mate. Concise coverage of this incident is given in Cedric Watts's 'Introduction' to his edition of *Typhoon and Other Tales* (2002). For more extensive coverage see Norman Sherry *Conrad's Eastern World* (1966).

Leggatt, the Chief Mate of the *Sephora*, has 'killed a man' (101) and, escaping from his ship, has swum the 2 miles to the narrator's vessel, where he is observed hanging onto the ship's ladder. The narrator immediately feels as if some 'mysterious communication was established' (99) and invites Leggatt aboard and hides him in his staterooms whilst he listens to his story. The narrator decides early on that this man is 'no homicidal ruffian' (102) and when Leggatt's own chief officer comes looking for him, he hides the fugitive and with 'punctilious courtesy' (120) faces the *Sephora*'s Captain Archibold who 'was a little disconcerted by . . . something in me that reminded him of the man he was seeking – suggesting a mysterious similitude to the young fellow he had distrusted and disliked from the first' (120).

Having seen off Captain Archibold, the narrator agrees to maroon Leggatt, having 'understood' (132) that his crime is one that is beyond the ken of land men's law (133). The narrator steers his ship close into the isle of Koh Ring, allowing Leggatt to escape with a chance of reaching shore. The crew, unaware of the Captain's motives, fear for the safety of the ship, but he pulls off the tricky manoeuvre and turns the ship away from the shore at the last minute despite being 'a total stranger to the ship' and unaware of how she would handle (141). In doing this, the narrator demonstrates his mastery and achieves communion with his ship, 'the perfect communion of a seaman and his first command' (143), and gains authority over his crew. Conrad suggested that he pulled off a similar manoeuvre, for purely nautical reasons, whilst 'amongst the islands of the Gulf of Siam' when he was Captain of the *Otago* (*The Mirror of the Sea*, 19).

'Freya of the Seven Isles'

'Freya of the Seven Isles', the final story in the collection, was begun in December 1910 and completed in February 1911. Conrad described it as an 'Eastern seas tale – quite a novel in character and quite suitable for serialising' (CL4: 417). The story mixes issues of trade and colonial politics in its account of old Neilson, a planter, and his daughter Freya. Neilson is caught up in the rivalry between the Dutch and British authorities for control of the Malay Archipelago, and whilst he mistrusts the Dutch, he takes care 'not to give even the shadow of offence' (149) to them. His daughter is renowned as a beefy beauty and is in love with Jasper Allen, a 'much too enterprising' (154) trader who is beginning to attract the attention of the Dutch authorities in the person of Heemskirk, Commander of the Dutch patrol boat in the region. Heemskirk is also interested in Freya, something that Nielsen tolerates in the hope of a quiet life. Conrad further points up the contrasts between the two men by having Allen's ship sail-powered whilst Heemskirk's is steam-driven. Allen and Freya plan to elope as soon as she is twenty-one. Meanwhile Heemskirk, frustrated by Freya's lack of interest, is making himself 'disagreeable' to Nielsen by 'expressing a sinister wonder at the Government permitting' him to remain on the Seven Isles (175). Things come to a head when the two rivals arrive at Nielsen's and Heemskirk witnesses Freya and Allen 'carrying on' which prompts him to confront her. Attempting to steal a kiss (184), Heemskirk is walloped by Freya, but his resulting 'incoherent imprecations' are interpreted by the guileless old Neilson as toothache (198). A simple comedy ensues as Freya and her father talk at cross-purposes about Heemskirk's behaviour. The two rivals depart early the next day, leaving Old Neilson worrying over Heemskirk's intentions. Heemskirk contrives to arrest Allen and impound his brig, which he takes in tow for Makassar but then cuts it adrift so that its momentum carries it onto Tamissa reef. Allen's stranded brig is looted and he remains in Makassar, mooning over his loss and the failure of his plans. News of his plight finds its way to the Seven Isles and Freya falls ill and has to be taken to Singapore for treatment. Here more is learnt of Allen's predicament and of Heemskirk's meddling, and Old Neilson is sent to find Allen only to discover him looking like 'a skeleton in dirty clothes' (236), gripped by the belief that with the loss of his beloved brig he no longer has any hold over Freya. Neilson reports this to Freya, whom he persists in seeing as 'too sensible' (237) to continue to love Allen, but she dies regretting that she was too 'selfish or afraid' (238) to go with him.

The story's narrative is typically Conradian in its use of a frame narrator who pieces the tale together on the basis of a 'long chatty letter' which sparks recollections of his own time in 'the Eastern Archipelago' (147). Also typical is the subversion of genre expectations as what starts off as magazine-ish tale of love rivalry becomes something far bleaker with the death of Freya, Allen's descent into madness and the grisly suicide of Allen's first mate: altogether what Conrad called doing 'a magazine-ish thing with some decency' (CL4: 464).

Early reviews

The collection was generally well received by the critics, with 'The Secret Sharer' being seen as the strongest tale and 'Freya' generally regarded as the weakest. The *Daily News* praised 'The Secret Sharer' as 'surely a masterpiece' of 'marvellous psychological insight' (Sherry 1973: 253) but suggested that the other stories supported the notion that Conrad's 'characters have frequently something of the character of victims' (Sherry 1973: 252). The *Manchester Guardian* made some rather lazy comparisons between the stories and some of Conrad's earlier work – seeing 'A Smile of Fortune' as similar to 'Heart of Darkness' in its presentation of 'a veil of mystery' about its central character (Sherry 1973: 254). The review suggested that Conrad's strength as a writer rested on his presentation of 'unusual people outside of the settled orders' (Sherry 1973: 255). *The Standard* was lavish in its praise, describing him as 'king . . . of story tellers' who 'combine the sense of life proclaimed by the great mid-Victorians with the sense of form discovered here in England somewhere about 1890' (Sherry 1973: 256). The review singled out 'The Secret Sharer' as 'the most perfect of all Mr Conrad's stories' (Sherry 1973: 257).

Later critical response

'A Smile of Fortune'

Lawrence Graver reads the story as fatally flawed by the demands of the magazine market and whilst accepting that Conrad 'describes the love affair in the fervid vocabulary of romance and the corruptions of trade realistically', argues that its two subjects are too disparate, creating 'moments of unintentional and almost ruinous comedy' in which Conrad mishandles the Captain's obsession with Alice in his focus on Burn's feelings about the potato transaction (1969: 160). William Lafferty, in 'Conrad's "A Smile of Fortune": The Moral Threat of Commerce' (1965) also examines the tensions between the narrator's personal and commercial interests. William Bonney, *Thorns and Arabesques* (1980) develops a reading of Jacobus's attempts to entangle the Captain in 'economically and emotionally compromising situations' (73), whilst Daniel Schwarz argues that the story has been overlooked and that 'we should view the tale as a dramatic monologue in which the speaker's tormented conscience gradually reveals a far different version of his relationship with Alice' (1982: 10). Cedric Watts, in 'The Narrative Enigma of Conrad's "A Smile of Fortune"' (1985) also argues for the story as one of Conrad's 'most brilliant yet most neglected and under-rated works'. Ted Billy reads the story as a study of 'drastic inversions' in which 'Conrad converts the narrator's naïve optimism into cynical self loathing, his romantic infatuation into monetary lust, and his inexperience with trade into an indoctrination in unscrupulous business practices' (1997: 91). Jeremy Hawthorn posits an influence of the reporting of the Dr Crippen murders on Conrad's understanding of the nature of male sexuality in his essay 'Conrad and the Erotic: "A Smile of Fortune" and "The Planter of Malata"' (2003a).

'The Secret Sharer'

There is a useful general survey of early critical responses in Bruce Harkness (ed.) *Conrad's Secret Sharer and the Critics* (1962). The story has been a productive quarry for psychoanalytic studies through its use of the motif of the double. Barbara Johnson and Marjorie Garber's 'Secret Sharing: Reading Conrad Psychoanalytically' (1987) provides an overview of major psychoanalytic readings.

Lawrence Graver suggests that the text brings about its own critical misrepresentation because 'its details are at times so vaguely portentous that readers are seduced into hunting for a complex symbolic consistency which the work does not possess' (1969: 152). Norman Sherry' *Conrad's Eastern World* (1966) surveys the ways in which Conrad draws upon the murder of a crewman by the first officer of the *Cutty Sark* in September 1880. Daniel Schwarz's study stresses the need to focus on the narrator, arguing that 'the captain is as much Legatt's secret sharer as is Legatt's the captain's' (1982: 6). Jakob Lothe traces 'how the ambiguous thematics of the short story' are 'shaped through its interplay of narrative devices, functions and effects' (1989: 58). Ted Billy argues that 'Conrad's narrator never fully comprehends the secret self who seeks immersion in the destructive element of the sea' and suggests that the story's ending 'leaves us grappling with a mystery rather than a revelation' (1997: 27). Vulcan draws on theoretical material from Lacan and Bakhtin to examine the story's reflections on the 'process of subjectivity' in relation to *Under Western Eyes*, 'its "other"' (1999: 35).

'Freya of the Seven Isles'

Lawrence Graver dismisses the story as 'clumsily protracted' and stricken by 'narrative blunders' (1969: 163, 164), but Daniel Schwarz makes a case for it as 'an artistic laboratory' for *Chance* and *Victory* (1982: 18). He argues, however, that the narrator is 'tediously loquacious' and that the tale lacks 'moral and artistic depth' (Schwarz 1982: 21). Vulcan treats the tale as an 'anti-romance', emphasising the role of the narrator who 'wishes to become a character in his own story' (1999: 152). In 'Territorial Vision and Revision in "Freya of the Seven Isles"' (2003), Mark D. Larabee argues that 'Conrad's topographical alterations lend this undervalued tale considerably more stylistic subtlety and richness than critics have recognised' (2003: 96).

Chance (1914)

Chance was the novel that finally saw Conrad secure a popular success and has been variously viewed as the first major work of his late phase or as evidence of the onset of his decline. The novel saw the return of Marlow, narrator of 'Youth' and 'Heart of Darkness' (see Works, **pp. 48–9, 49–52**), who presents much of the story in a notably misogynist and sardonic fashion. Conrad told an American journalist that the novel was 'rather a discursive sort of thing – by no means what the reviewers call "a well told story"' (CL3: 508). The book's complex narrative organisation makes its popular success even more surprising. Conrad had begun the germ of the novel in 'Dynamite', a short story whose title at least had been written in 1898 (CL2: 62). A year later Conrad referred to an untitled story 'about a Captain's wife' (CL2: 169), and in 1904 he sought to placate his agent with references to a number of new projects, including one 'about a voyage with a cargo of explosives' (CL3: 126); a year later he was still dangling 'a short story . . . about a dynamite ship' (CL3: 228). By May 1904 he reported to his agent '"Explosives" ready' (CL3: 243) but in September he writes of it being 'ready by the end of the year' (CL3: 280), and the novel was repeatedly set aside for work on *The Secret Agent* and then *Under Western Eyes*. When he did work on it, Conrad found it an effort, at one point lamenting, 'I go on with *Chance* convulsively as a jaded horse may be made to gallop – and I fear it's all extravagant trash – the trash and the extravagance of despair' (CL3: 504).

Initially Conrad seems to have conceived of *Chance* as a sea novel, promising Pinker in 1908 that it would offer the 'old effect – analysis applied to the life at sea' (CL4: 106). In March 1911 he wrote to Ford Madox Ford, with characteristic evasiveness, of making 'a fresh start with a thing called *Chance* I began some time ago' (CL4: 433), and by September he had completed about 60,000 words of his 'long (and stupid) novel' (CL4: 510). As the work drew to a close and serial rights were secured for the USA, Conrad seems to have turned his tale to focus more upon Flora.

In her detailed study of the novel and its development, Susan Jones has argued that the serial text highlights 'the constructions of female identity imposed upon the heroine by the male narrators [and] encompasses a generic shift towards forms favoured by a popular readership' (Jones 1999: 149). Writing to the *New York Herald* in an effort to promote his work to a wider readership, Conrad cannily commented that 'I aimed at treating my subject in a way which would interest women. That's all. I don't believe that women have to be written for specially as if they were infants' (CL4: 531–2). Conrad completed the manuscript in March 1912 and *Chance* was serialised in the *New York Herald* between January and June 1912: the manuscript bears the title 'Explosives: A Ship-Board Tale'. The novel was due to be published in the UK by Methuen in 1913 but was delayed by a printers strike. A few pre-publication copies, dated 1913, survived. The novel was published in the USA by Doubleday, Page in October 1913 and by Methuen in the UK in January 1914.

Commentary

As with other Marlow narratives, we are treated to many meditative asides, to convoluted accounts of how and where he obtained the information from which he builds his narrative, and, unique to *Chance*, to increasingly bitter and often fiercely misogynistic outbursts that are frequently countered by the frame narrator who interrupts to express his disbelief at Marlow's remarks. The careful disruption of chronological order means we have learnt more about Flora than any individual character save Marlow and, as such, are able to keep abreast of the tale and enjoy its ironies, despite its convolutions. Marlow presents himself as 'an investigator – a man of deductions' (326) and much of the narration can be seen as a modernist detective story in which the narrator not only pieces together evidence but also calls into question the very nature of evidence itself (Hampson 1980). Marlow's asides also work to question his capacity to narrate a love story since he appears to be deeply cynical about romantic love. Critics have noted Marlow's reliance on 'conjectural omniscience' to provide information on characters of whom he has no direct knowledge (Knowles and Moore 2000: 60).

Conrad once glossed the novel as 'the history of a luckless girl (with a good ending)' (CL5: 16). Writing to the editor of the *English Review*, he described the story as 'simple and biographical', 'a close-knit *intrigue* that is difficult to follow in all the varied episodes it presents' (CL5: 44). This is perhaps overstated but, on a first reading, the narrative organisation can seem ponderous. The novel makes use of a frame narrator who describes a chance meeting over supper in a riverside inn where he and Marlow happen upon 'a fellow yachtsman' (3) and 'the conversation took a special turn relating exclusively to sea-life' (4). The yachtsman, Powell, relates the tale of how he came to serve on the *Ferndale* with its cargo of dynamite – a story full of fortunate occurrences which sets the theme of the workings of chance underway. Powell and Marlow discuss the *Ferndale*, and Marlow begins to tell the tale of how he knew of its Captain Anthony via his acquaintance with Anthony's brother-in-law, Fyne. At this point, the narrative pauses, resuming via a series of conversations between the frame narrator and Marlow in which he tells the story of the Fynes and Captain Anthony. These conversations occur 'in several stages, at intervals which are not indicated here' (41). Mrs Fyne is a famous advocate of the rights of women, and the Fyne household has a succession of young women who come to visit – 'they were like disciples' (42). Marlow meets one of these women on the lip of 'a high quarry' (43) near the Fyne's house: later we learn that this woman is Flora de Barral whom Marlow casts as both a 'victim' (46) and 'a minx' (53). We learn that she is the daughter of the disgraced financier de Barral, a man who is described as an 'absurd monster' whose greed is 'incalculable, unfathomable, inconceivable' (69–70).

Flora's mother – an 'unassuming woman . . . with a fund of simple gaiety' (71) – has died 'from neglect' (72) and Flora was raised by a callous governess. Marlow details her father's rise and fall with Dickensian glee, showing him to have been a fool who has 'handled millions without ever enjoying anything of what is counted as precious in the community of men' (84). This twenty-page excursion into the background of Flora's case is typical of Marlow's narration, which might be characterised as a rolling analepsis in which the 'narration returns, as it were, to a past point in the story' (Rimmon-Kenan 1983: 46. Also see Lothe 1989: 25, note 10). As soon as de Barral's imprisonment is announced, Flora's governess abandons her, her schemes for living off de Barral's daughter being ruined. Marlow's narration again wrings every detail out in his account of the calculating governess's behaviour. What begins as a critique modulates, against the tenor of his telling, into something marginally more sympathetic as he relates the woman's life of 'constant self-repression' (104). After the governess has left, Flora runs from the house and is met by Fyne who takes her to his wife to care for her. Flora is then taken away by her uncle, an implacably lower-middle-class man whom Fyne regards as possessing a 'conceited satisfaction with his own respectable vulgarity' (129). The horrified Fynes reluctantly gives Flora up to the care of her relatives. In a conversation with the Fynes at his lodgings near their home in the country, Marlow learns more about Captain Anthony and Flora's relationship, or, as Marlow, alluding to the Edgar Allen Poe (1809–49) story, punningly terms it, the 'affair of the purloined brother' (148).

Flora is eventually dumped on the Fynes by her relatives who have failed to get on with her. The Fynes help her find work as a companion for an elderly woman, but this fails because she is too morose (179). She is then found work as a governess to a German family but leaves when the husband flirts with her and her true parentage is discovered. Flora has clearly become something of a problem for

the Fynes, and Marlow cynically suggests that she has taken 'a particularly feminine' approach to her predicament by casting her lot in with Anthony. Marlow
finally meets up with Flora again in person in a chance encounter on the pavement
outside the Eastern Hotel where Anthony is staying. Here Flora reveals her earlier
despair on the quarry edge and the fact that the day after her thwarted suicide
Anthony arrived at the Fynes' and the two lonely people quickly developed a
'tentative, uncertain, intimacy' (207). Marlow finds Flora oddly composed and
comments that she 'was not so much unreadable as blank; and I did not know
whether to admire her for it or dismiss her from my thoughts as the passive butt of
ferocious misfortune' (207):

> That girl was, one may say, washing about with slack limbs in the ugly
> surf of life with no opportunity to strike out for herself, when suddenly
> she had been made to feel that there was somebody beside her in bitter
> water. A most considerable moral event for her; whether she was aware
> of it or not.
>
> (222)

Flora accepts Anthony's love as an expedient way out of her predicament and as a
means of providing a home for her father away from public scrutiny. Marlow
later suggests that she is, in fact, 'abandoning herself passively' (331).

At the beginning of Part 2, Marlow explains to the frame narrator how he
'chased the mystery of the vanishing Powell' (258), following him as he cruised
the Thames, visiting Flora in her 'rural-retreat' (382) Essex home. As in *Lord Jim*,
Marlow's narrative frequently draws upon the perspectives and perceptions of his
interlocutors, and this reliance upon the views of others adds further layers to the
narrative. In order to present details of Flora's time aboard the *Ferndale*, he draws
on Powell's perceptions of Anthony and Flora in what Marlow cynically describes
as 'the floating stage of that tragic-comedy' (272). Powell's reading of the situation aboard ship is, according to Marlow, shaped by his inexperience, his youth
and even his inculcation of the trite tales of 'our light literature' (288): these
factors encourage us to question the basis of Marlow's narration and are part of
the way that the novel's narrative organisation works for a modernist emphasis
on indeterminacy and uncertainty. The Ferndale's crew are astonished by their
captain's marriage and the first mate, Franklin, pours scorn on it and the changes
it has brought to the ordered life aboard ship (286). Powell is just as astonished
when he finally sees Mrs Anthony, since he imagined a woman of far more mature
years than Flora. As the voyage progresses, Powell learns that Flora's father, now
released from prison and forced to accompany his daughter, is unhappy with his
life on board. A near collision at sea brings Flora and Powell together, and he
admires her 'pluck' and 'wonderful self-restraint' (320) in the face of danger.

Marlow tries to tease out the cause of the evident disquiet that exists between
Anthony and his wife and, in another analepsis, narrates the scenes immediately
after his meeting with Flora outside the Eastern Hotel to reveal that Anthony
accepted that Flora did not love him and understood that her acceptance of him
was expedient. The narrative then moves to Flora's meeting with her father on the
day of his release from prison in which he is revealed by turns as obsessed with his
trial and jealously outraged by her marriage. De Barral accompanies Flora to the

Ferndale 'under protest' (372) and this pollutes the atmosphere aboard ship as he plots how to get Flora 'away from that man' (377) and from the ship that he feels is little more than a second prison. Yet it is Flora, caught between her father's bitter sniping and Anthony's distant 'magnanimity' (389), who is shown to be truly trapped. Powell becomes irritated by the constant complaints of Franklin and the steward against Flora, who question whether the Anthonys are in fact married, and becomes seen by them, in an extension of the book's chivalric imagery, as her 'champion' (391). Anthony, noting that Flora seems to welcome talking to Powell, magnanimously engineers situations that ensure they are often together. The novel moves into melodrama as it reaches its conclusion, with Powell witnessing de Barral tampering with Anthony's drink. Anthony is reluctant to confront de Barral in front of Flora and threatens to leave her and her father at the next port but she, surprisingly, resists being cast off and is taken to her room. De Barral then kills himself in front of Powell with the poison he hoped to use on Anthony. Powell colludes with the Captain in putting de Barral's body into its bed so that the death appears natural when it is discovered by the steward. What seems surprising, to say the least, is that after this event Powell remains with the ship and the Anthonys for a further 'six years' (437). Powell reveals to Marlow the fate of the *Ferndale* and that Anthony 'went down with her' (438) when she collided with another ship. Marlow tells of his third and last meeting with Flora during which she revealed that she did eventually grow to love Anthony. In these closing scenes, Marlow plays an unlikely matchmaker, seeking to bring Flora and Powell together.

Early reviews

Henry James's famous late essay on 'The New Novel' offers a powerful analysis of Conrad's narrative strategy in *Chance*. Having discussed the shortcomings of the modern novel as manifested in the work of Arnold Bennett, H. G. Wells, Gilbert Cannan and Hugh Walpole, James turns to the question of what he personally wants from fiction. This centres upon the need for evidence of the 'touch of the hand of selection' (James 1963: 377), for whilst he is in favour of fiction being a 'slice of life', he argues that a slice is not amorphous but something defined and limited. Whilst the 'happy-go-lucky' incorporation of everything does produce some 'aesthetic pleasure', 'it takes method, blest method' to shape an incident in such a way that it can be shown to determine action (James 1963: 378). James then turned to Conrad's *Chance* as 'a supreme specimen of the part playable in a novel' (1963: 379) by method, approvingly noting Conrad's use of multiple narrative perspectives as a transgression of 'the general law of fiction' (380–1) which posits that narrators are subservient to the story they tell. James's account of Conrad's narrative technique as 'a prolonged hovering flight of the subjective over the outstretched ground of the case exposed' (1963: 381) has been influential. He argued that because of it, *Chance* was overwrought, compromised by:

> the Marlows . . ., the Powells, the Franklins, the Fynes, the tell-tale little dogs, [which form] the successive members of a queue from one to the

other of which the sense and the interest of the subject have to be passed on together, in the manner of the buckets of water for the improvised extinction of a fire, before reaching our apprehension.

(James 1963: 383)

The result of this method is that the reader's grasp of the importance of a given event is often tentative; as James puts it, a portion of the reader's apprehension has 'to be allowed for as spilt by the way' (1963: 383). James's stress on technique as central to any account of this novel was profitably taken up by later critics. The *Manchester Guardian* commented on 'Mr Conrad's unmistakable method of telling a story' (Sherry 1973: 274):

He keeps out of sight; he hides behind one man at first and then puts a second in front of the first, a perhaps a third in front of the second. Some shadowy figure of a narrator opens the tale and then melts into dimness behind it and lets the bulk of it come as a tale told by one of the persons whom he has mentioned, and this second narrator, in turn, hands over the job, for a time, to one of his own creatures. So that the core of the story is, in one sense, like a picture within a frame which itself is painted – It is within a frame too, and that frame within another, again.

Whilst not a wholly accurate account of the narrative organisation of *Chance*, this captures well the period's sense of its narrative complexity. Edward Garnett, writing in *The Nation*, notes 'the design or intellectual pattern which runs through the story – i.e. the infinite permutations out of which chance relations weave people's destinies – is one especially in keeping with the author's gift of philosophic irony' (Sherry 1973: 277). Garnett goes on to suggest that the method 'of telling his story through the mouths of three or for people, intermittently assisting in the drama, who unbosom themselves to a chief inquisitor, Marlow, is exceedingly artful, though occasionally a trifle artificial' (Sherry 1973: 278).

For Garnett, the tale 'is a masterpiece of indirect narrative' (Sherry 1973: 278). The *Glasgow Herald* was one of the few dissenters, complaining that 'Somehow *Chance* suggests a formidable scaffolding that people watch being constructed intricately for days, only to find that at the end it was designed for nothing more than placing a weathercock on a steeple' (Sherry 1973: 283).

Later critical response

The novel, although praised by Leavis in *The Great Tradition* (1948), suffered during the general downgrading of the later work which was a feature of Conrad criticism in the 1950s and 1960s. Gary Geddes' *Conrad's Later Novels* (1980) offers an early sympathetic account of the narrative organisation, commenting on its 'remarkable rhythm and symmetry' in which 'what may appear to be digressions' are 'very crucial to our understanding' and what 'seems to be background . . . turns out to be foreground' (1980: 20). Geddes defends the novel from those critics who decried its romance superstructure, suggesting that they had missed its 'ironic portrayal of the contemporary jungle of human relations and the shallowness and hypocrisy of religious and commercial motivations' (1980: 30). Daniel Schwarz's *Conrad: The Later Fiction* (1982) speculates that the return to the use of Marlow was a product of the writer's block that beset Conrad in the completion of the novel, since via Marlow's piecing together of the story 'he can transfer the problems of writing and understanding to an alter ego within the world he has been trying to create' (1982: 41). In *Chance*, however, Marlow has become 'a mere garrulous device to tell a tale' and 'a surrogate for Conrad's middle aged prejudices' (Schwarz 1982: 42). Schwarz suggests that the novel offers an 'unintentional parody of the self-conscious narrator' which 'teaches us something about the limitations and possibilities of the form that is caricatured' (1982: 45). Four important essays on the novel appeared in the special issue of *The Conradian*, 17, 2 (1993), including Laurence Davies' 'Conrad, *Chance*, and Women Readers' (1993: 75–88), which examines the factors that helped make the book a popular success, and Andrew Michael Roberts subtle reading of the figuration of women in 'Secret Agents and Secret Objects: Action, Passivity, and Gender in *Chance*' (1993: 89–104). Scott McCracken's 'Postmodernism, a *Chance* to Reread?' (1995) examines the novel's engagement with New Woman fiction. Susan Jones *Conrad and Women* (1999) is the most detailed study to date, providing an account of the novel's debt to Polish themes, speculating on the influence of Conrad's 'aunt' Marguerite Poradowska, and offering a detailed study of the book's development along with an account of the ways in which its marketing contributed to its success.

Within the Tides (1915)

Conrad aptly termed this volume 'not so much art as a financial operation' (CL5: 455). The stories which make it up are generally poor and for many commentators this is one of Conrad's weakest collections.

Commentary

'The Planter of Malata'

Conrad wrote this story whilst working on *Victory* in late 1913 (see Works, pp. 107–13). Begun as 'The Assistant' (CL5: 299) in early November, the tale 'gave me a lot of trouble for a good six weeks' (CL5: 313). By December he was discussing its inclusion in a proposed volume to be called *Tales of Hearsay*. Once the story was published, Conrad was dismissive of it, calling it 'well bungled' (CL5: 455, note 1).

Beginning in the offices of an Australian newspaper, the tale concerns Geoffrey Renouard's unrequited love for Englishwoman Felicia Moorsom. Renouard – the planter of the title – has lived a life of 'adventure and exploration' (5) but has spent the past five years in solitude at his silk plantation, a venture run along modern scientific lines and with some ruthlessness as regards its workers. At dinner he meets the striking redhead Felicia and promptly conceives a passion for her. She is the daughter of a famous physicist and philosopher whose ideas are '[q]uite the fashion in the highest world' (15). The Moorsoms have come 'looking for a man' (17), Felicia's fiancé Arthur had been caught up in a financial scandal in London and had come to Australia to avoid further disgrace. Arthur's name has recently been cleared, and the Moorsoms have come to find him. It is discovered that Arthur has been working under the assumed name of H. Walter as Renouard's assistant.

Arthur is in fact dead but Renouard 'would give the last shred of his rectitude to secure a day more' (56) with Felicia and does not reveal this fact, giving rise to some wooden comedy as they travel to Malata. Arriving at night, Renouard persuades his guests to delay disembarking so that, when all are asleep, he can swim ashore to brief his servants, advising them to pretend that Mr Walter has left on a trading trip. As he swims back to the ship, in a clumsy foreshadowing of the ending, we are told he 'had a sensation of eternity close at hand, demanding no effort – offering its peace' (62) but at this stage he rejects suicide. Next morning the party arrive on shore and Renouard sets his deception in motion, gripped by 'the intensity of his desire' (64). Taking Felicia for a walk, he is challenged by her assertion that 'there is something strange in all this' (73) and reveals that Arthur is dead. After a scene in which he professes his intense passion only to be rejected by a disgruntled Felicia, the Moorsoms arrange to depart aboard the trading ship *Janet*. Renouard pays off his workers and arranges for them all to be sent away on the ship, leaving him alone on the island. The tale ends with a coda in which Renouard's friend and backer, the newspaper editor, travels to Malata to search for him only to discover his clothes on the beach. The narrator coyly suggests that Renouard has swum 'beyond the confines of life' (85).

'The Partner'

Written in late 1910, the tale turns around a plot for a shipwreck recounted in a yarn by a dockworker. Conrad called the narrative style 'peculiar' (CL4: 421), perhaps alluding to the self-referential aspects of the tale's first-person narrator who is 'a writer of stories' (90) and is on the look out for inspiration. The docker tells him the story of George Dunbar's involvement with the duplicitous Yankee Cloete, who hatches a scheme to sink the *Sagamore*, captained by Dunbar's brother Harry, in order to raise money for a patent medicine business. Cloete arranges for an accomplice, Mr Stafford, to 'go to sea as mate of the *Sagamore*' (107) from which position he will be able to wreck the ship. The plot fails as Stafford takes matters into his own hands by murdering the Captain, whose death leaves Cloete with insufficient funds to invest in the booming stock of Parker's Lively Lumbago Pills, since a share of the ship's insurance money is passed to Harry Dunbar's widow.

'The Inn of Two Witches: A Find'

This story was written in late 1912 and is set in northern Spain during the Peninsular war fought between Britain and France over Spanish and Portuguese territories from 1808 to 1814. Using the familiar Gothic formula of a found manuscript, the tale recounts the experience of naval officer Edgar Byrne who comes to the inn in search of his mentor and crewmate Tom Corbin after he fails to return at the appointed time from a rendezvous. The inn does indeed contain witch-like women as well as a wild girl, and Byrne soon discovers the body of his friend, deducing that he 'had died striking out against something which could be hit, and yet could kill one without leaving a wound' (159). He discovers that the killer is a bed equipped with a mechanism that lowers its canopy onto the sleeper and suffocates them. Byrne is rescued and his friend's body is buried at sea. In his 'Author's Note', Conrad sought to fend off accusations that he took the idea of a murderous bed from Wilkie Collins's story 'A Very Strange Bed' (1852); a claim that has not convinced many critics.

'Because of the Dollars'

This story was written between December 1913 and January 1914 and features Captain Davidson who appears in *Victory* and Hollis from 'Karain' who acts as the reporter of events to the unnamed narrator (see Works, **pp. 107–13, 36–7**). Conrad told his agent that the story was 'nothing second class' but admitted that it was 'a queer thing – a little savage in parts' (CL5: 168).

Davidson, we are told, is a 'really *good* man' (169), and the story concerns his defeat of a plot to rob him of the dollars he has been collecting from traders to exchange on their behalf for new issue notes. Davidson's 'goodness' extends to helping the 'unique loafer' Bamtz (177), who is living with one-time prostitute Laughing Anne. Fector, a journalist of dubious character, overhears Davidson talking about his dollar-collecting trip and encounter with Laughing Anne and teams up with two villains, one of whom is 'the Frenchman without hands' (186) who knows of Bamtz's location. The ruffians await Davidson at Bamtz's, but Anne reveals their plot to him and that the maimed Frenchman plans to kill him with the iron weights he has made Anne tie to his stumps. Forewarned by Anne, Davidson watches the Frenchman attack his hammock and then opens fire, driving the robbers away. The Frenchman kills Anne and is then shot by Davidson, who takes her body and her child back to port with his cargo of dollars. Davidson's wife assumes the worst and refuses to have Anne's child in the house, arranging for the boy to be sent to a mission school (210) before she abandons her husband. Davidson's compassion has left him isolated and 'without a single human affection near him' (211).

Early reviews

The early reviews were mixed, with *The Spectator* paying the backhanded compliment that the collection bore witness to Conrad's 'aristocratic disdain for convention' (6 March 1915, pp. 338–9). *The Athenaeum* praised Conrad's artful rendering of 'the futility, irony, and melancholy of this limited world' (6 March 1915, p. 211). The US *Nation* declared 'The Planter of Malata' a failure but argued that the other stories 'show Mr Conrad at his best as a story teller pure and simple' (10 February 1916, p. 164), but the *New York Times Book Review* (16 January 1916, pp. 17, 22) felt that with the exception of 'The Partner' the collection was a failure.

Later critical response

Edward Said's *Joseph Conrad and the Fiction of Autobiography* (1966) argues that 'The Planter of Malata' was Conrad's most pessimistic story, a masterpiece (1966: 162) and a key point in his perception of himself as a writer. Lawrence Graver's *Conrad's Short Fiction* (1969) suggests that 'The Planter of Malata' suffers from Conrad's failure 'to make the passion convincing in its own terms (1969: 177). Graver sees 'Because of the Dollars' less as a simplified *Victory* and more as a reworking of 'a familiar Conradian theme: the perils of simpleminded altruism' (1969: 173). Daniel Schwarz, in *Conrad: The Later Fiction* (1982), argues that Conrad uses 'the melodramatic episodic plot of romance to demonstrate the kind of transparent moral scheme that he believed would have an appeal for the periodical audience' (1982: 24). He regards much of the collection as complete failures of imagination but sees 'The Planter of Malata' as a more complex work in which 'we are not always sure whether Conrad is debunking his protagonist or sympathising with him' (Schwarz 1982: 31). Ted Billy's *A Wilderness of Words* (1997) examines 'The Partner' in terms of its playing off of the rough and ready narration of the dockworker with the more polished response of the writer to whom he tells his tale, reading in this a satire of 'the aestheticism of Pater and Whistler' (1997: 133). In his account of 'The Inn of Two Witches', Billy concentrates upon what he sees as the tension between the frame narrator and narrator of the embedded tale, and he reads 'The Planter of Malata' as 'simultaneously a parody of the quest for knowledge, a satire on the romantic idealization of womanhood, a burlesque of the estranged loner, and a *reductio ad absurdum* of the doppelganger theme' (Billy 1997: 150). Daphna Erdinast Vulcan's *The Strange Short Fiction of Joseph Conrad* (1999) offers an account which, informed by earlier psychological and psychoanalytic readings, presents 'The Planter of Malata' as 'an unconscious self-reflexive parable on Conrad's own art, a projection of his subconscious anxiety about his conscious artistic choices' (1999: 155).

Victory (1915)

Conrad began the novel as a short story called 'Dollars' in April 1912, but the *Titanic* disaster, in which Conrad lost some manuscripts sent to the collector John Quinn, interrupted early progress. By June, the story of Augustus Berg – as Heyst was called in the manuscript – had grown in Conrad's conception to 'nearer 18 than 10 thousand words' (CL5: 73 and note) and by October it had become the basis for the novel, as Conrad's letter to his agent made clear:

> It has a tropical Malay setting – an unconventional man and a girl on an island under peculiar circumstances to whom enters a gang of three ruffians also of a rather unconventional sort – this intrusion producing certain psychological developments and effects. There is philosophy in it and also drama – lightly treated – meant for culture people – a piece of literature before everything – and of course fit for general reading. Strictly proper. Nothing to shock the magazine public.
>
> (CL5: 113–14)

A period of illness delayed the novel, with 50,000 words completed by early December when, by Conrad's reckoning, the final manuscript would be 116,000 words. Conrad was still struggling with it in April 1913 – 'I seem unable to get into a proper swing with this thing' (CL5: 216) – and soon became caught up in revising *Chance* for novel publication. By August he was still not much advanced, with around 660 pages of manuscript completed (CL5: 273). In October, serialisation was being discussed with various journals, and Conrad was plugging the story's 'sensational ending' (CL5: 288): he had completed about 60 per cent of the novel. At this stage, Conrad fluctuated between using the title 'Dollars' and *An Island Story*. In November, he broke off from *Victory* to start work on 'The Planter of Malata', spending the next six weeks completing this text before returning to the novel (see Works, **pp. 104–5**). Instead of returning to *Victory*, however, he worked on 'Because of the Dollars' – perhaps trying out in miniature some aspects of the larger project, given that both works share a trio of villains, a self-sacrificing heroine and the presence of Captain Davidson (see Works, **p. 106**). Finishing this story in January 1914, Conrad began work on the novel again in February, and by mid-month told his agent that work was 'well in hand' (CL5: 350), although to others he wrote of the slog of finishing the 'long dreary machine' (354) and by early April Conrad confessed that the book would not be complete by the time the serial starts in May (371): the serialisation was delayed in consequence. The book was finished on 28 June and on 10 July Conrad began revising the typescript. He had completed his work by 18 July (406). The novel, cut about by the magazine editors, was serialised in the USA in the February 1915 edition of *Munsey's Magazine*. It was first published in book form by Doubleday in the USA, appearing in March, and by Methuen in England, where it appeared in September. Unusually, the novel appeared with an 'Author's Note', which reflected on the irony of publishing a book with this title in the midst of war and went on to comment disingenuously on the character of Schomberg. Whilst the note made it clear that the character was created long before the war, by asserting that the scheming Schomberg is 'indubitably' Teutonic, Conrad was also playing to public sentiment (*Victory*, xxxii; cf. CL5: 467).

Commentary

Whilst pointing towards the romance themes of Conrad's later fiction, *Victory* returned to the Malay settings of his earlier work and, in its central character Axel Heyst, offered readers another study of idealism and isolation. It contains two memorable villains – the repellent Schomberg, who also features in *Lord Jim* and 'Falk', and the world-weary Mr Jones, a queer version of Jim's nemesis Gentleman Brown (see Works, **pp. 43–7**). The novel is organised around several paired and triadic character groupings; between Lena and Heyst; Schomberg and Lena; Jones and Ricardo; Jones and Heyst; Jones, Ricardo and Pedro; and Wang, Heyst and Lena. A common thread between nearly all the characters is their isolation – be it moral or emotional – and their related inability to read the motivation of others in anything but their own terms. By responding to Lena's plight, Heyst becomes engaged with a woman in ways that he had hitherto shunned, and this leads to him feeling 'enveloped in the atmosphere of femininity as in a cloud, suspecting pitfalls and afraid to move' (221–2). Lena and her desires are unread-able to him – 'like a script in an unknown language, or even more simply mysteri-ous: like any writing to the illiterate' (222). Whilst social class and culture divided his protagonists, Conrad is interested in more elemental differences between men and women here. Heyst's problem is his inability to express his feelings for Lena; whilst he decides that she has a central place in his thoughts, it is one that he has only 'secretly given her' (254), and he is unable to articulate his emotions. As Robert Hampson has suggested, Lena's problem is that her limited education ill equips her to deal with the situation she finds herself in – falling back on Sunday school platitudes regarding Heyst's noble sacrifice, she can only see her plight in binary terms in which 'the enchanted dream' of life with Heyst is threatened by the 'embodied evil' of Ricardo whose arrival represents 'cruel catastrophe' (*Victory*, 298) (Hampson 2000: 159). Whilst Heyst is dismissive of 'what you have been told – as a child – on Sundays', Lena recalls this epoch with nostalgia as 'the only decent bit of time I had when I was a kid' (359), and for her, God is 'to do with everything – every little thing. Nothing can happen'. For Heyst this is a belief of 'the old days', and he argues against the biblical notion of God's hand in all things by suggesting that, contrary to Matthew 10:29, that 'sparrows do fall to the ground, that they are brought down to the ground' (360). His stance of 'universal unbelief' (199) sits uneasily with Lena's reliance on well-worn ways of seeing, and Conrad uses the difference between their two perspectives as a means of critiquing the simplistic morality of the romance genre which his novel know-ingly draws upon (Erdinast-Vulcan 1991: 172–85). Despite her reliance upon the hackneyed and mundane, Lena is, however, far more willing to attempt to control her fate through action in stark contrast to Heyst's detached scepticism – a stance that makes him passive to an extent that, in Lena's conventional terms at least, unmans him, Like Jim, Heyst has allowed a philosophy of conduct to dictate the terms of his life and, like Jim, it is only through the conscious act of suicide that he – too late – takes some control of his destiny.

In *Victory*, Conrad was not writing a strictly realist novel – the playful allusions to *The Tempest* and the Eden myth, coupled with Heyst's philosophic angle of vision and the running meditation on the tension between dream and 'reality' clearly point to a work where allegory dominates. In allegory there is less emphasis on characters as psychologically true to life and more on their symbolic function, and this genre convention can be used to explain the somewhat two-dimensional presentation of all the characters apart from Heyst. As a latter-day atheistic *Pilgrim's Progress, Victory* tells the story of his struggles to accom-modate the trials and tribulations of life to his worldview. The novel's philo-sophical concerns mean that it is a work often studied as a late expression of the Conradian themes of isolation and human solidarity.

The narrative quickly establishes Heyst as an outsider – a 'queer chap' (4) and a man who is described by various, often conflicting, epithets – 'Enchanted Heyst' (7), 'Hard Facts Heyst' (8) – and drunken Captain McNab calls him 'a puffect g'n'lman' and a 'ut-uto-utopist' (8). Heyst's meeting with the impecunious Morrison reveals one facet of this utopianism – he bails him out without any hope of seeing a return on his money. In his relationships with others, Heyst shows all the signs of a classic version of the emotionless male – he is 'incapable of outward cordiality of manner' (18). For outsiders, the relationship that develops between

Heyst and Morrison is inexplicable – the world imagines 'some mysterious hold' (20) and there is a notion of parasitism ('sucking him dry'), which prompts the malign gossip Schomberg to create a new nickname – 'Heyst the Spider' (21). Following Morrison's death, Heyst becomes Manager of the Tropical Belt Coal Company's new station at Samburan which, for a time, looks like it might be profitable – prompting the gossipers to come up with the epithet 'Enchanted Heyst' (24). But, as the provider of coal to the new steamships, Heyst's success could ruin others who rely on slower sailing ships to make a living, and so Schomberg – whose hotel trade might suffer – starts to describe him as 'the Enemy' (24). The coal company fails but Heyst remains on the island, 'a hermit in the wilderness' (31). Coming to Sourabaya to collect his mail, he encounters Lena in Zangiacomo's travelling orchestra. Despite being 'detached from feminine associations' (60), Heyst takes her away with him to Samburan. Part 1 draws to a close with further reflections on the events leading up to Heyst and Lena's elopement – an action about which Captain Davidson cynically remarks, '[f]unny notion of defying the fates – to take a woman in tow' (57).

Part 2 then opens with a more detailed omniscient account of these events. Heyst's encounter with Lena is an experience that makes him 'positively forget where he was' (71). He intervenes in Lena's mistreatment by the Zangiacomos and she is stunned by his gentlemanly manner whilst he is 'seduced' by the 'amazing quality' of her voice (74). Heyst is motivated to intervene out a gentleman's sense of duty to the less fortunate – this is not a man smitten with passion; he saves Lena because he feels compassion (79) – *not* passion. Lena hints that she will be willing to sleep with Heyst – '[y]ou'll never be sorry' (84) – to repay him for his kindness, but he recoils 'from the idea of competition with fellows unknown' (85). Lena becomes irritated by Heyst's hesitations: 'I know what sort of girl I am; but all the same I am not the sort that men turn their backs on – and you ought to know it, unless you aren't made like the others' (86).

Schomberg has been pursuing Lena and is humiliated and full of 'shocked fury' (94) when her liaison with Heyst is discovered. It is this rivalry which contains the seeds of Heyst's downfall, because it spurs Schomberg's dislike into a hatred so intense that it 'seemed to him that he could never be himself again till he had got even with that artful Swede' (96). It is this state of mind that will lead him to direct Jones and his followers to Samburan. Jones is introduced as 'a wanderer . . . even as Heyst was, but not alone and of quite another kind' (98), and this notion of similarities between the two men will be developed as the novel unfolds. Jones is a parody of a gay man who barely troubles to disguise the true nature of his relationship with Ricardo – 'there was nothing secretarial about him' (100) – and is so misogynist that women make him sick: his appearance reveals 'a used up, weary, depraved distinction' (102). If Jones is the dark double of Heyst, then Ricardo seems to be cast in the role of a male Lena. Like her, he has a wide-ranging experience of men which makes him 'a connoisseur in gentlemen' (128), having been 'employed in that there yacht – schooner, whatever you call it – by ten gentlemen at once. That surprises you, eh? Yes, yes, ten' (126). Jones and Ricardo are stage-villains and their dealings with Schomberg are presented in a rather magazine-ish fashion that relies on them tediously recounting their previous exploits. Schomberg seeks to rid himself of these desperadoes by setting them off after Heyst whom he alleges is living alone on Samburan with 'all that plunder' (156).

Part 3 sees a shift of focus to Samburan as we learn briefly of Heyst and his life on the island prior to Lena and in more detail of their life there together. We also discover more about the influence of Heyst's philosopher father, whose beliefs inform his son's decision to be an onlooker to life. It is clear that deciding to save Lena marked a significant 'departure from the part of an unconcerned spectator' (184). Lena wants to 'give herself up to him more completely' but Heyst is 'a strange being without needs' (202). This conversation concludes with Heyst kissing Lena and the narrative discreetly breaks off until the aftermath of what seems to have been love-making. It is not the spur to any outpouring of affection since, on returning to the house, Heyst immerses himself in reading his father's pessimistic philosophy. Lena suggests that he 'should try to love' her, but the '[s]imple words . . . died on his lips' (221). Heyst feels trapped by Lena, '[a]ll his defences were broken now. Life had him fairly by the throat' (221), because he has no experience of women she is seen as unreadable (222).

Heyst seeks to calm Lena by reassuring her that he has no intention of dealing with the world at large and insisting that '[n]othing can break in on us here' (223) at the very moment when his servant arrives to tell him of the approach of the boat containing Jones and his followers. Heyst is particularly 'startled' (247) by the 'prodigious improbability of the arrival of the boat' and is 'aware that this visit could bode nothing pleasant' (248). A rather stagey plot device of a missing revolver seeks to add additional menace and a further twist is that Ricardo, in tempting Jones to seek for Heyst's plunder, has neglected to tell this arch misogynist of Lena's presence. Conversations between Ricardo and Jones reveal that they have swallowed Schomberg's calumnies whole and believe Heyst to be a solitary killer – 'a cold blooded beast' (276) – guarding a horde of swag.

Part 4, two days after Jones's arrival, details the final day in thirteen chapters. Ricardo steals into Heyst's bungalow only to come across Lena, whose violent reactions and refusal to cry out encourage him to ask her to help him find Heyst's swag. She pretends to ally herself with him in order to protect Heyst and helps him escape when the Swede returns. Heyst's servant, Wang, frightened by the strangers' servant Pedro and by Ricardo's visit, announces, without explaining why, that he is leaving. Heyst informs Jones of this who views it as a stratagem, especially since Heyst mentions that his servant's departure came after he had 'missed something' from amongst his possessions (323). Heyst is forced to accept the services of Jones's servant Pedro who spies Lena and goes to report her presence to Jones but is intercepted by Ricardo who, like Heyst, is beginning to act with Lena in mind and sends Pedro away before he can inform Jones of Lena's presence. Meanwhile, Heyst and Lena go to Wang to ask him to take the girl with him to the other side of the island where she will be safe, but he refuses and Heyst momentarily despairs over his inability to protect her. Trapped by circumstances, without any weapon save a penknife, Heyst, like many of Conrad's heroes, is faced with a predicament for which his belief system simply fails to equip him. So long an onlooker, Heyst is unsure of his capacity for action and, like Jim, finds himself trapped between his own values and the public perception of his actions. Forced to act, Heyst instructs Lena to don dark clothes and slip away under cover of night to the forest whilst he confronts Jones. The second meeting between Jones and Heyst sees Jones playing on the apparent similarity between himself and the Swede – an echo of Jim's encounter with Brown (see Works, **pp. 43–7**). Jones discounts Heyst's claims that there is no treasure and his protests that tales of him killing Morrison are mere lies – Jones's experience of the world means he believes these lies more readily than the truth. Heyst reveals rivalry over Lena as the source of Schomberg's jealousy, and Jones is horrified to learn that there is a woman on the island and that Ricardo knew of it all along. Jones actually proposes 'a truce' (388) with Heyst to enable him to deal with the unfaithful Ricardo. As they set off in search of him, Heyst is shocked to see Lena still at his bungalow and Jones assumes that Ricardo has formed an alliance with Lena. Of course, Lena has remained so as to secure Ricardo's knife for Heyst – a risky stratagem which the narrator suggests is like trying to 'disarm murder itself' (397). In a scene pregnant with sexual symbolism, the unsuspecting Ricardo lets her feel his knife whilst he kisses her feet. Heyst and Jones arrive, and Jones shoots at Ricardo but hits Lena. The ending is a fine piece of narrative delayed decoding in which Heyst is initially unaware of her fatal wound – Lena's 'victory' (405) in wresting the knife from Ricardo is a hollow one. The final pages of the novel are given over to Captain Davidson who arrives in the midst of these events and reports them later to a 'high official' (408). Davidson was despatched in timely fashion by Mrs Schomberg who overheard her husband's scheming and wished to prevent Lena being brought back. He reports that Jones shoots Ricardo and that Heyst kills himself by immolation in the burning bungalow in which Lena died. Wang shoots Pedro and cuts the villains' boat adrift and Jones drowns when he fall from the jetty whilst searching for it – Davidson suggests that Jones may have committed suicide. Heyst is summed up as 'a queer chap. I doubt if he himself knew how queer he was' (408).

Early reviews

The novel received good reviews, and in the UK two editions were sold out on publication day (CL5: 514). The novelist Jack London wrote from Waikiki Beach in Honolulu after a night's reading to say that *Victory* has swept him off his feet (CL5: 507 note 2). The *New York Times* suggested that in Heyst Conrad had created a south sea Hamlet (Carabine 1992: I, 380) whilst in the *Times Literary Supplement*, Walter de la Mare called it a 'little dish of diamonds' (Sherry 1973: 290), comparing Conrad to Flaubert. In *The Nation*, the reviewer praised the novel's narrative for its focus and the New York *Bookman* also commented on the more direct narrative style, noting that 'the greater directness of attack may win some friends for this gifted writer who have found him too elusive hitherto' (Carabine 1992: I, 380). Writing to Ford Madox Ford, Conrad suggested that most reviewers had missed the point of the novel, highlighting the review in *Truth* as the one which came 'nearest to the idealistic core of it' (CL5: 519); perhaps because it emphasised the book's modernity via its account of the novel's exploration of the nature of evil and the role of sexuality in modern minds (on this see Saveson 1974: 111–29). Reviewing the initial coverage, Conrad concluded that 'I've had a wonderful press on the whole' (CL5: 524).

Later critical response

Although Thomas Moser's *Joseph Conrad: Achievement and Decline* (1957) influentially sees *Victory* as the first work of Conrad's failing later canon, a view supported in Albert Guerard's *Conrad the Novelist* (1958), the weight of more recent criticism has tended in the book's favour. Sharon Kaehle and Howard German's 'Conrad's Victory: A Reassessment' (1964) offers an early account of the work's continuities with the preoccupations of Conrad's earlier work. Robert Secor's *The Rhetoric of Shifting Perspectives: Conrad's* Victory (1971) examines the text's use of the romance form. Jeffrey Meyers' essay on the novel in his *Homosexuality and Literature* (1977) studies the book's handling of same-sex desire.

An influential defence of the work is mounted in Frederic Karl's *Joseph Conrad: The Three Lives* (1979) which draws on the novel's lengthy manuscript to show that through the process of revision for publication, 'Conrad moved towards a more symbolic presence' (1979: 765), and Karl follows this reading up in more detail in his '*Victory*: Its Origins and Development' (1983). Gary Geddes argues that the novel is 'a continuing exploration of the aesthetic and philosophical concerns given shape in *Chance*', noting that critical disdain for the text has stemmed from an inability to understand its 'aesthetic variety and complexity' (1980: 42, 69). Daniel Schwarz sees the work as engaged with 'Conrad's recurring fear that the thoughtful intellectual man would prove inadequate to the demands of action', reading the novel as a bleak work which 'implies the triumph of materialism and greed over feeling and personal relationships' (1982: 61, 75). Schwarz concludes, however, that the work 'is not among Conrad's major achievements' and criticises its narration for failing to probe 'the meaning of Heyst's impressions' (1982: 78, 79). Tony Tanner wrote two essays that dealt with the novel's representation of the gentleman: 'Gentlemen and Gossip: Aspects of Evolution and Language in Conrad's *Victory*' (1981), and 'Joseph Conrad and the Last Gentleman' (1986).

Keith Carabine has reprinted a representative range of critical essays on the novel from the 1950s to the late 1980s (1992: 3). In addition to Karl's later work on the manuscript revisions, these include David Lodge's study of the relationship between the novel and Shakespeare's late play *The Tempest*, Suresh Raval's study of the novel's articulation of 'the tragic implications of a sceptical attitude to life' (1980) and Terry Collits's political study which draws upon the work of Fredric Jameson to examine the racism inherent in Heyst's existence on Samburan (1989). Robert Hampson, in *Cross-Cultural Encounters in Joseph Conrad's Malay Fiction* (2000), studies the novel in terms of the narrative's use of gossip and its the use of the intertext of *The Tempest*. Andrew Michael Roberts, in *Conrad and Masculinity* (2000), examines the role of vision in the text's figuring of masculinity, arguing that the presentation of the heroine in *Victory*, as in other late Conrad works, shows a combination of fetishization alongside certain hesitant signs of 'an understanding of what might underlie the male need . . . to fetishize a heroine' (2000: 189).

The Shadow Line: A Confession (1917)

This novella was written during the First World War and can be read as a response to wartime fears but may also be seen as a continued engagement with the theme of isolation which draws on an allegorical mode that we have seen in *Victory* (see Works, **pp. 107–13**). Conrad mentioned a story on the theme of 'First Command' as early as 1899 (CL2: 167) and returned to this 'old subject ... I've carried in my head for years' (CL5: 441) in February 1915. Given the similarities in theme, it is interesting to note that he turns to this story immediately after completing work on the proofs for the American edition of *Victory*. 'The Shadow Line' has its roots in Conrad's own 'early personal experience' (CL5: 441). In January 1887, he took up command of the *Otago*, and his first voyage as Captain, from Bangkok to Sydney (9 February–7 May) was beset by illness amongst his crew and tricky calms in the Gulf of Siam. Conrad would later declare the book to be 'strict autobiography' (CL6: 37), but hinted that he had left out aspects of his own experience since it 'was not an experience to be exhibited "in the street"' (CL6: 37). He summed it up as 'experience transposed into spiritual terms' (CL6: 37) and would stress that he did not 'really want that little piece to be recognised *formally* as autobiographical' (CL6: 41). There is detailed coverage of the autobiographical background in Sherry, *Conrad's Eastern World* (1966: 211–49).

By March 1915 Conrad had settled on the title, suggesting that the work would have 'a sort of spiritual meaning' (458). On 6 May he noted that the story was 'nearly finished' (CL5: 474) but he would not actually complete it until 15 December (CL5: 536), delayed by ill health and domestic matters. Of the finished manuscript, Conrad stated that it 'is by no means bad for what it is' (CL5: 541), but later in the year he expressed doubts about the work's ability to stand alone (CL5: 688). The novella was serialised in England in the *English Review* between September 1916 and March 1917 and in America in the *Metropolitan Magazine* (October 1916). It was published, despite Conrad's misgivings, in book form by Dent in March 1917 and in the USA by Doubleday, Page in April 1917. By late March, the English edition had sold 5,000 copies (CL6: 55) but wartime paper shortages meant that no more could be printed. The novella was dedicated to Conrad's son Borys and others serving at the Front in France. In August, Conrad was pleased to learn that the story had featured in a prize-winning essay on 'The Tendency of English Fiction in 1917' (CL6: 115).

Commentary

The story begins with the narrator recounting his impetuous resignation from a steamer and his plans to travel back to England. Taking up residence in the Singapore sailor's home whilst awaiting a ship, he comes under the care of the avuncular Captain Giles who ensures that he learns of the opportunity of a command. Captain Ellis, the Harbour Master, is presented as a 'deputy-Neptune' who 'pretended to rule the fate of the mortals whose lives were cast upon the waters' (30) – he informs the narrator that he is the 'only man fit for the job' (31) of taking command of a British ship whose captain has died. The narrator suggests that his first command has arisen 'as if by enchantment' (39) and equates himself with 'people in fairy tales', fancifully casting Captain Ellis as 'a fierce sort of fairy' godmother and imagining his ship, 'like an enchanted princess', awaiting him 'spellbound, unable to move, to live, to get out into the world (till I came)' (40). Like some fairy-tale hero, the narrator receives warning of the perils of his route from wise old Captain Giles who comments that the Gulf of Siam is a 'funny piece of water' (44) and warns him to keep to its east side (45). Once on board, the narrator makes his way to the Captain's cabin and sits looking at himself in his new guise in a mirror:

> It struck me that this quietly staring man whom I was watching, both as if he were myself and somebody else, was not exactly a lonely figure. He had his place in a line of men whom he did not know, of whom he had never heard; but who were fashioned by the same influences, whose souls in relation to their humble life's work had no secrets to him.
>
> (53)

This can be read as a both a paean to the solidarity of the craft of seamanship and as an astonishing act of youthful arrogance. The narrator has spent some time reflecting on what he believes a captain to be but, as his reception by the crew soon shows, there is more to being in command than a title. Conrad presents the narrator as acutely conscious of his age when faced by the older first mate Mr Burns who tells him of the previous captain's eccentricities (violin-playing and rather slack management). The previous captain seems to have been entangled with a Vietnamese women who is described as a 'professional sorceress of the slums' (59). Burns describes this man's unprofessional wish to 'cut adrift from everything' and go 'wandering about the world till he lost her with all hands' (62), a sentiment which perhaps echoes the caprice of the narrator in giving up his previous berth. The narrator doesn't see this, persisting with the metaphysical line he has been taking so far:

> That man had been in all essentials but his age just such another man as myself. Yet the end of his life was a complete act of treason, the betrayal of a tradition which seemed to me as imperative as any guide on earth could be. It appeared that even at sea a man could become the victim of evil spirits. I felt on my face the breath of unknown powers that shape our destinies.
>
> (62)

The ship is delayed in port by illness amongst the crew: the steward dies of cholera and then Mr Burns succumbs to fever. Even the apparently healthy cook, Ransome, has a heart complaint. Whilst in the grip of fever, Burns makes a 'rambling speech' in which he blames the dead captain, 'ambushed down there under the sea with some evil intention' (74), for delaying the ship. Once at sea, the narrator sees this fever spread amongst the crew and privately he insists on seeing this in meta-physical terms as 'the last desperate pluck of evil from which we were escaping into the clean breath of the sea' (79), yet when Burns repeats his fear that the spirit of the dead captain is hampering their progress, the narrator is quick to dismiss 'this insane delusion' (82). A few paragraphs later, however, the narrator is referring to 'the evil spell' that holds the ship back and comments to Burns that their hesitant progress is 'like being bewitched' (84).

As the sickness of the crew develops, the ship's stock of quinine is found to have been tampered with – Burns accuses the dead captain of selling it. The narrator shoulders the blame for failing to check the supplies prior to departure and immediately alters course for Singapore, the nearest port, but to reach it involves sailing on the west side of the Gulf of Siam. During the voyage, the narrator comes to doubt his own sanity but is kept going by dint of his service ethic – 'the seaman, the officer of the watch, in me was sufficiently sane' (101). Sailing practically single-handed, when a squall threatens, the narrator fears that he will be unable to reduce the amount of sail the ship carries since the crew are too weak to help him. Yet by his leadership, he rallies the few men able to work and they successfully adjust the sails. Burns drags himself on deck, railing against the maleficence of the dead captain and has to be restrained but faints away and at this moment the 'barrier of awful stillness which had encompassed us for so many days as though we had been accursed was broken' (121). The weather remains favourable and, despite a weakened crew, the ship makes good progress. Burns makes a 'wonderful recovery' (124) and with his help and that of Ransome the ship is finally brought to harbour. Coming ashore after his ordeal, the narrator meets Captain Giles and over tea tells him the tale. He asserts that he is 'no longer a youngster' (132), and, returning to the ship, he prepares to set sail with a new crew to complete the terms of his command.

The novella is a concise encapsulation of several Conradian themes: the role of duty, the earning of authority through a rite of passage, the recognition of the fellowship of the craft that unites crew and officers, its contrasting of shore life and sea life. For all the supernatural machinery put in play, it is clear that the narrator, whilst seeming initially to share Burns's supernatural reading of their predicament, manages the squall by dint of rational seamanship. Just as Ransome acts despite his heart condition and so earns the narrator's respect, it is because the narrator can act despite his fears that he earns Captain Giles's gruff praise – 'you'll do' (132). As Conrad's 'Author's Note' made plain, this is a tale about the giving up of childish things, and he deliberately emphasised the ease with which the narrator can fall into supernatural and metaphysical explanations of his experience only to show how inadequate they are as accounts of 'the visible and tangible world of which we are a self conscious part' (xxxvii).

Early reviews

Conrad was put out by his old irritant Robert Lynd's review, which criticised the book's reliance on the supernatural (CL6: 51) (see Works, pp. 78–9). In general, however, the reviews were good, with *The Nation* calling Conrad 'one of the great ones, not of the present, but of the world' (Sherry 1973: 305), classing him 'the greatest living psychologist writing in English, partly because of his method of revealing a personality from every possible angle of vision' (1973: 306). The *New Statesman* and *The North American Review* made flattering comparisons with Romantic poet Samuel Taylor Coleridge's 'The Rime of the Ancient Mariner'

(Sherry 1973: 310; CA: 385). Conrad told a friend that he 'never meant or "felt" the supernatural aspect of the story while writing it' (CL6: 64), a point he would return to in his 1920 'Author's Note' where he commented that:

> [w]hat did worry me in reality was not the 'supernatural' character but the *fact* of Mr Burns' craziness. For only think: my first command, a sinister, slowly developing situation from which one couldn't see any issue that one could *try for*; and the only man on board (second in command) to whom I could open my mind, not quite sane – not to be depended upon for any sort of moral support. It was very trying. I'll never forget those days.
>
> (CL6: 64)

Later critical response

The critical consensus suggests that the story represents the final flowering of Conrad's art. Edward Said's *Joseph Conrad and the Fiction of Autobiography* argues that the tale dramatises the entry into 'a sort of restricted, terrible reality' (1966: 186), and Ian Watt examines the moral initiation at the centre of the story in his 'Story and Idea in Conrad's "The Shadow Line"' (1960). Lawrence Graver reads the tale in terms of its staging of a conflict between altruism and egoism, dubbing it 'the communal counterpart' to 'The Secret Sharer' (1969: 192) (see Works, pp. 94–5). Gary Geddes argues that 'Conrad's preoccupation with the moral question of responsibility and with work as a technique of survival informs *The Shadow Line* at every level' (1980: 83). Daniel Schwarz examines the ways in which the novel shows that 'the viability of an ethical tradition depends upon its being continually reinvigorated by individuals who believe in it and live by its demands' (1982: 86). More recently, Ted Billy has read the tale as a study of an 'incomplete initiation' in which adherence to 'the practical matters of existence' is required 'to forestall disintegration' (1997: 37, 38).

The Arrow of Gold (1919)

As gout began to severely restrict Conrad's ability to write for sustained periods, he began to make greater use of his secretary in the direct dictation of his fiction. *The Arrow of Gold* was the first of Conrad's novels to be largely dictated, with only ninety-four of the 519 manuscript pages in his hand (CL6: 324, note 2). In February 1915, around the time he started work on *The Shadow Line*, Conrad had told his agent of another idea for a story based on a 'Carlist war episode from my *very* young days' (CL5: 441) (The Carlist war over the succession to the Spanish throne was fought between 1872 and 1876.) Conrad had already presented aspects of this material to the public in 'The "Tremilino"' chapter of *The Mirror of the Sea* (1906). By December 1916 he was still talking about the work as a 'a 10–12 thou.' short story (CL5: 688), but very slow progress was made as it developed over the next eighteen months. Conrad reflected on the irony that when finished this novel – 'the thinnest possible squeaky babble' – would be sold 'for twenty times the money' he received for *The Nigger of the 'Narcissus'*, deeming this 'a horrible prospect' (CL6: 164). In February 1918, Conrad rather tetchily wrote some notes on the novel for his American publisher. At this point he had no definitive title in mind but noted that:

> the novel may best be described as the Study of a woman who might have been a very brilliant phenomenon but has remained obscure, playing her little part in the Carlist war of 75–76 . . . The book, however, is but slightly concerned with her public . . . activity . . . What it deals with is her private life: her sense of her own position, her sentiments and her fears. It is really an episode, related dramatically and in the detailed manner of a study, in that particular life. That it is also an episode in the general experience of the young narrator . . . serves only to round it up and give it completeness as a novel.
>
> (CL6: 185–6)

Originally conceived as 'R. T. Fragments' (CL6: 9) or 'R.T. Selected Passages from Letters' (CL6: 24) Conrad added the two notes that begin and end the novel only after he had written the main body of the text. He completed the novel on 4 June 1918, and serialisation began in *Lloyd's Magazine* in December 1918 and would run until February 1920. The book was published in the USA by Doubleday, Page in April 1919 and in the UK in August by T. Fisher Unwin.

In the USA, the novel sold out its first print run of 15,000 in a fortnight (CL6: 411), and the US sales were better than those of *Chance* and *Victory* (CL6: 437). Conrad summed the novel up as consisting 'not of action but of shades of intimate emotion' (CL6: 454), but the critics gave the book what Conrad described as 'a very unsatisfactory send off' (CL6: 459), and he grumbled about the propensity of the critics to hark back to *Lord Jim* – 'I couldn't go on writing *Lord Jim* all my life' (CL6: 465).

Commentary

The novel is elaborately framed, first by two notes written by the unnamed editor of Monsieur George's recollections of a twelve-month period in his younger life which formed 'his first great adventure' (4) and the basis of the novel that follows. The first note tells us that the work it frames has been 'extracted from a pile of manuscript which was apparently meant for the eyes of one woman only' (3) – this woman, the childhood friend of M. George, is the addressee of the original text, but the editor of the first note tells us that he has cut out all reference to this person. Parts 1–4 are George's edited narration, based on his recall of events some thirty-five years after they took place. The work is – literally and in its narrative framing – an old man's work of recollection, and much of the novel's character comes from its nostalgia-driven self-indulgence. Many of George's asides are about writing, and this adds further to the self-reflexive character of a work which it is tempting to read as a wryly satirical (self-)portrait of the artist as a naïve young man. By relying so heavily on George's narration, we do not have any relief from his often-tedious account of his youthful experiences and, without any real incidents to speak of, the book stands or falls on our interest in George and his naïve engagement with his surroundings. He is clearly an unreliable narrator, describing his own telling as shaped by a 'refreshing ignorance' (31), but this is not enough, in my view, to make us interested in his account of his life.

Part 1 spans three chapters and gives us details of George's first meeting with the Carlists Mills and Blunt. These men tell George about Rita and her involvement with Don Carlos and the painter Allègre who plucked her from obscurity to make her his model and later his heir (Rita will later argue that she chose to be plucked). Part 2, covering four chapters, continues from where Part 1 ends and details George's first and subsequent meetings with Rita and his preparations for his involvement in a gunrunning expedition. Part 3, also four chapters, opens with George returning from his first trip, learning more of Rita, and realising that he is falling love with her. It ends with him witnessing a row between Blunt and Rita which reveals 'something more close in their intercourse than I had ever before suspected' which makes him 'profoundly unhappy' (148). In Part 4, George is described by one of the Marseilles Bohemians as an artist who:

> has broken away from his conventions. He is trying to put a special vibration and his own notion of colour into his life; and perhaps even to give it a modelling according to his own ideas, And for all you know he may be on the track of a masterpiece.
>
> (166)

There is, perhaps, a distant echo here of Stein's wisdom about man not being a masterpiece because his maker was 'a little mad' (*Lord Jim*, 208) and also of his sense of the human need to pursue a dream until the very end: the dream which George pursues is Rita and his unexpressed feelings for her leave him unable to sleep. Over an awkward lunch, George meets Blunt's mother who has plans for her son to marry Rita. George then visits Rita and declares his love but leaves for a further gunrunning trip. Part 5 opens with him returning to Marseilles to discover that Rita has left for Paris. George spends the next three months running guns, but the situation in Spain is deteriorating and their involvement ends when the ship is wrecked (256). George returns to Marseilles, arriving, as he did at the opening of the novel, in carnival time. Reporting on 'the sudden ending of my activities' to the local Carlist agent, he is advised to meet another agent at the railway station who will pass on his news to Rita. The man he meets, Ortega, is well known to Rita since as an adolescent he persecuted her (110–13), demanding that she agree to marry him once she was of age. Ortega the man is a cynical revolutionist who challenges George's idealised view of Rita, asking him how long Rita has been his mistress (271), and George resolves to protect her from this man (272). On returning with Ortega to his lodgings, George discovers that Rita has already returned from Paris. During a difficult night-time meeting, he accuses her of being 'insensible' (298) to his feelings and then reveals, to her despair, that Ortega is in the house. By now Ortega knows of her presence, and he hammers on the door and rails at her. Rita, rather hysterically, responds to this with fits of giggles (319) that appal the anxious George. In his frenzied assaults on the doors of the room, Ortega injures himself and subsequently dies. After a doctor has called to see to him, George and Rita talk, and Part 5 ends with them kissing. In a second note, the narrator glosses the next six months in which George and Rita leave Marseilles for a love-nest in the mountains. On a visit to the town, George hears that Blunt has been slandering him and Rita, suggesting that he is 'a young adventurer' who is 'exploiting her shamelessly' (344). George challenges Blunt to a duel in which both men are wounded. Both Rita and Blunt vanish from the region, and Mills, summoned by Rita, comes to care for George. Mills tells him that Rita declared that until she met George she had known 'nothing of love' and, rather ambiguously, that he had been 'in more senses than one a complete revelation' (349).

Early reviews

The book was widely reviewed, perhaps more so than any of Conrad's previous works. The *Morning Post* called the novel's story 'very vague' and laid this at the door of Conrad's 'processes of elimination, of glosses and glazes' but went on to praise as the 'high-water mark' of 'Mr Conrad's peculiar art of ironic exposition' the presentation of the maid Rose, Therese and Mrs Blunt (Sherry 1973: 315). The *New Statesman* suggested that Conrad 'has exhumed a manuscript of earlier days' (Sherry 1973: 321) which was not 'equal of his later works' (1973: 322) but offered qualified praise for the creation of Rita. The *Daily Telegraph* described the book as a test case, with Conrad's supporters suggesting that the work is evidence of his talent whilst his detractors cite it as evidence of their conviction that 'Mr Conrad never has been able to tell a story' and that 'in this long-dragged-out romance there is a great deal that is tedious' (Sherry 1973: 325). *The Nation* was firmly on the side of the detractors, aligning the novel with other writers' experimental works, alluding to Hardy's *A Pair of Blue Eyes* (1873) and Shakespeare's *Pericles* (written between 1606 and 1608).

Later critical response

The novel's focus on the folly of youth not only echoed *The Shadow Line* but also harked back to earlier work like *Lord Jim* and 'Youth' itself. Viewed in this way, it can be seen as a work on the subject of initiation – political and personal. Rita is a female character of a type we meet in *The Secret Agent, Chance* and *Victory* – hemmed in by the limited options available to women in a male-dominated society, she is presented as striking a fine balance in adopting aspects of the role of femme-fatale as a strategy to manipulate the social codes that seek to frame her. As several commentators, starting with Guerard, have suggested, the novel shared with these earlier texts the theme of sexual repression and its consequences (Guerard 1947).

The novel is only today beginning to recover its critical standing from the damning assertion by F. R. Leavis that it is Conrad's worst book (1948: 210), Jean Aubry's erroneous claim in *The Sea Dreamer* that the facts presented in the novel are true (Aubry 1957: 68), and Thomas Moser's citing of the novel as evidence of Conrad's decline in *Joseph Conrad: Achievement and Decline* (1957). The negative view of the late fiction dominated Conrad studies from the 1950s and, a few lonely champions notwithstanding, did not begin to change until the early 1980s, helped by Gary Geddes' *Conrad's Late Novels* (1980) which explored the role of visual metaphors in the text. Daniel R. Schwarz's *Conrad: The Later Fiction* (1982) does not spare *The Arrow of Gold* from its by-now-habitual critical drubbing, declaring it to be Conrad's 'least successful novel', citing 'its unexplored and undeveloped mythic pretensions, its confused characterisations, its discontinuous narrative, its strained imagery and its shrill tone' (1982: 132). Daphna Erdinast Vulcan's powerful reading 'Conrad's Double Edged Arrow' in *Joseph Conrad and the Modern Temper* (1991), also does not seek to rescue the novel but argues instead that it is 'an important autobiographical document' because it 'exposes the psyche of its author and sheds some light on the dynamics of his work in ways which were probably only dimly suspected by Conrad and entirely out of his control' (1991: 196). In the same year, Pamela Bickley and Robert Hampson developed an account of Conrad's creation of the text as 'an aesthetic object' in their ' "Lips that Have Been Kissed": Boccaccio, Verdi, Rossetti and *The Arrow of Gold*' (91). Hampson, in his chapter on the novel in *Joseph Conrad: Betrayal and Identity* (1992), offers a corrective to the decline camp claiming that the novel's investigation of George's 'initiation into passion . . . is combined with renewed technical inventiveness' (1992: 251) and develops an argument for the novel's sensitive depiction of Rita's predicament, in which she is seen as a female Heyst, unable to love and exposed 'to scepticism at an impressionable age' (1992: 256). More recently, Andrew Michael Roberts has explored the novel in terms of its emphasis on the visual in Conrad's late representations of masculinity (2000: 163–85).

The Rescue: A Romance of the Shallows (1920)

The novel was begun in March 1896 as *The Rescuer: A Tale of Shallow Waters* and, after interminable stops and starts, was eventually completed in May 1919. The novel is the first book in the so-called Malay Trilogy, dealing with Tom Lingard's early years prior to *An Outcast of the Islands* and *Almayer's Folly* (see Works, pp. 22–7, 28–31). Critically, it occupies an interesting position since Conrad's inability to work on it in the 1890s led him away from the East to the English concerns and narrative innovations of *The Nigger of the 'Narcissus'* (see Works, pp. 31–5). In 1916, when Conrad returned to the novel with renewed commitment, he again struggled with the book and broke off to write what became *The Arrow of Gold*.

Conrad's initial phase of work on the novel was undertaken in 1896 during his honeymoon in Brittany; by early April Conrad had written '11 pages' (CL1: 271). A few days later Conrad sent Edward Garnett '24 pages' of manuscript, anxious for his views and 'ready to cut, slash, erase, destroy; spit, trample, jump, wipe my feet on that MS at a word from you' (CL1: 273) (see Life and Contexts, pp. 11–12). Later that month, Conrad wrote to his publisher asking for a Malay dictionary in order to add 'language-colour' to the book. Conrad soon became blocked on this novel, noting in June that it 'crawls a page forward' each day whilst he was gripped by 'long fits of depression, that in a lunatic asylum would be called madness' (CL1: 284). He complained of using '103 pages of manuscript to relate the events of 12 hours' (CL1: 286) and feared that despite his plan to 'present to the reader the impression of the seas – the ship – the seamen . . . I doubt having conveyed anything but the picture of my own folly – I doubt the sincerity of my own impressions (CL1: 287). Conrad laid his inability to write on his reliance upon 'impressions and sensations of common things' (289). During this early period of block, he wrote 'The Idiots' (April) and 'An Outpost of Progress' (July), 'The Lagoon' (August) and during the autumn worked on *The Nigger of the 'Narcissus'*. In November 1896, plans for serialisation of *The Rescuer* were mooted but Conrad did no work on the story again until October when he has a further 'tussle' with it (CL1: 396). In fact it was not until June 1897, having written 'Karain' and *The Nigger of the 'Narcissus'*, that he sent the first part out for consideration by Heinemann and in August hoped to interest Blackwood in a serialisation (CL1: 376). He wrote a synopsis for Blackwood in September, stressing that for this novel, 'the effect must be produced in the working out – in the manner of telling' but also noting the 'human interest' arising from the encounter between his primitive adventurer Lingard and the 'complex type' of civilised woman represented by Mrs Travers (CL1: 381). Whilst noting that 'the paraphernalia of the story are hackneyed', Conrad suggested that by 'stimulating vision in the reader', he 'can present it in a fresh way' (CL1: 381) that 'is not pure story-telling' (382). Blackwood decided against serialisation since the book rights had already been allocated to Heinemann.

Conrad struggled on with the novel through the autumn and winter of 1897, writing to Garnett that now his 'ambition is to make it good enough for a magazine – readable in a word' (CL1: 417). By January 1898 Conrad had written about 30,000 words and was still seeking serial publication, and in February he learnt that the US serial rights had been purchased (CL2: 42). In March, Garnett's feedback on Part 2 made Conrad feel that one and half pages in every two 'are too bad for anything' and he declared that 'I hate the thing with such great hatred' (CL2: 46–7); he was soon badly blocked (CL2: 49) and stayed that way for most of the summer. Conrad turned to more congenial subjects, writing 'Youth' and making a start on *Lord Jim*, but by late June he had begun Part 3 of *The Rescue* even though he lamented that 'the end is not in sight' (CL2: 74) for this 'infamous pot-boiler' (CL2: 76). In August he began work on proofs for its impending serialisation in the *Illustrated London News* but was anxious about the sudden shift in deadline arising from the unexpected sale of serial rights, feeling he 'must write or burst' (CL2: 85). Later in the year, he lamented that:

> Attempting to tell romantically a love story in which the word love is not pronounced, seems to be courting disaster deliberately. Add to this that an inextricable confusion of sensations is of the very essence of the tale and you may judge how much success material or otherwise I may expect. The reader wants an obvious predicament and clear cut motives. He will not find it in the *Rescue*.
>
> (CL2: 122; the penultimate sentence is in French in the original.
> I take the translation from CL2: 122, note 1)

In November, Conrad arranged for the publication of the UK serial of the novel to be put back until April 1899. By December, he had begun Part 4 but had also made a start on 'Heart of Darkness' which would absorb his interest until well into the new year. In February 1899 he agreed to the cancellation of plans for serialisation in the UK, but plans for US serialisation were still being mooted in March. Over the summer, Conrad pressed ahead with *Lord Jim* and by January 1900 he expressed doubts as to 'when and how I will ever fight my way back to the *Rescue*' (CL2: 241). In April, however, he optimistically claimed that the book would be 'finished before long' (CL2: 260), but no progress was made by July 1900 when 'much remains to be done' (CL2: 336). From now on, Conrad's work on the book was little more than 'tinkering' (CL2: 368). In January 1903, Conrad sent the novel to Ford Madox Ford for comments but any plans for it were laid to one side as work progressed on *Nostromo* (see Works, **pp. 63–8**). In late 1904, Conrad mentioned a possibility of serialising the work in *Pall Mall Magazine* (CL3: 194), but this came to nothing. References to the work crop up now and again in Conrad's letters and having the manuscript to hand seemed to act as a comfort to him as he could always dangle it in front of his agent when the latest project was grinding to a halt.

In 1915, Conrad returned to *The Rescue* but progress was slow and he spent much of the year working on *The Shadow Line* (see Works, **pp. 114–17**). He did not return to the novel again until June 1916, predicting that it would be 'an immensely long book' (CL5: 606). Little work was done on the 'wretched story' for the remainder of the year (CL5: 679, note 1) and it was not until summer 1918 that Conrad once more took it up, 'reading it over for the 20th time at least' in June in the hope of capturing 'the old style as much as possible' (CL6: 239). He did not start dictating new material until late August (CL6: 272) and then made only limited progress. In October, serialisation was arranged for *Land and Water*, commencing in January 1919, and in November he finally completed the end of Part 4 of the novel and finished nearly three chapters of Part 5 (CL6: 307). In early December, Conrad wrote to express his outrage at the standard of illustrations which were to accompany the serial edition of the novel, complaining that aside from the artist's lack of finesse when it came to drawing the boats, there was 'gross contempt' in his depiction of Lingard:

> What does he mean by sticking a fur cap on the head of Lingard? What is it – a joke? Or is it to display a fine independence in a story whose action takes place in the tropics? And what is that face? (Lingard is a man with a beard – I say so.) – that face which says nothing, which suggests no type, might belong to a hotel waiter or a stock broker.
>
> (CL6: 328–9)

The worst offences in the illustrations were corrected prior to publication. Towards the end of the month, Conrad offered his agent a synopsis of the ending of the novel, noting that the denouement 'must depend on the success of the romantic presentation' (CL6: 340), which in January 1919 he would describe as 'picturesque' and 'conventional' (CL6: 353). In February he wrote rather optimistically of the book gaining him the Nobel Prize for its 'concentrated colouring and tone' which, in his view, made it the 'swan song of Romance as a form of literary art' (CL6: 362). By March, Conrad had completed Part 5 and made a start on Part 6 (CL6: 376), and April saw him starting 'the penultimate chapt' (408). On 25 May 1919, he declared that the work was now finished. The book was published by Doubleday, Page in the USA in May 1920 and in August by Dent in England.

Commentary

Part 1 works to establish Lingard's character and sets the plot underway as well when the gig of the yacht *Hermit* arrives in search of aid. The yacht has become stranded on a sandbank and Lingard agrees to go to its rescue. His motives are not humanitarian since its presence threatens a scheme of his to meddle in native politics on behalf of his friend Hassim. The reader is presented with this information in Part 2 via an analepsis which reveals that, as part of his plans to work with the native leader Belarab to aid Hassim, Lingard has arranged for a large shipment of arms to be stored under the guard of old Captain Jorgensen aboard the *Emma*, a derelict ship in a native harbour adjacent to where the *Hermit* has become stranded. In Part 3, Lingard encounters the yacht's passengers, the worldly D'Alacer, the patronising Mr Travers and the disenchanted Mrs Travers. Mr Travers is frightened by Lingard who looks 'as if he had stepped out from an engraving in a book about buccaneers' (126) and the two men are immediately antagonistic 'as if they had been life long enemies' (129). Tensions rise when Hassim and his sister arrive and demand that Lingard kill the yacht's people to prevent the well-laid plans from going awry. That evening, whilst Mr Travers, D'Alacer and the sailing master leave the yacht to walk on the sandbank, Lingard reveals their predicament to Mrs Travers. Meanwhile, Mr Travers and D'Alacer are captured by native pirates, and Part 4 begins with Lingard taking Mrs Travers and the remaining crew from the *Hermit* aboard the *Lightning* for their protection. The following day, he and Mrs Travers go onto the island in search of the captives where they meet up with Jorgensen who tells them that the white prisoners are being held in a nearby native stockade. Jorgensen's perspective is used by Conrad to suggest to the reader the extent to which Lingard is behaving oddly:

> What is the world coming to? Hasn't King Tom a mind of his own? What has come over him? He's mad! Leaving his brig with a hundred and twenty born and bred pirates of the worst kind in two praus on the other side of a sandbank. [. . .] Has he put himself in the hands of a strange woman?
>
> (256)

Part 5 begins with Travers and his wife reunited, but he spends most of the conversation upbraiding her for her 'wilfulness' (269) and revealing his unshaken elitist attitudes. Lingard arranges that Travers and D'Alacer are to be placed in his care and gives his word that the pirates will be safe if they do not attack the yacht. Unfortunately, Carter, the resourceful second mate of the yacht, has taken command of both ships in Lingard's absence and sunk the pirates' boats – this has broken Lingard's promise and the agreement under which he has custody of the white men is therefore negated (326–8). Mulling over his predicament, Lingard is shocked to realise that his 'secret enemy' (329) is himself, for in allowing his fascination with Mrs Travers to sway him he has brought the scheme to restore Hassim into jeopardy. His only option is to give up the white men and, much to his astonishment, Mrs Travers agrees and the men are returned to Belarab's stockade. Part 6 sees news of Hassim and his sister's capture by a rival to Belarab, but they manage to send a call for aid back to Lingard in the form of an emerald ring. A messenger brings this token to Jorgensen who gives it to Mrs Travers to take to Lingard since he believes she is the only person present who has a chance of crossing to Belarab's stockade without being killed (383). Unfortunately, Jorgensen is reluctant to trust Mrs Travers with the full story of the ring's importance and this means that once she has met with Lingard she does not give him the token and, therefore, he is unaware of Hassim's predicament. Meanwhile, the chief who holds Hassim captive has come to Jorgensen to open negotiations with Lingard. Jorgensen refuses to leave the *Emma* and insists that any negotiations take place on board. Chapter 6 jumps ahead thirty-six hours and then tells in retrospect of Jorgensen's destruction of both the *Emma* and Belarab's rivals. Also on board are Hassim and his sister, who die believing Lingard has failed them. With the blowing up of the stored weapons, Lingard's power to influence events is lost and Belarab has him and all the other white people returned to their ships. Carter sees in Lingard a man who has 'lost his own soul' (453). Lingard meets Mrs Travers one last time on the sandbank, proclaiming that 'the world is dead' (463) but explains that he will not criticise her failure to alert him to Hassim's plight. The two part in 'invincible solitude' (466).

Early reviews

The reviewers expressed reservations about Conrad's handling of the romance between Lingard and Mrs Travers. The *Morning Post* noted that he struggled to present 'the quality of his emotions' and wondered if 'the object is accomplished to which all this beautiful and impressive artistry is bent' (Sherry 1973: 331). It suggested that it was a 'weakness' that Mrs Travers was made 'symbolic of Western civilisation at the expense of her individuality' (Sherry 1973: 331). Virginia Woolf's anonymous review in the *Times Literary Supplement* was published under the title 'A Disillusioned Romantic' and argued, rather facilely, that Conrad was too old to write romances. Woolf also lamented the presentation of Mrs Travers, noting that as the novel unfolds, 'it becomes more and more difficult' to believe in her as 'a living person' (Sherry 1973: 334). Writing in *The Nation*, Edward Garnett wondered if 'Mr Conrad does not at times carry his mystification too far' but suggested that his 'love of mystification' and 'sense of the mysterious' are also amongst 'the crowing qualities of his genius' (Sherry 1973: 338). He claimed that the story showed that 'Mr Conrad has no confidence in love, save as a passing event' (Sherry 1973: 339) and commented that 'we are not sure we like Mr Conrad best as a novelist of love', describing the narrative as 'something of a maze' (1973: 340).

Later critical response

F. R. Leavis dismisses *The Rescue* as 'boring in its innocence ... calculated to engender more deference than thrill' (1948: 210–11). Albert Guerard's 'Joseph

Conrad' (1947) offers some material on the novel's depiction of sexuality and the presentation of Lingard across the Malay Trilogy. Vernon Young's 'Lingard's Folly: The Lost Subject' offers an early account of the trilogy and presents *The Rescue* as 'a concession to criticism of the heroic ideal' (1971: 341). Thomas Moser's ' "The Rescuer" Manuscript: A Key to Conrad's Development and Decline' (1992) argues that 'The Rescuer' was abandoned because Conrad was unable to write about love and suggests that the final text 'obscures the most important and interesting facts of Lingard's psychology' (1992: 568). Moser suggests that the revised text presents an emasculated Lingard, shorn of his original capacity for self-destruction: he expands on his claims in his later work *Joseph Conrad: Achievement and Decline* (1957). Adam Gillon's *The Eternal Solitary: A Study of Joseph Conrad* (1971) fits the novel into a schema in which Conrad's depiction of sexual love is shown to lead to increased isolation and solitude; Lingard is seen as exemplifying 'the paralysing power of the romantic dream' (cited in Teets and Gerber 1971: 432). John D. Gordan, in *Joseph Conrad: The Making of a Novelist* (1940) develops an account of the ways in which Conrad draws on the historical figure of James Brooke, the white Rajah of Sarawak in his creation of Lingard. In Eloise Knapp Hay's *The Political Novels of Joseph Conrad: A Critical Study* (1963), there is further discussion of the role of Brooke as a model for Lingard. Hay reads the novel as Conrad's first political work for its exploration of the contrast between 'two sorts of Westerner', those like Travers who are 'effete' and dominated by 'shallow pride in their cultural superiority' and men of 'ungovernable energy' such as Lingard (1963: 89). Noting the ways in which the novel can be seen as an anticipation of aspects of *Lord Jim* and 'Heart of Darkness', Hay offers a strong account of the novel's critical engagement with imperialist culture and provides a suggestive reading whose concerns anticipate more recent criticism. Norman Sherry's *Conrad's Eastern World* (1966) examines the ways in which Conrad draws upon shore gossip rather than first-hand knowledge of William Lingard as the prototype for his Rajah Laut. Geddes, in *Conrad's Later Novels* (1980) examines the theme of diplomacy and the novel's interest in 'the psychology of speech and communication' (1980: 158). Schwarz, in *Conrad: The Later Fiction* (1982), also considers the role of language in the novel.

The Rescue has been subjected to the same fate as the other late novels, often being cited as evidence of decline. In Stape (ed.) *The Cambridge Companion to Joseph Conrad* (1996), the essay on the late novels contains only incidental comments on the book. Much modern criticism treats the book only in relation to the other works in the Malay Trilogy. Heliéna Krenn's *Conrad's Lingard Trilogy: Empire Race, and Women in the Malay Novels* (1990) examines the way in which Lingard moves to a central role as the trilogy develops. In *Joseph Conrad and the Modern Temper* (1991), Vulcan saw the text as evidence of Conrad's depiction of the failure of paternalistic imperialism and her study carefully detailed the ways in which Lingard's world can be read a mythic one, whose codes are disrupted by the arrival of the representatives of modernity in the guise of the yachtspeople (1991: 52). Christopher GoGwilt's *The Invention of the West* (1995) examines the novel in the wider context of Conrad's work on the Malay Archipelago, highlighting the ways in which a rescue motif permeates the texts set in this region. GoGwilt argues that the text 'spectacularly misrepresents its Malay subject' in an attempt to 'shore up a coherent idea of European culture' (1995: 75), suggesting that in *The Rescue* Conrad is consciously reorienting his Malay Trilogy 'toward the sort of English perspective that emerged in the Marlow tales' (1995: 76). Geoffrey Galt Harpham's *One of Us: The Mastery of Joseph Conrad* (1996) examines the ways in which Conrad's impasse with the novel chimes with his anxieties about his developing status as a writer. Harpham regards the portion of the novel written in the 1890s as 'bad early Conrad' with the sections written after 1916 being dismissed as 'bad late Conrad' (1996: 101). Robert Hampson's *Cross-Cultural Encounters in Joseph Conrad's Malay Fiction* (2000) offers a critique of GoGwilt via an account of the ways in which Conrad's deployment of European strategies of representation shape the 'situated misrepresentation' that characterises the narrative of *The Rescue* (2000: 162). Hampson points up the way the novel foregrounds the European's dilemma whilst relegating those of the Malays to the background, drawing out parallels here between the novel and *Lord Jim* (2000: 163). His analysis does not fall back upon simplistic binary thinking as he carefully traces Lingard's misreading of cross-cultural encounters and the ways in which Conrad's narrative incorporates Malay perspectives on the Europeans. Hampson also examines the ways in which Conrad uses metaphors from drama and opera, as European modes of representation, to configure the Malay world as 'imperial spectacle' (2000: 181).

The Rover (1923)

Conrad's last completed novel began, as so many of his works had done, as an idea for a short story. Conrad had begun work on *Suspense*, his incomplete novel of the Napoleonic era in May 1920, shortly before the publication of *The Rescue*, but in October, struggling to make any headway with *Suspense*, Conrad began *The Rover*. As was the case with his two previous novels, the text was largely dictated, but even with this assistance, Conrad made slow progress, with only 5,000 words produced by December. By April 1922, he had completed the first six chapters and between May and June he would create a further ten, bringing the book to a close in late June. Characteristically, Conrad then amended the text, adding material before finishing his work on the manuscript by July. Conrad stated that this novel was 'perhaps my only work in which brevity was a conscious aim. I don't mean compression. I mean brevity *ab initio*, in the very conception, in the very manner of thinking about the people and the events' (Aubry 1927: 326). Conrad noted that the book sold well and its publishers were clearly confident since the first edition ran to a remarkable 40,000 copies (Watts 1994: 44). In his creation of Escampobar Farm and its environs Conrad drew upon his own experience of the landscape of the Giens Peninsula, near Toulon, which he had visited in 1921 whilst en route to Corsica.

Commentary

The novel is set in the late eighteenth and early nineteenth centuries during the rise of Napoleon. Britain and France are at war, but Master Gunner Jean Peyrol is retiring after 'nearly fifty years of lawful and lawless sea life' (8). Turning his back on the port of Toulon, secretly carrying a hoard of treasure, he returns to the 'region of his boyhood days' (6) and takes up residence in a farmhouse on the Giens Peninsula. The farm is owned by Arlette, the psychologically damaged daughter of royalist parents who were slaughtered during the revolutionary terror. Her Aunt Catherine cares for her and the farm is managed by a previously ardent revolutionary, a man called Scevola who harbours affections for Arlette. Chapter 4 jumps forward eight years from the novel's opening to a time when Peyrol has become a part of the community at Escampobar Farm and 'all in it are like shipmates' (44). Scevola, however, is shown to be a marginalised figure, clinging to his revolutionary ardour long after the surrounding villagers have embraced change. Peyrol has been restoring Arlette's father's ship and has taken under his care Michel, a homeless fisherman. He has learnt more of Arlette's past and of Scevola's hand in the mob violence that gripped Toulon during the revolution. Peyrol constantly frames his feelings for Arlette as paternal, but the narration suggests that he is aware of and attracted by her nascent sexuality.

The English place a naval blockade off Toulon where the French Navy are fitting out a fleet and Lieutenant Réal comes to stay at the farm whilst he monitors the English vessel. Increasingly, he visits during his periods of leave since Arlette fascinates him. The English ship puts a party ashore at the prompting of Mr Bolt, the first mate, who had dealings with Arlette's parents. Bolt is disturbed to see Arlette walking at night – 'she made me cold all over for a moment' (62) – and, woodenly concluding that there have been many changes since his last visit, he beats a hasty retreat. In leaving, however, one of the crew becomes lost and plans are laid to recover him the following night. The crewman has in fact been knocked out by Peyrol and is locked in the cabin of his ship under the watchful eye of Michel. Peyrol learns that Réal is on a secret mission from Napoleon designed to dupe Nelson into believing that the French are preparing a fleet for the East. He has a package of fake documents which he has been charged to ensure fall into English hands. Réal seeks to persuade Peyrol to help him undertake this mission and he returns to Toulon to make further arrangements, promising to return that night, Meanwhile Arlette, awakening to her self through her love for Réal, goes to confess her past deeds at church. She tells of seeing the bodies of her murdered parents and then of being caught up in the mob – 'the pavements, the arms and faces, everything was red. I had red splashes all over me. I had to run with them all day, and all the time I felt as if I were falling down, and down, and down. . . . And suddenly I heard myself yelling exactly like the others' (154). It has taken her years to overcome the horror of what she witnessed and became involved with, but Réal has made 'my heart beat' (156) and 'her true self had returned matured in its mysterious exile, hopeful and eager for love' (159). Scevola is growing jealous of Arlette's interest in Réal, and Catherine fears for her niece's restored health should anything happen to the lieutenant.

The novel moves into its closure with a night of flurried action. Scevola, believing Réal to be aboard Peyrol's ship, sets off with jealousy-driven murderous intent but is overpowered by the captive English sailor who makes good his escape and is rescued by Blunt who has come under cover of darkness to search for him. Meanwhile, Réal returns from Toulon and finds Arlette in his room and, in a rather overblown scene, she declares her love and alerts him to Scevola's plans, but the two are parted by Catherine. The next day, Peyrol gets the ship ready for

Réal but Arlette begs him to leave her beloved behind, fainting in her desperation. Peyrol helps Réal carry her part way back to the farm and then asks the lieutenant to take her the rest of the way whilst he continues to prepare the ship. He then sets out to sea with Scevola and Michel on board and leads the English ship into pursuit. Peyrol has decided that the only way to make the plan convincing is if he gives his own life and he allows himself to be killed – along with Scevola and Michel. He dies smiling at a vision of 'the days of his manhood, of strength and adventure' (269). Napoleon's plot works and the captain of the corvette takes the fake despatches to Admiral Nelson. The corvette's captain then arranges for Peyrol's ship to be sunk by gunfire. The novel ends with a coda that reveals the marriage of Réal and Arlette and reflects on Peyrol as 'not a bad Frenchman' and a man of 'great heart' (286).

Early reviews

The reviews were mixed. The *New York Tribune* liked the story's simplicity and the absence of 'disquisitions on ethics and psychology' but felt it was 'too long' (Sherry 1973: 352). The *Times Literary Supplement* called the book 'straight-forward Conrad' and praised its evocation of the Mediterranean coast, glossing it as an 'honestly thrilling tale of action' (1973: 355). The *Glasgow Evening News* noted Conrad's effective use of his 'trick of suspense, of delayed explanation' (Sherry 1973: 356) but concluded that the work was 'a disappointment', especially for what it diagnosed as 'a lack of conviction about the latter half of the book' (1973: 357). The *New Statesman* saw the book as typical of his late work and went on to criticise the plot, characterisation and descriptions, lamenting that:

> the reader has to construct for himself all the relations between the characters. Throughout the book Mr Conrad relies on us to do the work. With some knowledge of his earlier books, we can do it. An image here, a familiar rhythm there, and our memories will lend these faint beings a greater sonority than they possess. But it is doubtful if a critic who had read nothing of Conrad's except *The Rover* would realise that this vague and ill-considered book was the work of an important writer.
> (Sherry 1973: 359–60)

Later critical response

There are many echoes of the other late fictions in this novel: Arlette, the damaged heroine, is a variant of *Victory*'s Lena and *The Arrow of Gold*'s Rita, and Scevola is kin to *The Arrow*'s villain Ortega or *Victory*'s Ricardo (see Works, pp. 107–13, 117–20). Geddes *Conrad's Later Novels* (1980) considers Conrad's depiction of post-revolutionary France and comments upon the ways in which the novel is 'replete with specific images' that lend it a cinematic concreteness. Schwarz's *Conrad, The Later Fiction* (1982) sees the book as 'a minor masterpiece', and a 'synopsis of a number of major themes in his previous work' (1982: 139). Two important essays on the novel are David Leon Higdon's 'Conrad's *The Rover*: The Grammar of Myth' (1992) and Avrom Fleishman's 'Conrad's Last Novel' (1992).

Higdon examines Conrad's use of a particular myth – in which the nymph Galatea attracts the love of a young prince Acis and a cyclops whom she rejects in favour of the prince. The cyclops 'torments her with his attentions' and, happening upon the couple, kills Acis with a boulder (1992: 626). Higdon draws out the ways in which this myth can be read as a template for Conrad's late fiction, with its 'immature, inexperienced men' who are 'rendered immobile by the power of an idea or a woman' (1992: 626). His essay also looks at the ways in which Conrad portrays women as *la belle dame sans merci*, discussing Arlette's figuring as queen, siren and idol in relation to this figure. Finally, he analyses the novel's use of the Eden myth, pointing out similarities between the farm and the mythical garden.

Fleishman offers a comparative reading of the novel and *The Secret Agent*, identifying points of comparison in terms of theme – 'political-historical subjects lead them both into the realm of revolutionary terrorism' (1992: 634) – and (rather less convincingly) character, comparing Heat with Réal as 'stiff young men', Winnie and Arlette as 'long-suffering women', and Verloc and Scevola as 'faintly comic' revolutionaries (1992: 634). Whilst he concedes that the book 'is not Conrad's greatest novel', he concludes that 'its thoroughness of execution and consistency of theme put it in the same camp with his finest achievements, and belie any generalizations about his late falling off' (1992: 638). More recently, Robert Hampson's *Joseph Conrad: Betrayal and Identity* (1992) has offered a reading of the novel as a work of initiation. Building on Schwarz's account of the book, which stresses its focus on 'coming to terms with age and dying' (Schwarz 1982: 145), Hampson examines the way in which 'Peyrol's life of unreflecting, unselfconscious action is beginning to give way to reflection and the consciousness of his own declining powers' (1992: 278). Hampson notes that in this novel, the father–daughter–suitor triangle we see in works ranging from *Almayer's Folly* through *Lord Jim* to *Chance* is also present, but here 'the "father" sacrifices himself, and his efforts are directed towards the liberation of the younger generation from the burden of the past' (1992: 280).

POSTHUMOUSLY PUBLISHED WORKS

Tales of Hearsay (1925)

In 1925, four short stories were published under this posthumously published title by T. Fisher Unwin in England and Doubleday, Page in the USA. Conrad had mooted the collection in 1922 as one that would bring together the earliest and latest works of short fiction from his career. The volume comprised (with dates of first publication in the UK) 'The Warrior's Soul' (1917), 'Prince Roman' (1911), 'The Tale' (1917) and 'The Black Mate' (1908).

Commentary, early reviews and later critical response

'The Warrior's Soul'

Begun as 'The Humane Tomassov' in early 1916, Conrad completed the story in late April by when it was 'quite sufficiently developed for Mag^{ne} Pub^{on}'

(CL5: 583). The title was changed to 'The Warrior's Soul' as Conrad worked on the typescript in May – he felt it was 'a better one' (584). The story appeared in the 29 March edition of *Land and Water*, and Conrad referred to it as a 'pot-boiler (CL6: 91). The story was drawn from Conrad's interest in Napoleon and is set during the retreat from Moscow in the winter of 1812. Narrated by an old Russian soldier, it tells the story of young Tomassov, 'inexperienced, unsuspicious, and unthinking' (7), who has spent his youth in Paris as part of a Russian diplomatic mission where he became besotted by a 'highly civilized woman' (10). As relations between Russia and France sour, he is saved from arrest by the warning of a French officer, De Castel, who also courts the lady. Tomassov returns to Russia, grateful for the warning and in his debt. In the course of the conflict that follows, he captures a French prisoner only to discover that it is De Castel. The Frenchman feels that his capture has robbed him of his honour and he requests that his captor 'do him the favour to blow his brains out. As a fellow soldier ... As a man of feeling – as – as a humane man' (22–3): Tommasov is horrified but eventually shoots the man. Later he resigns his post and 'went away to bury himself in the depths of his province, where a vague story of some dark deed clung to him for years' (26).

Early reviewers such as Edward Garnett praised the story, 'almost at his best', but the work has received very little critical attention (cited in Teets and Gerber 1971: 147). Lawrence Graver's *Conrad's Short Fiction* lumps it with 'The Tale' as 'slight "war-time products"' (1969: 193) noting that it is characteristically Conradian in its dramatisation of 'the ordeal of a hero pressed to choose when every choice is frightful' (1969: 194). Graver is dismissive of the old Russian narrator, criticising the way in which he 'continually harps on his own inadequate powers of explanation' (1969: 196). Daniel R. Schwarz's *Conrad: The Later Fiction* sees parallels with Cain and Abel, noting that in this story Conrad conflates the roles so that Tomassov, in acting to pay his debt of honour to a brother soldier, is both keeper and killer. G. W. Stephen Brodsky's '"What Manners!": Contra-Diction and Conrad's Use of History in "The Warrior's Soul"' (2001) provided a detailed account of the military and historical background.

'Prince Roman'

This story was based on material originally intended for *A Personal Record* but Conrad turned it into a 'long short story', completing it in late September 1910 (CL4, 366). It is unusual in Conrad's canon for its direct engagement with Polish material. Drawing upon his Uncle Bobrowski's *Memoirs*, Conrad created a tale drenched in what one commentator has called his '[h]opeless, mourning fidelity to the memory of Poland' (Najder 1964: 26), which the narrative figures as '[t]hat country which demands to be loved as no other country has ever been loved, with the mournful affection one bears to the unforgotten dead' (51). The story was published in serial form in the *Oxford and Cambridge Review* in October 1911 and in the USA in *Metropolitan Magazine* in January 1912.

The story is based on episodes in the life of nineteenth-century Polish patriot Prince Roman Sangusko, described by Bobrowski as a man 'of unrivalled integrity, noble mindedness and strength of character' (Najder 1983b: 8). The story details Prince Roman's grief at the loss of his wife and tells of his involvement in the Polish rising of 1831 to which he is called by patriotism – 'something louder than my grief' (42). Disguising his origins, he enlists and as Sergeant Peter 'became famous for his resourcefulness and courage' (46). Finally captured, he risks death by firing squad since, as an ex-Russian guardsman (the Polish aristocracy were required to make allegiance with the Tsar) he has transgressed by fighting for 'the enemy'. He is arrested and tried but refuses to express any remorse, declaring that he 'joined the national rising from conviction' (52). He is exiled 'for life to the Siberian mines', but after twenty-five years 'stone deaf, his health broken', he is permitted to return to Poland (53) where he becomes active in 'the private and public life of the neighbourhood' (54).

Edward Garnett, writing in *The Nation* called it 'a charming souvenir of Conrad's boyhood' (cited in Teets and Gerber 1971: 147). The story has tended to receive most coverage from those critics interested in Conrad's engagement with all things Polish; André Busza's 'Conrad's Polish Literary Background and Some Illustrations of the Influence of Polish Literature on his Work' (1966) includes material on the tale's links with Polish Romantic literature, and he has also written on its debt to Flaubert in 'St Flaubert and Prince Roman' (1980). Adam Gillon has also written on the Polish context for the story in 'Some Polish Literary Motifs in the Works of Joseph Conrad' (1966). Eloise Knapp Hay proposed 'Prince Roman' as a fictionalised self-portrait of the artist in her essay 'Conrad's Self-Portraiture' (1975).

'The Tale'

Conrad's only story to deal directly with the First World War was written in autumn 1916. Prior to writing it, as part of his research for government-commissioned propaganda articles, he had spent time on a minesweeper. The story opens with a frame narrative in which a couple converse as night draws on. The man is on leave from the war and the opening scene is washed with 'crepuscular light . . . dying slowly' (59). The woman asks the man for a tale of the kind he told her 'before the war' when he had 'a sort of art' (60). He proceeds to tell the story of 'a Commanding Officer and a Northman' (61), which he suggests is comic in 'a very grim way' (62). The Commanding Officer's ship patrols the coast and one foggy night comes across a neutral ship laid up in a cove, which he suspects has been involved in replenishing enemy submarines (66). The ship is investigated and whilst its '[p]apers and everything' are all in order the mate is 'surly' and its Northman captain is semi-drunk (71), so the Commanding Officer decides to look into the matter himself. The two captains meet and the Northman tells the same story of engine trouble, compounded by fog on an unfamiliar voyage as his crew have done, but the Commanding Officer is put out by the Northman's willingness to make a profit by trading as a neutral during the war, thinking of him as a 'moral cannibal' (74). He cannot discover any evidence that the Northman is lying other than that of his own misgivings. Confronted by the navy man's suspicions, the Northman reflects on neutrality and the temptations of money for poor sailors but asserts that for him 'the risk is too great' (79). The Commanding Officer does not believe him, declaring that he will 'clear all you fellows off this coast' and demands that he leave. Grudgingly he give the Northman a course that he claims will allow him to make his way despite the fog.

The story shifts back to the frame in which it is revealed that the storytelling man is the Commanding Officer and that he gave a false course which led 'straight on a deadly ledge', thus ensuring that the Northman's ship went down with all hands (80). Since the Northman followed this course, it appears that he was telling the truth, but the Commanding Officer believes 'it proves nothing' (80). The narrator declares that he does not know 'whether I have done stern retribution – or murder' and the story ends with him leaving for active duty.

'The Tale' has attracted a good deal of critical attention for its focus on morality in wartime and for its narrative structure. Edward Garnett calls it Conrad 'almost at his finest' and praises the organisation of the narrative (cited in Teets and Gerber 1971: 141). David Harrington and Carol Estness's 'Aesthetic Criteria and Conrad's "The Tale"' (1964) explores the parallels between the presentation of the woman and Northman in a New Critical account of the story's organic unity. Bonamy Dobrée's *Rudyard Kipling: Realist and Fabulist* (1967) offers a brief but illuminating comparison with Kipling's 1915 depiction of a neutral in his story 'Sea Constables'. Porter Williams, in 'Story and Frame in Conrad's "The Tale"' (1968), speculates that the narrator was involved in an illicit affair and reflects on the way the frame story, seen in this light, can illuminate the moral issues faced by the Commanding Officer. A later account, based on a similar hunch, is to be found in William Bonney's *Thorns and Arabesques: Contexts for Conrad's Fiction* (1980). Lawrence Graver's *Conrad's Short Fiction* (1969) dismisses 'The Tale' as a minor work whilst noting that 'the officer is left in ethical limbo' (1969: 194). He was critical of the interplay between frame and embedded narrative, lamenting the reliance upon allegory in the latter (1969: 197). Jakob Lothe's detailed study of the story's presentation of epistemological uncertainty declares the narrative method 'exceptionally sophisticated for late Conrad' (1989: 72) and examines the ways in which the text foregrounds the epistemological problem of 'whether knowledge is possible at all' (1989: 84), thus setting the story in the larger context of Conrad's scepticism and of modernism's interest in 'conflicting interpretive possibilities' (86). In *Joseph Conrad: Narrative Technique and Ideological Commitment* (1990), Jeremy Hawthorn notes a parallel between the reader's sense of ambiguity at the end of the story and the Commander's desire for the truth of the Northman's actions. More recently, Vivian Rundle has focused on the ways in which the tale figures and problematises the role of the reader in her essay ' "The Tale" and the Ethics of Interpretation' (1992). This approach is also adopted in Daphna Erdinast Vulcan's account of the story in *The Strange Short Fiction of Joseph Conrad: Writing, Culture and Subjectivity* (1999), making a bold claim for the work's 'subversion of the most fundamental Platonic paradigm, the cultural episteme which equates knowledge with instrumental mastery ... so central to Modernity itself' (1999: 174). In a powerful reading, Vulcan suggests that this tale 'is an episode whose significance is produced in the act of telling' (1999: 182).

'The Black Mate'

It seems likely that this story, or at least a portion of it, was written in summer 1886 for a competition in the mass-circulation *Tit-Bits* magazine where a prize for sailor's tales was advertised (Carabine 1988). Conrad told his agent that the story was 'supposed to be funny' (CL4: 26) and the tale has a simplistic comedy inherent in the deception in which Mr Bunter, mate of the *Sapphire*, dyes his hair black to disguise his age. His Captain is obsessed with spiritualism and his belief in the supernatural irritates Bunter. Spiritualism had been a popular craze in the later part of the nineteenth century, but medical scepticism and high-profile public trials in the early 1880s had begun to limit its popular appeal: Conrad's captain is, thus, written with an eye on the views of *Tit-Bits* mass readership (Owen 1989, Oppenheim 1985). During a gale, Bunter's supply of hair dye is spilt and, later, when he accidentally falls, he is quick to think up a story that will enable him to explain away his gradually fading hair colour. He tells the gullible captain that he fell because he saw a ghost and when his bandaged head is later revealed and his hair gradually whitens, his story is accepted. The Captain reads his hair as evidence of 'the anguish of the supernatural' (113). Bunter inherits money from a relative and this enables him to give up the sea and the story ends with Bunter giving his side of the story to the narrator.

Conrad ruled out including the story in the English edition of A *Set of Six* (CL4: 43) but he considered putting it in the US edition (CL4: 317, 506–7). Early reviewers were dismissive of the story and most modern critics have ignored it. Of the limited critical work available, Dale Kramer's 'The Maturity of Conrad's First Tale' (1983) and Keith Carabine's '"The Black Mate": June–July 1886; January 1908' (1988) can be recommended.

UNCOLLECTED WORKS

'Laughing Anne' and 'One Day More' (1924)

'One Day More' is a one-act stage version of the short story 'To-morrow' from the collection *Typhoon and Other Stories* (1903) (see Works, **pp. 57–62**). Conrad wrote the adaptation in 1904, breaking off from work on *Nostromo*. Ford Madox Ford helped Conrad to revise the dialogue (CL3: 236) and he also had advice from J. M. Barrie, Arnold Bennett and George Bernard Shaw. Despite their aid, the adaptation only ran for three performances at the Royalty Theatre in London (25–7 June 1905) and whilst it was performed intermittently during Conrad's life, it was not a critical or commercial success. It was first published in the *English Review* (August 1913), and in the USA appeared in *Smart Set* in February 1914. Limited editions designed for the burgeoning collector's market in Conradiana appeared in 1917, 1919 and 1920. It was published commercially with 'Laughing Anne' in an edition introduced, rather critically, by John Galsworthy in 1924. Alison Wheatley's 'Conrad's *One Day More*: Challenging Social and Dramatic Convention' (1999) provides a detailed account of the work's history and argues that the work anticipates 'elements of absurdist tragicomedy' (1999: 3). The adaptation simplifies relationships and puts less emphasis on explaining motives for action, and this means that 'the audience is frequently in the dark, both literally and figuratively' (Wheatley 1999: 13). Wheatley argues that in 'transforming the story into drama, Conrad developed new methods of dramatising noticeable gaps in coherent behaviour, requiring his audience to strain at the boundaries of perception and comprehension' (1999: 15).

'Laughing Anne' is a two-act version of the short story 'Because of the Dollars' from the collection *Within the Tides* (1915) (see Works, **p. 106**). Conrad worked on the stage version towards the end of 1920, shortly after completing work on a script for a silent film adaptation of 'Gaspar Ruiz' entitled *Gapsar the Strong Man* (see Works, **pp. 74–5**). It is also worth noting that earlier in the same year Conrad had commented on a professional dramatisation of *The Secret Agent*. *Laughing Anne* was written with one of the most experimental theatre companies in England in mind and Conrad described it as 'a play for Grand Guignol', alluding to the late nineteenth-century French vogue for violent and melodramatic dramas (Najder 1983a: 457, Hand 2002: 45). The script was published by *Metropolitan Magazine* in September 1914 and in a volume with 'One Day More' in 1924. It was not performed during Conrad's lifetime and received its world premiere at Texas Tech University, Lubbock, Texas, during a Conrad conference in August 2000. Richard Hand, the director of this premiere, argued that 'we should see the play as a masterful understanding of a quintessentially French genre of theatre, a dramatic form which is avant-gardist and distinctly experimental in a 1920 London context' (2002: 52). As with 'One Day More', Conrad simplified the story and characters, condensing its time span and range of locations. Alison Wheatley's '*Laughing Anne*: "An almost unbearable spectacle"' (2002) traces the history of Conrad's interest in dramatisation. She notes that he 'recast the story to focus on the lone female character' (2002: 65) and argues that Conrad's interest in dramatisation in the period 1919–1920 reveals a writer 'remarkably interested in experimenting with new genres and new aesthetic strategies' suggesting that 'he was evolving as a creative artist' (2002: 74).

Suspense (1925)

Conrad's final novel was unfinished at the time of his death, with only the first two parts complete in draft form when he died. At some 80,000 words, however, this is more than a fragment. The work appeared in various serial versions during 1925 and was published in volume form by Doubleday, Page in the USA and Dent in the UK in September. The novel drew on Conrad's interest in Napoleon and is set in Genoa in 1815, where it weaves a romance plot of political intrigues and mistaken identities. Conrad had mentioned his desire to write a Mediterranean novel as early as 1902 (CL2: 423), and by 1911 had the story in mind, but at this stage mixes material that would form *The Rover* with that which ended up in *Suspense* (CL3: 409). Critical work has tended to focus on Conrad's sources and settings: see, for example, Hans van Marle and Gene Moore, 'The Sources of Conrad's *Suspense*' (1997) and Urgo Mursia's 'Notes on Conrad's Italian Novel: *Suspense*' (1992).

The Sisters (1928)

This was the novel that Conrad began working on in late 1895 after completing *An Outcast of the Islands*. He set it aside on the advice of his mentor Edward Garnett (see Life and Contexts, **pp. 11–12**) and the work remained an incomplete fragment of seven chapters which tell two as yet unrelated stories. One strand concerns a young eastern European painter whilst the other focuses on two Basque sisters. Najder noted that the second strand is very reminiscent of aspects of *The Arrow of Gold* (1978: 40). The fragment was published in the New York *Bookman* in 1928 and then appeared in a limited edition of 935 copies published by Crosby Gaige in New York (Najder 1978: 44). Najder reprinted it in *Congo Diary and Other Uncollected Pieces by Joseph Conrad* (1978).

3

Criticism

The study of Conrad's work is now a major industry, supporting three scholarly societies, two academic journals, an annual round of specialist conferences, and major publishing ventures such as the Cambridge University Press *Collected Edition* and *Collected Letters* series. Conrad's fiction is studied on most twentieth-century literature survey courses and, thanks in part to work by scholars who have brought perspectives from gender studies and post-colonial studies to bear upon his works, has become a relatively popular area for graduate student dissertations and theses. All of this activity generates a huge number of publications: a search in the Modern Language Association database in summer 2005 revealed nearly 4,000 items devoted to the author and, in marshalling this diversity for an introductory book, a high degree of selection is necessary if readers new to the study of the author are to be helped to steer their way through the enormous range of work available. Whilst Part 2 offered information on some of the major studies of individual texts, this section will provide outline details of some of the milestones in the critical history of Joseph Conrad from 1914, the date of the publication of the first book-length study of his works, through to the present day. As was the case in Part 2, I have devoted some time to the early critical studies since these, coupled with the review material discussed earlier, enable readers to access key facets of the period's perception of Conrad in ways that chime with the dominant 'texts in context' approach of many survey courses offered by universities in the UK and USA. In this section's selective overview of main currents in the field, the focus will be on significant general studies that are generally agreed to be of lasting value or of literary-historical significance for the field: coverage of key texts means that readers can use this section as an annotated bibliography to the main currents in Conrad studies. My outline of the critical history of Conrad studies concludes with concise overviews of four major areas of critical inquiry which continue to animate the field in ways that have a bearing on the work of readers at the beginning of their engagement with the author.

Early studies: 1914–30

Richard Curle, *Joseph Conrad: A Study* (1914)

This was the first book-length critical study of Conrad and for some time it remained, for all its omissions, an important reference point in the study of the author. Written by an acolyte with assistance from Conrad, the study was thematic and offered chapters with generalising titles such as 'Conrad's Atmosphere' and 'Conrad's Women'. The book appeared in a series entitled *Studies of Living Writers*, which had previously published works on major British authors, including Arnold Bennett, George Bernard Shaw and H. G. Wells. Curle sees Conrad's fiction as marking a 'new epoch' (1914: 1) in prose, largely because of the role which is afforded to imagination in his work (1914: 3). Curle's discussion of 'Conrad's Novels and Stories' (1914: 27–65) is little more advanced than the criticism found in the periodical press – 'Heart of Darkness', for example, is glossed as a 'sombre story of the dark forests of the Congo' and the tale 'of the darker hearts of men', in which Kurtz is cast as 'the embodiment of that lawless and unhappy land' (1914: 51). Curle's limited understanding of narrative technique is evident in his claim that 'the creation of Marlow would seem a mistake' (1914: 25). Whilst Curle praises *Nostromo* and presents Conrad in the tradition of European writers such as Flaubert and Turgenev, his inability to grasp his author's narrative strategies suggests both his limitations as a critic and, more interestingly, something of the way in which in 1914, some nineteen years after he had begun his career, Conrad's work was still technically challenging for mainstream criticism. Curle's book panders to a readership that seeks uncomplicated storytelling, and research has shown that Conrad encouraged this portrait of the artist as accessible old master, since he clearly saw a critical introduction in this anodyne vein as a valuable part of his bid for popular success with *Chance* (CL6: 274). He described Curle's book as 'complementary' to *A Personal Record* (CL6: 280), his own attempt to position himself for an English readership, and saw several sections in draft, offering comments and advice (see Works, **pp. 88–92**). For a study of Curle's relationship with Conrad, see Raymond Brebach, 'Conrad and Curle' (1996).

Wilson Follett, *Joseph Conrad: A Short Study of his Intellectual and Emotional Attitude towards his Work and of the Chief Characteristics of his Work* (1915)

Wilson Follett's *Joseph Conrad: A Short Study of His Intellectual and Emotional Attitude Towards His Work and of the Chief Characteristics of His Work* (1915) is a key text in understanding the growing popular success of Conrad's work in the USA. It was privately printed by Doubleday, his American publishers, as part of their campaign to boost his standing in that marketplace. Although designed with marketing in mind, Follett was an academic by training, and whilst the study was not free of hagiographic overstatement, there was what contemporaries might have seen as a Jamesian concern with a novel's formal arrangement which makes this short book a far more progressive account of Conrad's technique than

Curle's. Follett's work begins by isolating two areas in which Conrad's significance as a writer could be established. The first rests upon what he terms 'his
special contribution to the body and permanency of the short story as a form' and
the second is his 'probable importance to modern realism' (1915: vii). Follett's
analysis of Conrad's life as a construct of three distinct lives (1915: 27–9) offers a
schema which rapidly became dominant in Conrad studies. He argues that the
shifts from Pole to sailor to writer are to be understood as expatriations – a strong
term that contained the idea of renouncing one's allegiance to a country (*OED*).
Follett asserts that each remove – from Poland to sea career to fiction writer –
'was not improvement, but enrichment' (1915: 31). Developing a case for Conrad
as a modern realist, whose work is concerned with the psychological rather than
the social, he argues that whilst his fiction offered readers detail 'as sharply as the
professional notebook realist' (1915: 91):

> his fancy is ever constructively out working upon the finer congruities
> that subsist between the aspect observed and the sensitised observing
> faculty; so that . . . he is not to be confounded with the globe-trotting
> realists who have offered their memoirs and confessions under the guise
> of fiction.
>
> (Follett 1915: 92)

His account of Conrad's method stresses that the technique described enables a
more accurate depiction of life since 'in the overpowering culmative effect of a
story, we see a score of minor episodes and a hundred tangential meanings
brought into alignment, reduced to a fine organisation, all made to count, and
count simultaneously' (1915: 96). Follett manages to raise questions about
Conradian textual practice which very few British critics had asked, and Conrad
was fulsome in his praise for the book, suggesting that '[n]othing ever written
about be me had come anywhere near it, in tone, in discernment, in comprehension' (CL6: 575).

The growth of Conrad criticism in the period 1916–30 brought with it an increasing focus on four major areas: Conrad as Slav, Conrad as pessimist, Conrad as
technical innovator and Conrad as precursor to the modern tradition. What is
strikingly evident in the work of Conrad's critics in this period is the extent
to which the issues of technique that vexed his earliest commentators slowly
but surely become accepted as evidence of his artistic merit. Throughout this
period there was a steady decline in the number of articles on Conrad written
by literary journalists and men of letters and an increase in pieces written by
and for academics, especially in North America. The critical machine was fuelled
by G. Jean Aubry's two-volume *Joseph Conrad: Life and Letters* (1927) and
Edward Garnett's *Letters from Conrad* (1928) along with Ford Madox Ford's
entertainingly unreliable memoir of collaboration, *Joseph Conrad: A Personal
Remembrance* (1924), and Jessie Conrad's self-serving *Joseph Conrad as I knew
Him* (1926). From this period, I will outline three works that were milestones in
the developing critical reputation of Conrad's work.

Ruth Stauffer, *Joseph Conrad: His Romantic-Realism* (1922)

Stauffer's short study, based on her MA thesis awarded by the University of California in 1919, sets out to prove an explicitly stated theory about Conrad's conflation of the genres of romance and realism. Her work relies heavily on Conrad's 'Preface' to *The Nigger of the 'Narcissus'*, leavened by quotations from authoritative writers and critics ranging from Aristotle to Zola. Stauffer suggests that in Conrad one could identify a combination of 'the poetic imagination of the Romanticist and the minute observation of the Realist' (1922: 27), arguing that the often startling juxtapositions of the 'mundane and the marvellous', of the 'incongruous' and 'matter of fact' (1922: 27), which readers find in his work are motivated by 'the high purpose of presenting life as it actually is' (1922: 28). Stauffer 'discovers' that Conrad, by his own admission, is readily to be located in the context of the literary history of romantic and realist modes but is also a writer whose work, by fusing realism with a dominant romanticism, adds to that history. Her work was the first sustained study of the relationship between romantic and realist worldviews in Conrad's fiction, and this is an area of inquiry which has continued to be the focus of study for critics interested in Conrad's position in literary history: questions of Conrad's debt to Romanticism are central to Ian Watt's influential *Conrad in the Nineteenth Century* (1979) and, in a somewhat different vein, to Daphna Erdinast-Vulcan's *Joseph Conrad and the Modern Temper* (1991).

Ford Madox Ford, *Joseph Conrad: A Personal Remembrance* (1924)

This was a key work in English Conrad criticism in the 1920s, one of a number of texts prompted by Conrad's death. Ford's stylistic idiosyncrasies energise his rather biased examination of Conrad's technique, and the work offers an after-the-event explanation of the foundations of Conrad's greatness which some have seen as an attempt to underline Ford's own significance for the modernist avant-garde with whom he was working in Paris during the early 1920s. The book examines Conrad's life and work through a series of anecdotes illustrating what Ford regarded as typical Conradian behaviour. Ford does not stray from received opinion in emphasising the aesthetic credo advanced in the 'Preface' to *The Nigger of the 'Narcissus'* in his account of Conradian technique. He examines the importance of beginnings and goes on to offer an insight into the 'formulae for the writing of the novel at which Conrad and [he] had arrived . . . in 1902' (1924: 179). Under an impressive range of headings covering 'Impressionism', 'Conversations', 'Style', 'Cadence', 'Structure', 'Progression d'Effet' and 'Language', among other areas, Ford suggests his version of a Conradian poetics. Ford's first heading, 'General Effect', is taken up with an examination of the maxim that 'the general effect of a novel must be the general effect that life makes on mankind. A novel must not be a narration, a report' (1924: 179). Ford's next point is the Jamesian one that 'the whole of Art consists of selection' (1924: 182), and he argues that the impressions a writer selects are chosen according to the extent to which they will 'carry the story forward or interest the reader' (1924: 183). Ford extends his discussion of selection to the incorporation of speech since, for Ford, a fiction driven by a desire to render impressions faces a particular problem with dialogue because 'the object of the novelist is to keep the reader entirely oblivious of the fact that the author exists' (1924: 186) and the mechanics of dialogue – 'he said', 'she interjected', etc. – shatter the dramatic illusion. Ford argues that Conrad found dialogue particularly problematic but solved his difficulties by 'the use of indirect locutions together with the rendering of the effects of portions of speech' (1924: 186).

Ford then turns his attention to 'the eternally vexed' subject of literary style (1924: 193). He begins by stating that the 'business of style is to make [a] work interesting' (1924: 193) and, after noting that Flaubert and Maupassant were the 'chief masters in style' (1924: 195), for him and Conrad, sums up their notion of Absolute Prose as follows: 'In writing a novel we agreed that every word set on paper – every word set on paper – must carry the story forward and, that as the story progressed, the story must be carried forward faster and faster and with more and more intensity. That is called *progression d'effet*' (1924: 210).

By 1924, the impressionist novel was a largely accepted form, one which was in the process of being challenged by newer modes of textual practice being developed by writers such as Virginia Woolf and James Joyce who had learnt from its revelation of the power of a narrative technique founded upon a concern to render the often incomplete impressions of individuals. Ford's book attempts, with some success, to characterise what was, at the time of writing, an almost historical mode and genuinely seeks to promote the work of Conrad as its greatest practitioner. Whilst some commentators have downplayed the book's account, it seems to me that Ford more often than not illuminates areas of Conrad's method by focusing on technique and providing quoted or created examples which support his claims. It is this combination of genuine insight and detailed examination that made Ford's work a landmark in early Conrad criticism. His study influenced later critics, notably underpinning F. R. Leavis's influential grouping of Conrad as part of *The Great Tradition* (1948).

Gustav Morf, *The Polish Heritage of Joseph Conrad* (1930)

Gustav Morf's book, a psychological biography rather than a work of literary-critical evaluation, draws on the theories of Freud and, in particular, those of Jung to examine Conrad's psychological traits as they are 'revealed' in his fictions. Morf's psychological approach is informed by a dominant trend in British Conrad criticism in the 1920s which saw his writing as shaped by Slavonic concerns and attitudes. Edward Garnett was, much to Conrad's exasperation, the first critic to suggest a Slavonic dimension to his work when, in his unsigned article in *The Academy* of 15 October 1898, he noted that Conrad's art was like the 'poetic realism of the great Russian novels' (Sherry 1973: 106). Morf's work develops this notion via an application of psychological theory to reveal a guilt complex associated with Conrad's departure from his homeland which, for Morf, shapes key moments in his fiction. The study adopts a somewhat pedestrian approach in which a Polish characteristic is delineated and then 'evidence' of its presence in Conrad's fictions is deemed to reveal Slavonic influences in his writing. Morf was one of the first critics to speculate on the extent to which tensions between the outlook of the Korzeniowski and Bobrowski sides of Conrad's family manifested themselves in his fiction. Thus, the influence of the rational and pragmatic Bobrowski was said to motivate what Morf sees as Conrad's hatred of idealists such as Kurtz or Decoud (1930: 22), a hatred which is complicated by the fact that it involves rejecting the Korzeniowski aspect of his character. Morf's account of Conrad's ironic angle of vision attributes Conrad's 'sarcastic mind' (1930: 37) to the influence of his father's distinctive outlook. It is this legacy that makes Conrad's texts 'sarcastic books, provocative books, they are pamphlets of seditious contents in the form of symbolic stories' (1930: 37).

Morf, somewhat simplistically, argues that Conrad's characters and narrators are versions of himself, presentations of an ideal self that enables him to work through problems in his inner quest for equilibrium: 'Marlow resembles Conrad in all essential traits of character. Besides being a cosmopolitan, he is a fascinating story-teller, with a strong sense of romance, and a marvellous power of intuition, observation and imitation. He is really the projection of Conrad's best qualities' (1930: 90).

In what was to prove an influential analogy, Morf suggests that Jim's jump from the *Patna* is to be equated with Conrad's decision to leave Poland. According to Morf, '*Lord Jim* is more than a novel, it is a confession' (1930: 149) in which 'Jim is the projection of Conrad's unconscious wishes for compensation. Mentally or morally, he is, . . . the projection of Conrad's repressed fears' (1930: 161). Reading his book today, it quickly becomes apparent that Morf's argument is overly shaped by the dictates of psychological theory when he goes on to argue that the evidence provided by the presence of narrators such as Marlow 'is certainly another proof of Conrad's deep introspection' (1930: 161). This notion is central to Morf's major thesis which posits Conrad as a Jungian 'intuitive type':

> The intuitive type possesses in a remarkable degree the faculty of putting himself in the place of others, or rather, of feeling as if he were some third person, of identifying himself with others, as the technical expression is. The consequence is that he adapts himself very easily to whatever appeals to his imagination and that he understands and penetrates and literally makes his the motives of all sorts of men.
>
> (Morf 1930: 90–1)

As Frederic Karl has argued, the label could equally be applied to any writer, but it is important to stress that this 'intuitive type' fitted with the period's dominant conception of what was to be expected from a great novelist (Karl 1979: 110). Morf is arguing for a reappraisal of Conrad which more fully comprehended the influence of his Polish background upon his way of seeing. His concern with this aspect of Conrad is the logical product of over twenty years of critical inquiry which turned upon the author's alleged Slavonic qualities, and in this self-consciously pioneering work, Morf's desire to set the record straight, perhaps, excuses his overemphasis. His approach provides critics with a model for understanding the deep psychological implications at stake in the notion of Conrad as Slav and his account of the psychological processes which Conrad focused on in his characterisation develops earlier critical claims for Conrad to be seen as a psychological novelist. His reading of Freud, whose *Interpretation of Dreams* is cited as a source in the analysis of *Lord Jim*, may be crude and unconvincing, but this book is notable as the earliest text to use psychoanalytic theory in Conrad studies, and it remains an important milestone in the maturation of Conrad criticism.

The changing critical reputation: 1930–60

Conrad's reputation waned during the 1930s – too much associated with the pre-war period and perhaps too gloomy for the hedonist spirit of the Jazz Age – and his work was not in critical favour again until the darker wartime days of the 1940s. This is not to say that that there were no significant works on the author produced in the 1930s. Joseph Beach Warren's essay 'Impressionism: Conrad', in his *The Twentieth Century Novel: Studies in Technique* (1932: 337–65), Edward Crankshaw's *Joseph Conrad: Some Aspects of the Art of the Novel* (1936), and David Daiches chapter on Conrad in *The Novel and the Modern World* (1939: 25–62), are notable exceptions to the general neglect of Conrad in this decade. The 1940s saw a number of significant works published, including J. D. Gordan's *Joseph Conrad: The Making of a Novelist* (1940) and Muriel Bradbrook's *Joseph Conrad: England's Polish Genius* (1941). R. W. Stallman (ed.) *The Art of Joseph Conrad: A Critical Symposium* (1960) contains a representative selection from many of the key works on Conrad produced in this period. Perhaps the most significant individual studies of Conrad in the period – in terms of his wider critical standing – are F. R. Leavis's 1941 essays in the influential journal *Scrutiny*, later reprinted in *The Great Tradition* (1948). In the 1950s, Leavis's view of Conrad's work would be supplemented by two major studies – Thomas Moser's *Joseph Conrad: Achievement and Decline* (1957), and Albert Guerard's *Conrad the Novelist* (1958) – and, between them, these would set the terms of debate within Conrad studies for many years to come. What all three works had in common was the placing of Conrad in a broadly realist novelistic tradition, from Leavis's claims for his 'moral realism' to Guerard's emphasis on his 'sincerity of expression', the criticism of this period could only see a tangential relation between Conrad and modernism.

F. R. Leavis, *The Great Tradition* (1948)

Leavis makes a case for Conrad as 'a master of the English language' (1948: 28), who could be ranked with Jane Austen, George Eliot and Henry James in his concern with form. These writers were the 'really great' since 'they not only change the possibilities of the art for practitioners and readers' but through this attention to form they promote 'awareness of the possibilities of life' (1948: 10). Leavis argues that James's American origins and Conrad's Polish background enabled them to develop radical solutions to their fictions' formal problems. Leavis emphasises Conrad's debt to Dickens, and it is clear from his work's footnotes that he has drawn on Ford Madox Ford's recollections of working with Conrad for many of his views about the author's notions of form and technique. Leavis's study is thematic, emphasising Conrad's alertness to the pressures of his epoch and to 'the stresses of the changing spiritual climate' (1948: 33). He sees Conrad's interest in depicting moral isolation as part and parcel of his relevance as a writer for 1940s readers – he is 'incomparably closer to us today than Hardy' (1948: 34). He critiques 'Heart of Darkness' for what he sees as its magazine-like overwriting, famously citing the 'adjectival insistence' of its narration's harping on the inscrutable (1948: 204) and the unspeakable (205) as the cause of a cheapening of tone that is 'little short of disastrous' (206). Leavis breaks with critical convention by rejecting the conventionally high ranking of Conrad's sea fiction and, *Typhoon* aside, he argues for the importance of his political fictions, praising *Nostromo* as 'one of the great novels of the language' (1948: 218) and *The Secret Agent* as 'indubitably a classic and a masterpiece' (239), though he also finds good things in *The Shadow Line, Victory, Chance* and *Under Western Eyes*. He is sceptical of the value of Marlow as a narrative device, seeing him as a temptation to authorial interjection, and he discounts the early novels and *Tales of Unrest* as 'excessively adjectival studies in the Malayan exotic' and downplays the importance of *Lord Jim*, influentially lamenting the shift to Patusan as 'decidedly thin' (1948: 218). He dismisses *The Rover* as the work of an old man and the other 1920s fiction as 'inferior novels' (1948: 257). Leavis's study constructs a Conrad canon that was to prove influential for over twenty years.

Thomas Moser, *Joseph Conrad: Achievement and Decline* (1957)

Moser's study draws upon the work of Leavis and that of Morton Zabel, whose essays and influential introduction to *The Portable Conrad* (1947) helped shape the terms of American Conrad studies in the 1940s with its emphasis on existential preoccupations. Moser echoes Leavis in his critique of the late fiction, and his study divides Conrad's output into two main phases. His early period (1895–1912) is seen as developing three character types – the simple, vulnerable, or perceptive hero – through tales centred on issues of fidelity to community values. The simple hero is a character such as Singleton from *The Nigger of the 'Narcissus'*, an 'unreflective, courageous, loyal seaman' (Moser 1957: 15). The vulnerable heroes are the men who fail, such as Willems in *An Outcast of the Island*, or Nostromo when he steals the silver for himself, and these represent 'Conrad's most difficult, most complicated' characters (Moser 1957: 16). Moser groups them into simple betrayers of trust such as Nostromo, and the more complex, ironic figures, such as Decoud or Jim. The perceptive hero is presented as an amalgamation of the first two types – 'the kind of man who follows the simple seaman's code, yet has the imagination, skepticism, and self-doubts of the betrayers' (Moser 1957: 23): for Moser, it is Marlow who fulfilled this role.

Moser goes on to influentially argue that much of the vitality of Conrad's early fiction stemmed from its exclusion of the theme of love, arguing that there 'is something about the theme of love that elicits only bad writing from Conrad (1957: 69). He offers an analysis of 'The Return', Conrad's unusual early tale of urban middle-class marital breakdown, as 'a kind of *locus classicus* for the near paralysis of Conrad's creativity when dealing with a sexual subject' (1957: 77) (see Works, **p. 39**). Moser speculates that Conrad's inability to draw scenes of love with any conviction stemmed from his worldview, which 'sees man as lonely and morally isolated, harried by egoistic longings for power and peace, stumbling along a perilous path, his only hope benumbing labor or, in rarer cases, a little self knowledge' (1957: 127). For Moser, the early Conrad is a writer interested in the psychology of moral failure whilst the later Conrad (1913–24) is seen as less preoccupied with moral dilemmas and more interested in the workings of chance. In Moser's account, works written in this phase show a diminishment in technical mastery and thematic complexity which he lay at the door of encroaching old age. Another cause of Conrad's decline is seen as his difficulty in handling the romance dimensions of his later works and a related failure to convincingly draw female psychology: only Emilia Gould from *Nostromo* is deemed wholly successful. Moser's chapter on Conrad's (non-)representation of women is still a rich source of insights that have profitably been taken up by later critics working on Conrad and gender.

Albert Guerard, *Conrad the Novelist* (1958)

Guerard's study offers an influential psychological approach to the writer, beginning with a bold rejection of New Critical orthodoxy by insisting on the relevance of the life to the art on the grounds that Conrad 'was one of the most subjective and most personal of English novelists' (1958: 1). Guerard's study focuses on the novels, covering *Almayer's Folly* through to the incomplete *Suspense*, via detailed close reading. He makes some fruitful comparisons between Conrad's work and that of French novelist André Gide (1869–1951) and British novelist and poet Thomas Hardy (1840–1928), and his work is notable for its pioneering work on the relationship between Conrad's fiction and that of American modernist novelist William Faulkner (1897–1962). Guerard concurs with Moser in downgrading the late fiction, arguing that 'Conrad's period of commercial success as a novelist exactly corresponds with his period of falling power' (1958: 257), and he identifies three facets which caused the late novels to be failures: a 'sentimental ethic' (1958: 257), a narrator 'or central consciousness as dullard' (258), and a failure of 'imaginative power and imaginative common sense' (258). Guerard seeks to place Conrad as a modern: he 'seems closer to the present – to Faulkner, Graham Greene, Malcolm Lowry, and others – than to the major figures who emerged just before and after the First World War' (1958: 300). Drawing upon psychoanalytic theory from Freud and Jung, Guerard's work remains valuable today for its close study of the major fiction and it has served as a starting point for many later studies.

Boom years: 1960–80

As the study of Conrad became firmly established as an academic field in its own right, the critical studies of his work show increased specialisation. Many of the key works from this period are covered in later subsections of this chapter, which examine particular themes and topics (see Criticism, **pp. 158–67**). Evidence of Conrad's significance in academia and of the variety of responses his work was generating, can be seen in the appearance during these decades of substantial critical anthologies. Marvin Mudrick's *Conrad: A Collection of Critical Essays* (1966) offers a selection that includes work from the 1960s by Jocelyn Baines (author of the first serious biography of Conrad) and others but concentrates upon essays from the 1950s. Frederic Karl (ed.) *Joseph Conrad: A Collection of Criticism* (1975) draws together work from the 1950s and early 1960s, whilst Norman Sherry (ed.) *Joseph Conrad: A Commemoration* (1976) reprints papers from a major international conference marking the fiftieth anniversary of Conrad's death. This volume provides modern readers with a good flavour of the variety that characterised Conrad studies in the mid-1970s, with essays on Conrad and philosophy and issues of speech and language to the fore. The growing student market also drove the appearance of a number of introductory guides during this period, ranging from Karl's *A Reader's Guide to Joseph Conrad* (1960) – which made a cogent case for Conrad as a modernist writer – through Neville Newhouse's *Joseph Conrad* (1966), and C.B. Cox's *Joseph Conrad* (1977).

Jocelyn Baines, *Joseph Conrad: A Critical Biography* (1960)

Amongst the most significant general works from the early part of this period is Jocelyn Baines, *Joseph Conrad: A Critical Biography* (1960), which brings a scholarly detachment to biographical matters that helps correct the excesses of earlier studies. Drawing upon a wide range of source material, Baines's study enriched the field and his critical assessments of the text, if somewhat cautious, remain reliable. The Malay fiction is crisply dealt with: *Almayer's Folly* 'is too self-conscious a literary creation, written according to a formula' (1960: 185) whilst *An Outcast* is hobbled by a prose style 'even more artificially literary' (200) and *The Rescue* is 'turgid with . . . exoticism' (216).

Baines rates *The Nigger of the 'Narcissus'* as 'the culmination of Conrad's apprenticeship as a novelist', noting that its prose style 'is far more flexible and the imagery, for the most part, more visually precise than that of Conrad's previous work' (1960: 222). He notes the importance of Marlow's narration in creating the 'moral elusiveness and ambiguity' that underpin 'Heart of Darkness' (1960: 273), but echoes Leavis's complaint about the narration's overuse of adjectives (275). He concludes, however, that it is 'one of the finest short stories ever written' because of its 'masterly' presentation of the enigma of Kurtz (Baines 1960: 275) and its 'creation of visual scene upon visual scene charged with emotive impact – from the French man-of-war shelling the coast, [to] the grove of death . . . – to attain the culmative effect of human imbecility, of evil and horror (281).

Lord Jim is described as rather overdone in terms of narrative method, 'as in "Heart of Darkness", one may be tempted to wonder whether even Conrad himself was always quite clear as to what he was trying to say or, in this case, whether there was not some unresolved ambiguity in his own attitude to the events he described' (Baines 1960: 295). *Nostromo* is praised as 'Conrad's most ambitious feat of imagination and is worthy of comparison with the most ambitious of all great novels, *War and Peace*' (Baines 1960: 358). Baines notes a shift in technique in the novel's use of anonymous third-person narration and the use of 'the characters to comment on each other and reflect events' (1960:

360). Baines's hesitation over Conrad's modernist narrative strategies impede his reading of the novel; his claim that the lack of a narrator 'exposed the weakness of Conrad's characterization' (1960: 36) leads him to the dubious notion that:

> It is evident that most of the characters, in particular the leading ones, exist for what they represent rather than for what they are. Although they play important roles in the development of the themes and are in that respect vivid and real, their psychology is on the whole crude, blurred, or even unconvincing. It is with the minor, picturesque characters such as Sotillo, General Montero, and Mitchell that Conrad succeeds best.
>
> (Baines 1960: 360)

Despite these problems, he regards the novel as 'almost without blemish' and praises the effect of the time shifts in enabling Conrad to

> approach the simultaneity of visual experience which a painting offers. The elimination of progression from one event to another also has the effect of implying that nothing is ever achieved. By the end of the book we are virtually back where we started; it looks as if the future of Costaguana will be very similar to her past.
>
> (Baines 1960: 362)

Baines does not rate *The Secret Agent* as high as some, suggesting that it lacks a unifying theme and 'when it is carefully examined falls apart into a succession of only superficially related scenes' (1960: 408). *Under Western Eyes* is praised for its subtle and convincing characterization (Baines 1960: 434), including that of Natalia Haldin whom Baines regards as 'Conrad's most effective portrait of a woman' (1960: 435). *Chance* is dismissed as 'one of Conrad's most imperfect novels' (Baines 1960: 459), whilst *Victory* is praised for the subtlety of its central character's consciousness (477).

The late novels were given reasonably even-handed estimates: *The Arrow of Gold* is described as a 'a failure of imagination' awash with 'overwriting and melodrama' (Baines 1960: 493), whilst *The Rescue* is 'a melancholy but a moving book' (502) and *The Rover* 'a worthy swan song' (506) which lacks the 'profundity or range of his major works' (506). As a whole, Baines reads these late fictions as evidence of a decline in literary power. His final chapter seeks to correct the period's growing tendency to read Conrad as a wholly sceptic or even pessimistic author, and he concludes with the claim that his 'achievement is an assertion of the indomitability of the human spirit', suggesting that whilst it is useless to look for 'consolation' in his fiction, 'his work does provide exhilaration; thirty years of dedicated effort had as their reward the presentation of depths of experience which few artists have been able to excel' (Baines 1960: 540). Baines's work was the standard biography until the late 1970s and, as such, shaped the work of many critics writing in this period.

Norman Sherry, *Conrad's Eastern World* (1966) and *Conrad's Western World* (1971)

Equally influential were Norman Sherry's studies of the sources and historical background to Conrad's work, collected in *Conrad's Eastern World* (1966) and *Conrad's Western World* (1971). The earlier volume offered source material relating to *Almayer's Folly, An Outcast of the Islands, Lord Jim*, 'The End of the Tether', *The Shadow-Line* and 'The Secret Sharer', whilst the later book covered 'Heart of Darkness', *Nostromo* and *The Secret Agent*. Although these works have been criticised for an over-simplistic equation of source with fictional character and incident, they extend Conrad studies by revealing an important facet of Conrad's working practice and emphasising the role of imagination in transforming these sources. Sherry also edited *Conrad: The Critical Heritage* (1973), which reprinted a large number of early reviews of the major fiction and remains a standard reference work (though one that needs updating).

Edward Said, *Joseph Conrad and the Fiction of Autobiography* (1966)

Another important overviews of Conrad's work produced in this period include Edward Said's *Joseph Conrad and the Fiction of Autobiography* (1966), which draws upon existentialist and phenomenological thinking to examine the ways in which Conrad presents himself as a writer via his short fiction. Said's study makes extensive use of Conrad's letters on the basis that 'if Conrad wrote of himself, of the problem of self-definition, with such sustained urgency, some of what he wrote must have had meaning for his fiction' (Said 1966: vii). Addressing the critical received wisdom head-on, Said argues that Conrad's overwriting, his excessive use of adjectives and the resulting passages of purple prose are not to be read as 'the unearned prolixity of a careless writer, but rather the concrete and particular result of his immense struggle with himself' (1966: 4) For Said, the writer's project is the rescue of meaning from experience, 'to make intellectual use of what he had known' (1966: 7), and he boldly claims that in the letters 'we are able to discover the contours of Conrad's mind as it engages itself in a partnership with existence (9). The analysis of Conrad's mind and art in the first part of Said's book is suggestive, especially his account of the artful creation of a public persona in *A Personal Record* (1966: 58–63), but despite its close engagement with the letters, the work suffers somewhat from a turn to abstraction: it is rich in speculation but poor in its application to specific textual examples. The second half of Said's work offers the first serious study of Conrad's short fiction, dwelling on previously derided work such as 'The Return', critiquing Jungian readings of 'The Secret Sharer', and identifying an overarching interest in the 'the intrusion of the past into the present and the intrusion of the present into the past (Said 1966: 93). Said provides illuminating discussion of self-presentation in the two autobiographical works, *The Mirror of the Sea* and *A Personal Record*, and a detailed reading of *The Shadow Line*. He concludes that 'Conrad's achievement is that he ordered the chaos of his existence into a highly patterned art that accurately reflected and controlled the realities in which it dealt (Said 1966: 196). Although this work is an important milestone in the psychological study of Conrad, its focus on the short stories has led one influential critic to suggest its limitations are analogous to those of 'a psycho-biography of Shakespeare which carries no reference to *Hamlet*' (Knowles 1992: 50).

Bernard Meyer's *Joseph Conrad: A Psychoanalytic Biography* (1967) probed the author's psychology to a far greater extent than Said's work. Meyer, a practising psychoanalyst, offers a provocatively speculative study of the author's life and works in the light of 'contemporary psychoanalytic knowledge' (Meyer 1967: 5). Meyer suggests that Conrad's fiction provided a means for him to work out deep-rooted psychological concerns, and whilst he influenced a number of further studies in the 1970s, his account has dated. His studies of the minor fiction can be illuminating and the work continues to be mined by those working on aspects of Conrad and gender.

Paul Kirschner's *Conrad: The Psychologist as Artist* (1968), further evidence of the 1960s vogue for psychological readings, offers a ground-breaking study of Conrad's debts to European writers Anatole France (1844–1924) and Guy de Maupassant (1850–93) and Russian authors Fyodor Dostoevsky (1821–81) and Ivan Turgenev (1818–83) (see Life and Contexts, **p. 9**). Kirschner argues that Conrad was attracted to these writers since they, like him, were 'psychological realists, combining a sympathetic understanding of romantic character with an objective and critical attitude towards it' (1968: 184).

Lawrence Graver's *Conrad's Short Fiction* (1969) builds on Said's work and on what he sees as the growing consensus amongst 1960s scholars that 'the highest level of Conrad's art exists in his short fiction' (1969: vii). Graver's study laments the influence of magazine publishing on Conrad's work, suggesting that his later stories attempted to apply 'the formulaic secrets of commercial fiction – and fail' (1969: 198). His work is still a starting point for more recent critics working on the short fiction.

Bruce Johnson, *Conrad's Models of Mind* (1971), also continues in a vein opened by Said in its careful study of the philosophical underpinnings of Conrad's conception of mind. His work provides a detailed account of the ways in which the fiction can be illuminated by the ideas of Schopenhauer and, retrospectively, by those of Jean-Paul Sartre. Johnson's study, which concentrates on the major novels but also includes serious discussion of *The Rescue* and the late stories 'Because of the Dollars' and 'The Planter of Malata', argues that Conrad moved away from the influence of Schopenhauer to explore 'the existential freedom of the will' (1971: 208). His study is complemented by Royal Roussel's Sartrean study *The Metaphysics of Darkness: A Study in the Unity and Development of Conrad's Fiction* (1971).

The late 1970s saw a number of influential works being published. H. M Daleski's *Joseph Conrad: The Way of Dispossession* (1977), which focuses on works from *The Nigger of the 'Narcissus'* to *Under Western Eyes* – the period when 'Conrad's best work was done' (1977: 19) – provides some admirably clear readings of these texts which continue to be of value. His study argues that 'self-possession may be seen as Conrad's obsessive preoccupation' and is manifested in 'repeated depictions of loss of self . . . in passion; . . . panic[;] . . . 'in a situation which demands physical self-possession; [in] 'nullity' arising from 'spiritual disintegration; and ... in suicide, the deliberate destruction of self' (1977: 20).

Jacques Berthoud's *Joseph Conrad: The Major Phase* (1978), which studies *A Personal Record, The Nigger of the 'Narcissus', 'Heart of Darkness', Lord Jim, Nostromo, The Secret Agent* and *Under Western Eyes*, finds in Conrad's sceptical accounts of the human capacity for self-deception a writer 'in the forefront of twentieth-century deflators of a naively self-confident nineteenth century idealism' (1978: 188).

Jeremy Hawthorn's *Joseph Conrad: Language and Fictional Self-Consciousness* (1979) studies the role of language and self-reflexive accounts of writers and writing in the major novels and novellas from 'Heart of Darkness' to *Under Western Eyes*, arguing that 'Conrad's novels concerned themselves with the nature of language, the status of fiction, and ... the whole question of self-consciousness, of man's ability to scrutinize himself and his activity' (1979: 2). Drawing on Marxist and sociolinguistic theory, Hawthorn offers an elegantly concise study of Conrad's 'obsessive attention' to the complex 'relationship between sign and referent' (1978: 6).

Two key works of criticism, which remain widely cited today, were published in 1979. Ian Watt's *Conrad in the Nineteenth Century* draws together work previously published from the late 1950s through to the 1970s, and Frederic Karl's monumental biographical study *Joseph Conrad: The Three Lives* provides a comprehensive account of the man and the art, though it would later be criticised for factual errors.

Ian Watt, *Conrad in the Nineteenth Century* (1979)

Ian Watt's study provides a detailed contextualised account of Conrad's early literary career, studying four texts – *Almayer's Folly, The Nigger of the 'Narcissus', 'Heart of Darkness', and Lord Jim* – in terms of the writer's life, his sources and the works' ideological contexts and interpretive cruxes. Watt's work is particularly significant in promoting a view of Conrad as impressionist, emphasising the modernist dimensions of his narrative art, especially in his account of the role of what he termed 'delayed decoding' (1979: 176), the narrative strategy that captured 'the disjunction between the event and the observer's trailing understanding of it' (1979: 177). Watt sees this technique as 'the verbal equivalent of the impressionist painter's attempt to render sensation directly (1979: 176). His work has been read as an attempt to provide a basis for a critical consensus on Conrad in the late 1970s, but already work was underway that would challenge the views Watt's work summed up.

Frederic Karl, *Joseph Conrad: The Three Lives* (1979)

Frederic Karl's study emphasises Conrad's Polish background as 'the matrix for his ideas, his attachments, his memories and nightmares' (1979: xiii) and proclaims itself 'a psychological study of the development of the man as much as of the development of the writer' (xiii), painting Conrad as a 'representative modern man and artist' (xiii–iv). Karl's speculations, whilst engaging, tend toward generality and are not always sustainable. We are told, for example, that Conrad's use of baffled voyeuristic external narrators may have its origins in childhood where, struggling to make sense of his disrupted family life meant that he was frequently 'attempting to put together a story whose parts did not quite fit' (Karl 1979: 16). He crudely asserts that Conrad believed that 'no matter what the state did – or how benevolent its intentions – it must deceive the individual to gain its goals and end in totalitarianism' (1979: 227). More insightfully, he suggests that the Marlow narrations represent 'an art structured on stasis, even as it tells of great movement, activity, and emotional turbulence' (1979: 246). Karl's study is more effective when highlighting contextual factors – of the experience recorded in the diaries written during his travels in the Congo, he comments:

> Conrad's immersion in language clusters once again intrigues us. In these diary entries, in English, Conrad was writing a kind of shorthand, with a phrase and sentence brevity. Yet at the same time he was jotting down his impression of African phenomena, he was writing in fullness of his Borneo memories, not at all in shorthand but in the roundness of paragraphs and pages [in the draft of what would become *Almayer's Folly*]. Almost simultaneously, he was writing in French to [his 'aunt'] Marguerite and commenting on her work, which was concerned with Polish scenes; and he was writing in Polish in and around this time to distant relatives or to his uncle.
>
> (Karl 1979: 291)

Karl also writes engagingly about the psychological roots of Conrad's illnesses (see, for example, 1979: 307–11) and about his literary relations and the ways in which his critical reception in general and supportive feedback from H. G. Wells, W. E. Henley and William Blackwood in particular encouraged his early artistic development (1979: 372, 344, 393). Karl highlights Conrad's literary innovations, noting that for 'an audience accustomed to Barrie or Kipling to come upon the nightmarish "Heart of Darkness" was not an easy experience' (1979: 393–4) and untangles Conrad's literary debts to Walter Pater, French nineteenth-century fiction, Edward Garnett and the work of Henry James in a shrewd reading of the 'Preface' to *The Nigger of the 'Narcissus'* (1979: 397–9) which concluded that it 'was more a point of demarcation for Conrad in the late 1890s than it was a directive' (399).

Karl devotes a whole speculative chapter to an attempt to locate Conrad's theory of imagination and its impact upon the works produced in the period 1899–1904, finding affinities between *Romance, Nostromo* and *The Rescue* in what he termed an art of 'the thwarted move, the inert, the immobile . . . retrieval of memory, convolution of time, creation of segregated temporal empires . . . passivity of character and observation' (1979: 455–6). This line of argument is central to Karl's overarching claim for Conrad as part of the modern tradition of 'Proust, Kafka, and Beckett' (1979: 461). Karl also develops a mythic paradigm for Conrad's work, suggesting that it rests upon a tension between 'Promethean and Orphic elements' (1979: 463):

> The Promethean strain . . . was attached to the doing, active life which

he had lived so elementally in ships and among seamen. Prometheus, traditionally, is the external hero, a rebellious, troublesome, inherently incontrollable force for change. Defying Zeus, stealing fire, he is a figure of action who brings change from without. . . .

The Orphic side, however, is equally compelling. Orpheus is our hero of internal change, since he is dedicated to transformations of self through meditation and contemplation. Orphism involves self-consciousness, inward turning . . . a romantic conception of the individual . . .

(Karl 1979: 463)

As with many of Karl's conceptions, this one is provocative but ultimately rather diffuse: a critical conceit of the kind that Conrad himself was quick to distance his work from.

Karl's study emphasises the personal factors at stake in Conrad's political fiction, noting that work from *Nostromo* through *The Secret Agent* and *Under Western Eyes* involved 'confronting the deepest and potentially most upsetting recesses of his own psyche' (1979: 577). Of *The Secret Agent*'s Professor, Karl suggests that all Conrad's 'conscious contempt for maniacal political activity is there; and yet he can comprehend the impulse that makes . . . [him] seethe. In a world without passion, craft, or values, mediocrity rules and men like the Professor become prophets' (1979: 599). Karl sees the novel as a deliberately provocative attempt to 'tell the English that their goals as well as the texture of their lives were melancholy matters, not reasons for celebration' (1979: 627). Whilst Karl notes that it was 'both dangerous and futile to read fiction as auto-biography', he suggests that it is 'very fruitful to read fiction for the psycho-logical preoccupations of an author at the time of composition' (1979: 668), seeing in Conrad's post-*Under Western Eyes* breakdown an unconscious playing out of 'what his imagination was projecting artistically' (681). The novel is a pivotal one for Karl, who sees it in psychological terms as representing for Conrad an exorcism of the views of his father (1979: 705) – a notion that later critics have taken up.

Of the then-dominant achievement-and-decline thesis, Karl suggests that one needs to include *Chance* and *Victory* in the achievement category and argues that *The Shadow Line* and *The Rover* also have strengths. He suggests that the popu-lar success of *Chance* and *Victory* cannot be taken as evidence of any 'concession to popular tastes' (1979: 725), noting a prototype stream of consciousness narra-tion at work in parts of *Chance* (744). He suggests that Conrad's literary status 'had reached a peak of sorts just before the new generation was to gain its own foothold' (1979: 748):

Yet what was to burst around him – Joyce's *Portrait*, Lawrence's *Rainbow* and *Women in Love*, Woolf's first fictional efforts, poetry by Pound, Eliot, and Yeats, vorticism, Marinetti's futurism, Dadaism, sur-realism – were . . . the major shift; and Conrad would himself lose esteem and reputation as a consequence of their efforts, although he would not be extinguished.

(Karl 1979: 749)

Karl sees Conrad as holding back from engaging with these new writers (unlike his one-time associate Ford Madox Ford) and argues that all of Conrad's work after *Victory* is 'an extension of *A Personal Record*: reminiscences, auto-biography, and memoir material' and:

> whereas earlier he had utilized mere hints and isolated details as the basis of his fiction, now he strained the past futilely to find imaginative structures for the detail. His work lost that very quality of symbolic overtone which had characterized his struggle not to be realistic; and once that symbolic overlay was lost, his language relinquished its bur-nish and vitality and he indulged in both flat and 'purple' passages.
>
> (Karl 1979: 777)

Although criticised for some factual errors and for its tendency to offer lengthy speculative readings that disrupt the work's chronological flow, the study remains a significant milestone in Conrad studies.

Zdzislaw Najder, *Joseph Conrad: A Chronicle* (1983)

In 1983, Zdzislaw Najder brought together the fruits of many years' painstaking study in his biography *Joseph Conrad: A Chronicle* (1983). The work's preface tells us that it was effectively completed in 1977 and draws on work undertaken from 1957 until the late 1970s. Originally published in Polish, it was only minim-ally revised for its English version and does not directly engage with Karl's study. Casting himself in the role of 'biographer as lexicographer' (1983: viii) seeking to explain Polish 'cultural and intellectual categories' (vii), Najder develops a detailed account, based on careful compilation of sources, which avoids the kind of speculation that often hampers Karl's work. As Najder commented, 'Auto-matically and uncritically linking the two spheres, literature and private life, . . . throws a distorting light upon their mutual relationship. Conrad used his own experiences as raw material, but the finished product shouldn't be treated in the same way' (1983: 493).

There is little in the way of sustained literary critical analysis of the works in this self-consciously restrained biographical study, but Najder offers a richly detailed contextual account of Conrad's life and develops a carefully evidenced portrayal of his personality and psychological outlook. Within the study, how-ever, there are clear pointers to Najder's views on the arts: these may be summed up in the notion that 'he wanted to be a writer of action, not of psychological dissections', one for whom a novel's overall structure is not 'determined by the plot, but that, conversely, the plot be subordinated to the overall artistic pur-pose' (1983: 282). The biography is also effective at seeing through Conrad's 'auto-mythological posturings', noting that psychologically they are symptoms of insecurity and uncertainty' (Najder 1983: 342): his account of *A Personal Record* is especially clear-sighted. Half the length of Karl's study, Najder's work is both more readable and more reliable and, for many scholars writing today, it is seen as the standard biography and one of the few indispensable books on Conrad.

Theory and after: 1980–present

The 1980s saw some concerted attempts to recast critical orthodoxies in the field of Conrad studies, whether via the application of the insights of literary theory or through more traditionally inspired scholarship. William Bonney's *Thorns and Arabesques: Contexts for Conrad's Fiction* (1980) builds on early philosophically based studies to develop a phenomenological grounded reading of Conrad as a nihilist. His work unashamedly studies hitherto-disparaged works such as 'The Return', 'The Planter of Malata', and 'The Informer' alongside the major fiction. At the centre of the work is an account of the ways in which Conrad uses romance paradigms in his fiction, providing an early account of the significance of this mode for a more positive evaluation of the late fiction.

Daniel R. Schwarz's *Conrad: Almayer's Folly to Under Western Eyes* (1980) and its companion volume on *Conrad: The Later Fiction* (1982) argue that Conrad's pessimism has been overemphasised and present him as a humanist. Schwarz offers a chronological study of all of Conrad's works, viewing each as 'a unique imagined world with its own aesthetic and moral geography' (1980: xviii). His 1982 study is an important re-evaluation of the later fiction, which can be viewed as part of a wider concern to review the critical orthodoxy, and further evidence of this trend was to be found in Gary Geddes *Conrad's Later Novels* (1980), which argues for the 'theme of solidarity or human community' (1980: 5) as a uniting feature of the late works. Geddes sees dangers in Conrad's use of 'the romance pattern of the rescue of the individual in distress' (1980: 6) but notes that he modified this pattern by presenting readers not only with 'rescues within rescues, but also various false "rescuers" against which the quality of the genuine rescuer can be measured' (6). Geddes also studies the role of the narration in undercutting 'the romance patterns and its potential for sentimentality and melodrama' and concludes that the late fiction saw Conrad creating a unique form of 'ironic romance' (Geddes 1980: 6).

The introduction of structuralist and, more significantly, post-structuralist theory into the academy generated as much furore in Conrad studies as it did in the wider field of literary studies. One of the most significant works on Conrad to be written by a major literary theorist is Fredric Jameson's important chapter in *The Political Unconscious: Narrative as a Socially Symbolic Act* (1981), which studies the function of romance in Conrad's fiction in a powerful theorised analysis of *Lord Jim* and *Nostromo* which has goaded and guided a number of later studies. Drawing on post-structuralist theory, Jameson provocatively argues that a case might be made for Conrad 'not as an early modernist, but rather an anticipation of that later and quite different thing we have come to call variously textuality, *écriture*, post-modernism, or schizophrenic writing' (1981: 219). Arguing against the notion of a straightforwardly modernist Conrad, Jameson sees him creating a new narrative mode in which

> what is essential to the production of the text is not . . . the construction of a central observational and psychic perspective within which one may for a time remain, but rather the quite different matter of inventing modulations, chromatic bridge-passages, cinematographic

fadeouts or montages, which allow us to slip from one point of view to another.

(Jameson 1981: 222–3)

He sees this mode as a precursor to the aleatory writing of Joyce and Woolf in its transformation of history and politics into something analogous to the unconscious for modernist textuality. In the camp of those goaded by this account is Jacques Berthoud, who offers a rebuttal of Jameson's position in the essay 'Narrative and Ideology: A Critique of Fredric Jameson's *The Political Unconscious*' (1985). On the guided front, one might cite Mark Conroy's *Modernism and Authority: Strategies of Legitimation in Flaubert and Conrad* (1985), which draws on post-structuralist theory to develop an account of the ways in which Conrad's writing mediates the 'profound tensions' between modernist textuality and the dominant values of the early twentieth century (1985: 156). Conroy studied *Lord Jim, Nostromo* and *The Secret Agent* in terms of their fashioning of audience and response to the ideological conditions dramatised in their narratives. The long-lasting influence of Jameson's study can still be seen today in work as recent as Andrew Michael Roberts *Conrad and Masculinity* (2000), and his emphasis on narrative modulation underpins many recent rereadings of the late fiction.

Aaron Fogel's *Coercion to Speak: Conrad's Poetics of Dialogue* (1985) draws on the work of Russian philosopher of language Mikhail Bakhtin to develop an account of the role of 'forced dialogue' within Conrad's major fictions. Fogel studies scenes in which speech is coerced to establish each work's 'distinctive "idea" of dialogue' and the development of dialogue across his work as a whole (1985: 12). He saw 'forced dialogue' as central to texts from Conrad's middle period and began his study with 'The End of the Tether' on account of its 'rich distribution of dialogue forms' (1985: 25), and went on to offer detailed studies of *Nostromo, The Secret Agent* and *Under Western Eyes*. This work represents a major advance in the study of Conrad's technique and paves the way for later studies. Suresh Raval, in *The Art of Failure: Conrad's Fiction* (1986), eschews adherence to any single set of theoretical principles but, informed by poststructuralist theories of language, offers an eclectic study of Conrad's scepticism as manifested in the major novels from 'Heart of Darkness' to *Victory*. He examines Conrad's 'enduring and fundamental critique of the central concepts and institutions of Western culture' (1986: 4), arguing that the power of Conrad's fiction 'does not derive from a skepticism verging on futility and despair, but, rather, from its radical confrontation with both hope and failure . . . [his is] a skepticism concretized in language, action, and character' (1986: 166). Jakob Lothe's *Conrad's Narrative Method* (1989) draws on Gerard Genette's narrative theory to provide a detailed account of narrative strategies. Although, in common with much narratology, the work is occasionally ponderous in its painstaking mapping of Conrad's texts, Lothe's study carefully established the 'wide-ranging, diverse, and thematically highly stimulating . . . narrative sophistication of his fiction' (1989: 303). His work is complemented by Jeremy Hawthorn's *Joseph Conrad: Narrative Technique and Ideological Commitment* (1990), which offers a detailed account of Conrad's use of free indirect discourse, a technique that provides sophisticated 'narrative flexibility' and whose use is read as evidence of 'the author's evaluative and moral commitments' (1990: xii). Building on work by Raval and sharing some interests with Fogel, Mark Wollaeger's *Joseph Conrad and the Fictions of Skepticism* (1990) draws on Bakhtin's philosophy of language and the tradition of philosophical scepticism in a subtle study of 'the peculiar relation between philosophy and literary form' (1990: 3) which ranged from the early *Tales of Unrest* through to *Under Western Eyes*. Finding affinities between postmodernist theory and Conrad's sceptical worldview, Wollaeger argues that 'Conrad's novels . . . defend against skepticism even as they express it' (1990: 5). He examines the ways in which 'Bakhtin's ideas of dialogic structure illuminates the relation between narrative form and the operations of skepticism' (1990: 20) in a study that regarded Conrad as a philosophical novelist in terms of his 'particular style of thinking' (1990: 194).

Yves Hervouet's *The French Face of Joseph Conrad* (1990), building on early work by Paul Kirschner and others, exhaustively details Conrad's debts to French writers throughout his career and carefully shows how Conrad drew on phrases, passages and themes from the work of Flaubert, Maupassant and Anatole France. Hervouet's study offers well-evidenced speculation on the centrality of borrowing to Conrad's literary technique and its role in underpinning the 'triumphant originality in his major phase' (1990: 230). The study reveals many of Conrad's works to be 'composed like mosaics from innumerable details drawn from a huge variety of sources (1990: 232) (see Life and Contexts, **pp. 8–9**). Hervouet's approach informs the individual studies collected in Moore et al. (eds) *Conrad: Intertexts and Appropriations* (1997).

Daphna Erdinast-Vulcan is one of the most influential Conrad critics to emerge in the 1990s. Her *Joseph Conrad and the Modern Temper* (1991) offers a sophisticated study which reads the fiction as a response to the cultural crises of late nineteenth-century Europe, focusing on 'the tension between the writer's temperamental affinity with the Nietzschean conception of culture as a set of fragile illusions imperfectly overlaid on a chaotic, fragmented, and meaningless reality, and his ideological need to reinstate the Ptolemaic [i.e. integrated and anthropocentric] universe' (1991: 4). Her study of the major novels extends to *The Rescue* and *The Arrow of Gold* a seriousness of scrutiny that most critics reserve for *Lord Jim* or *Nostromo*, and she develops an elegant reading which situates Conrad's work in terms of its presentation of 'The Failure of Myth' (*Lord Jim, The Rescue* and *Nostromo*), 'The Failure of Metaphysics' ('Heart of Darkness', *Under Western Eyes, The Shadow Line*) and 'The Failure of Textuality' (*Chance, Victory* and *The Arrow of Gold*). Her later study, *The Strange Short Fiction of Joseph Conrad* (1999) provides a sophisticated account of authorial subjectivity and modernist ethics which draws upon the work of Bakhtin and French philosopher Jacques Derrida in a series of close readings of ten short stories.

Somewhat more accessible, but no less influential or theoretically adroit, is the work of British critic Robert Hampson. His *Joseph Conrad: Betrayal and Identity* (1992) seeks to counter the achievement-and-decline thesis by developing a subtle and persuasive account of Conrad's use of late nineteenth-century psychological models of identity and of his engagement with early psychoanalysis. Drawing on approaches pioneered by Fleishman and Kirschner and the anti-psychiatry of R. D. Laing, Hampson offers a detailed study of Conrad's exploration of the nature of identity. The work's final chapters provide a powerful re-evaluation of the late fiction which has inspired much critical debate for its revisionist account of it as 'technical experimentation' and evidence of 'Conrad's artistic maturity rather than a decline in his creative power' (1992: 9). Like Hampson, Bruce Henricksen was also interested in Conrad's representation of subjectivity and his *Nomadic Voices: Conrad and the Subject of Narrative* (1992) draws on Bakhtinian narrative theory and the postmodernist thinking of Jean-François Lyotard to provide sophisticated and complex readings of the narrative organisation of *The Nigger of the 'Narcissus'*, 'Heart of Darkness', *Lord Jim, Nostromo*, and *Under Western Eyes*, tracing a movement from 'rigidness to openness, from the monologic to the polyphonic' and arguing for a Conrad who 'repeatedly challenges the notion of the . . . self-determining subject' (1992: 162).

Editions, guides and introductions

The continued vitality and importance of Conrad studies within the academy can be read in the ongoing investment in two major scholarly projects which began to bear fruit in this period. The first of these is the *Collected Letters of Joseph Conrad* (1983–), initially edited by Frederic Karl and Laurence Davies, and, following Karl's death, by Davies and a number of leading scholars (see bibliography). The collection is planned to run to eight volumes – though there is the possibility of a ninth – and will provide the text of over 4,000 letters hitherto only accessible via archive and private collections. The seven volumes currently available cover the period 1861–1922 and are an indispensable – if expensive – resource for any serious student of Conrad. The second project that is coming to influence modern studies, albeit rather slowly, is the *Cambridge Edition of the Works of Joseph Conrad* (1990–), which will provide a critical edition of the entire canon, including Conrad's non-fiction. At the time of writing, three volumes have appeared: *The Secret Agent*, edited by Bruce Harkness and Sid Reid (1990), *Almayer's Folly*, edited by Floyd Eugene Eddlemann and David Leon Higdon (1994), and *Notes on Life and Letters* (2004), edited by John Stape. These works are especially useful for their detailed account of the textual history of the work in question.

Student editions of the works of Conrad have been produced for some time – the first Norton edition of 'Heart of Darkness' appeared in 1963 and is about to go into a fourth edition in 2006 – but during the late 1990s and early 2000s a wide range of new paperback editions appeared. Everyman produced a number of revised editions in 1997; some, like Allan Simmons's edition of *The Nigger of the 'Narcissus'*, offered readers access to serial versions of the texts. A revised Oxford World's Classics edition of the major works was published in 2002, with some newly commissioned introductions from leading contemporary scholars, and these texts are highly recommended. Canadian publisher Broadview have produced student editions of *Nostromo* (1997), 'Heart of Darkness' (1999) and *Lord Jim* (2001), with introductions by leading scholars and a wealth of contextualising material.

Conrad's fictions are complex and challenging works of art which repay repeated reading and reflection. For those who lack the luxury of time for such things, a number of guides and introductions aimed at readers new to the study of

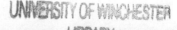

Conrad are readily available. Amongst these, one of the best short studies is Cedric Watts's booklet *Joseph Conrad: Writers and their Work* (1994). A rather fuller account is also offered by Watts in his concise *Joseph Conrad: A Literary Life* (1989), which offers a much-needed account of aspects of Conrad's finances and his complicated dealings with the literary marketplace. Brian Spittles' short contextualising study, *Joseph Conrad: Text and Context* (1992), helpfully locates Conrad's work in terms of period debates and cultural upheavals. Norman Sherry's *Conrad and his World* (1972) and Chris Fletcher's *Joseph Conrad (Writer's Lives)* (1999) are two good introductory biographical studies that provide a wealth of photographic material. An accessible short biography is John Batchelor's *The Life of Joseph Conrad* (1994), which provides clear contextual- ised readings of the fiction. John Stape (ed.) *The Cambridge Companion to Joseph Conrad* (1996) and Owen Knowles and Gene Moore (eds) *The Oxford Reader's Companion* (2000) bear testimony to the ongoing demand for reliable student-friendly guides to Conrad's work and have fast become key reference works. The web site of the Joseph Conrad Society (UK) at <http:// www.josephconradsociety.org> includes a section devoted to the needs of student readers.

Thematic studies

Conrad's fiction has generated a wide variety of critical responses, drawing from most of the major theoretical schools of the twentieth century. Within this range, several areas have formed the focus of repeated inquiry and are significant aspects of the modern critical understanding of the author. For the purposes of the present work, these may be glossed as the following fields on inquiry: nation and location, colonialism and post-colonialism, politics and revolution and gender and sexual- ity. It should be noted that these are not suggested as hard and fast demarcations but, rather, are offered as convenient labels under which to group some key works that approach the fiction with a more specialised focus than those discussed earlier in this section.

Nation and location

There is a significant body of criticism on the subject of Conrad's complex rela- tionship with a number of nation-states, including England, France, Russia and, perhaps most importantly, Poland. His vexed relationship with things Russian has long been a source of critical inquiry, and a special issue of the journal *Conradiana* (12, 1980) was devoted to the topic. A number of key essays, cover- ing issues ranging from the influence of Turgenev to the reasoning behind making the Harlequin figure from 'Heart of Darkness' a Russian, are collected in Carab- ine (1992, Vol. IV). This volume also collects a number of essays on Conrad's affection for and relationship to things French, including essays on the extent to which he uses French idiom and an account of the influence of Flaubert and Maupassant in the creation of Marlow's narrative technique in 'Heart of Darkness' (1992, Vol. IV). There has also been a vein of study which, following Conrad's lead in *A Personal Record*, has sought to explore his representation of and affinities with England, the country where he became a naturalised citizen in August 1886. Whilst Conrad declared that 'at sea and on land my point of view is English, from which the conclusion should not be drawn that I have become an Englishman' (CL3: 89) his artful memoir, *A Personal Record*, sees him purposely charting the inevitability of his coming to England and Englishness (see Works, pp. 88–92). Benita Parry has argued that Conrad's identification with England's dominant culture was informed by his perception of its 'respect for order and tradition, . . . cohesive civil society and . . . widely disseminated stance of self-assurance which the politically volatile continent lacked' (Parry 1989: 190). Keith Carabine writes on the figuring of England in 'Amy Foster' in his ' "Irreconcilable Differences": England as an "Undiscovered Country" in Conrad's "Amy Foster" ' (1989), and Allan Simmons has examined this topic in his short entry on 'England' in *The Oxford Reader's Companion* (2000: 100–1) and at more length in his essay 'The Art of Englishness: Identity and Representation in Conrad's Early Career' (2004), which studies 'Conrad's sense and self-fashioning as an English writer, and . . . his literary representation of Englishness' (2004: 1) from *Almayer's Folly* to *The Nigger of the 'Narcissus'*.

Whilst these engagements with other national traditions and scenes have been a productive vein of critical research, it is the study of the influence of Conrad's Polish heritage that has generated most work in the field of nation and location. Some early Polish critics were famously hostile to Conrad's decision to write in English, and the idea that his writing often deals with questions of guilt arising from his allegedly ambivalent feelings towards his native country was a staple of much of the early critical coverage of his Polish background. Gustav Morf's study *The Polish Heritage of Joseph Conrad* (1930), which mooted this notion, was followed by a number of works exploring this theme (see Criticism, pp. 141–2). Polish scholars have been keen to identify distinctive linguistic and literary antecedents as well as a characteristic turn of mind as the lasting legacy of Conrad's Polish childhood. Good starting points for work in this field are the collection of articles in Ludwik Krzyzanowski (ed.) *Joseph Conrad: Centennial Essays* (1960) and André Busza's 'Conrad's Polish Literary Background' (1966), which examines the influence of the political views of Conrad's father and uncle on his work.

The scholar most associated with the presentation of Conrad's Polish background as a crucial context for reading his work is Zdislaw Najder. His *Conrad's Polish Background* (1964) draws on Polish studies and original archive research to provide a wealth of translated letters to Conrad from his uncle Taduesz Bobrowski and other Polish correspondents; the work was a milestone in that it ensured English-speaking readers had access to work that had hitherto been inaccessible. This study was supplemented by *Conrad Under Familial Eyes* (1983b), which offers further material, including letters from Conrad's parents. Najder's *Conrad in Perspective* (1997) reprints a number of essays and conference papers from the 1960s to the mid-1990s, including his 1986 'Conrad's Polish Background: Or From Biography to a Study of Culture', which argues for the centrality of Polish cultural concerns in any understanding of the writer's work.

Conrad's Polish background has also remained a central facet in more general studies. Two recent examples are Christopher GoGwilt's *The Invention of the*

West (1995) and Geoffrey Harpham's *One of Us* (1996). GoGwilt examines the legacy of Conrad's Polishness in his persuasive study, arguing for the 'significant *lack* of national affiliation informing Conrad's imaginative and creative work' (1995: 7), whilst Harpham, having explored a psychological function for Polish memories, concludes that the case for Conrad's greatness as a writer rested on 'his willingness to think as a human being rather than as a citizen of some nation, a resident of some place' (1996: 185). Recently, Najder has written persuasively of Conrad as 'self-consciously a writer of many cultures, showing them in relief as well as analysing and contrasting them' (2003: 1) and it is surely as a writer whose work was shaped during an intensely nationalist and imperialist epoch that Conrad can speak to modern readers in our era of new imperialism and distorting nationalisms.

The allegiances and empathies that come together in a sense of national identity are also at play in one's identification with the locales one inhabits as part of daily life, and whilst Conrad is usually more interested in delineating the psychological than he is the geographical, his work contains some memorable evocations of place ranging from the creation of an imaginary South American republic in *Nostromo* to representations of cities such as Geneva in *Under Western Eyes*, Singapore in *Lord Jim* or London in *The Secret Agent*. As a child whose experience of place included the radical disjunction between the official maps of the Russian state and the fondly recalled and imagined maps of his parents' Poland, Conrad did not need contemporary cultural theory to tell him that identities and their conditions of existence are inseparable. It is not surprising, then, that critics have examined Conrad's representation of other cultures and his capacity to evoke place and the relationship between location and identity has long been a topic of interest, either as a subset of work on his engagement with questions of national identity or as a topic in its own right. Gene Moore (ed.) *Conrad's Cities* (1992) is an excellent starting point for essays on location and place in Conrad's fiction.

Colonialism and post-colonialism

As Conrad studies grew in an academy dominated by New Criticism's love affair with textuality, it is not surprising that for much of the twentieth century the dominant concern was the text rather than the context. In the 1970s and after, however, we can see the growth of studies that focus on contextual matters. Today it is a critical commonplace that many of Conrad's greatest works examine the interface between white and non-white in ways that frequently questioned his era's simplistic binaries and pointed towards the hybrid cultures of post-colonialism. Whilst Conrad has been praised for his coruscating assault on the mindset of the colonialist in works as different as 'Heart of Darkness' and *Nostromo*, many commentators have found that his work is less successfully critical of the situation of native peoples under colonialism. The topic has been controversial since African novelist and critic Chinua Achebe's denunciation of him as a bloody racist in his essay 'An Image of Africa: Racism in Conrad's "Heart of Darkness"' (1977) (see Works, **pp. 49–52**). The issue of Conrad's depiction of race and racism is also to be found in those works which treat

Conrad's depiction of imperialist and colonialist activity. Alan Sandison's chapter on Conrad in *The Wheel of Empire* (1967) draws out parallels with Kipling but suggests that he 'uses the ethnic conflict endemic in imperialism to explore the process of alienation more fully than Kipling' (1967: 121). Jeffery Meyers examines Conrad's humanistic approach to the problems of colonialism in his somewhat unconvincing chapter on Conrad in *Fiction and the Colonial Experience* (1973). Molly Mahood's essay on 'Heart of Darkness' in *The Colonial Encounter* (1977) locates Conrad's work in the context of historical theories of empire. Martin Green's chapter on Conrad in *Dreams of Adventure: Deeds of Empire* (1980) offers an overly anecdotal reading but includes an early reassessment of the Malay Trilogy. John McClure's *Kipling and Conrad: The Colonial Fiction* (1981) examines Conrad's detached critique of imperialism whilst Jefferson Hunter explores the ironic handling of adventure-story conventions in his chapter on 'Conrad and Adventure' in *Edwardian Fiction* (1982). Jacques Darras, in *Joseph Conrad and the West: Signs of Empire* (1982), examines Conrad's account of imperialism via a deconstructive approach, whilst Benita Parry's *Conrad and Imperialism* (1983) draws on post-structuralist Marxist theory 'to discuss how the interlocution of narrative discourses . . . transforms, subverts and rescues the established norms, values and myths of imperialist civilization' (1983: 7). Patrick Brantlinger has a useful discussion of 'Heart of Darkness' in *Rule of Darkness: British Literature and Imperialism: 1830–1914* (1988).

Robert Hammer (ed.) *Joseph Conrad: Third World Perspectives* (1990) offers an invaluable survey of responses to Conrad's representation of colonialism, though its title is slightly misleading since only nine of its sixteen essays are written by developing-world authors. Hammer reprints work on this topic from 1904 through to 1982 and provides a useful bibliography of key works. These include a number of essay on the Malay fictions, including D. C. R. A. Goonetilleke's concise analysis of Conrad's growing uncertainty in his handling of Malay material, a section on Conrad and Africa which focuses on 'Heart of Darkness' and reprints not only Achebe's important essay but also Guyanan novelist Wilson Harris's riposte which casts the novel as a frontier text which praises his 'crucial parody of the properties of established order' (1990: 163). The volume concludes with an account on Conrad's legacy for developing-world writers, which includes Peter Nazareth's passionate account of Conrad as 'a mental liberator' for both European readers and 'the colonized elite wearing the eyes of Europe' (1990: 221).

Heliéna Krenn's *Conrad's Lingard Trilogy: Empire, Race and Women in the Malay Novels* (1990) examines Conrad's ironic depiction of the role of the white man in colonial situations and suggests, perhaps a little problematically, that in his presentation of indigenous peoples can be found the seeds of a view of native culture which accepts difference as a source of resilience. Andrea White's *Joseph Conrad and the Adventure Tradition* (1993) offers a detailed study of the adventure-fiction genre and assesses how Conrad's demythologised the notion of the imperial adventure in his early fiction from *Almayer's Folly* to 'Heart of Darkness'. White's subtle and engaging study explores Conrad's apparent failure to question the 'sexist and racist biases' of the imperialist discourses his fiction deploys but concludes that his early works 'work towards a de-construction, a dismantling, of the imperial myth' which although rather modest' (1993: 194) by modern standards was, by the standards of the day, 'remarkable' (195). Edward Said's *Culture and Imperialism* (1993) argues that Conrad's self-conscious narratives of imperialist activity were inflected by his childhood experience of Russian imperialism and saw in his proto-modernist textual strategies 'an ironic distance' (1993: 27) from his epoch's dominant concerns. Whilst Said acknowledges that Conrad did not 'imagine a fully realized alternative to imperialism', his work is part of the what he termed the *dating* of imperialism; work that 'shows its contingency, records its illusions and tremendous violence and waste' (28).

Further powerful analysis of Conrad's role in undermining traditional assumptions about empire is offered in Christopher GoGwilt's *The Invention of the West: Joseph Conrad and the Double Mapping of Empire* (1995), which uses his ambiguous accounts of imperial and colonial activity to trace the emergence of the concept of 'the West' in the late nineteenth and early twentieth centuries. Focusing upon 'the Conrad who consistently sustains an ambivalent rhetorical position toward the larger cultural, historical, and political realities his fiction seeks to represent' (1995: 1), GoGwilt claims that 'Conrad's fiction traced the emergence of a global distortion of contemporary history' (1995: 2) as the seeds for imperialism's implosion were being sown at the turn of the nineteenth century. He offers a complex deconstructive reading of text and context, including a powerful account of *A Personal Record* (1995: 111–21), and a detailed examination of the literary and psychological issues at stake for Conrad in resisting the label of Slavonic writer in *Under Western Eyes* (1995: 130–55). He extends his coverage of this text in the work's seventh chapter where he offers a dazzling reading of it, along with *The Secret Agent*, as the culmination in 'Conrad's political evolution'. GoGwilt argues that in overcoming his distaste for revolutionary intrigue to produce a novel that 'more successfully subverts than affirms the invention of the West' (1995: 159), Conrad has fostered an 'oblique redefinition' (1995: 171) of the notion of Western identity. In the work's closing chapter he develops a reading of *Nostromo* as 'a paradigmatic Conradian problem of political form' (1995: 219) and identifies as the guiding concerns for his fiction a sense of 'the contingency of our European cultural identity on unpredictable national imaginings' and a related concern for the 'unpredictable ends of imperial imaginings' (1995: 219).

Elleke Boehmer's influential study *Colonial and Postcolonial Literature* (1995) treats Conrad as a writer whose works addressed the 'central preoccupations of colonialist writing under high imperialism' but who 'temperamentally belonged to a later historical moment – a moment in which colonial possession had become more problematic, raising spectres of European cultural failure' (1995: 61). Her study reads *Lord Jim* as a figure of fin-de-siècle early modernism and the novel in which he features as a vehicle for the exposure of 'the tautology of the colonial hero ideal' and the 'fundamental hypocrisy' of the colonial dream (1995: 64).

Simon Gikandi's *Maps of Englishness: Writing Identity in the Culture of Colonialism* (1996) also examines the relationship between modernism and colonialism, suggesting that Conrad was part of a colonial aesthetic 'generated by questions about empire as a cultural formation in crisis' (1996: 167). Gikandi suggests that 'Conrad's goal is to unpack the idealism that underlies both the colonial project and the claim that imperial spaces engender new subjects' (1996:

169). In similar vein, the essays which were collected in Gail Fincham and Myrtle Hooper's *Under Postcolonial Eyes: Joseph Conrad after Empire* (1996) demonstrates the ability of Conrad's fictions to 'interrogate and undermine the discourses of early modernism, particularly those constituted around colony and empire' (1996: xi). In addition to a valuable introduction to the field by the editors, the volume contains important essays by Paul Armstrong, Robert Hampson, Padmini Mongia and Andrea White and provides new material on Conrad and empire, and the representations of race, class and gender in his work. The volume concludes with a valuable section on Conrad's legacy for post-colonial literature. Andrea White's essay, a helpful summary of various responses to Conrad by later post-colonial writers, suggests that:

> it took an outsider to understand just how empty the categories of 'us' and 'them' are, for his concern about their instability undoubtedly reflected his own anxieties about identity made especially acute by contemporary uneasiness with 'difference'. But the frontier in fiction his own sense of difference enabled him to open helps explain why Conrad seems to have figured powerfully for those writers who have lived through colonial periods of linguistic and cultural disruption, and who carry with them the enduring complications of colonial identity.
>
> (White 1996: 208)

In the same year, Geoffrey Galt Harpham's provocative account of Conrad's relationship with discourses of imperialism and national identity, *One of Us: The Mastery of Joseph Conrad* (1996), suggests that Conrad's greatness rests on his key role in helping 'Western literature . . . to think of itself as deracinated, as properly belonging not to a national tradition but to a more comprehensively conceived human community that can best be represented by the exile or émigré' (1996: 184). Linda Dryden's accessible study *Joseph Conrad and the Imperial Romance* (2000) covers similar ground to Andrea White's work but also offers a focus on Conrad's depiction of Malaysia. Dryden, like White, argues that in 'some subtle and not so subtle ways, Conrad consciously manipulated the genre of imperial romance to force a reassessment of the imperial cause and its heroes' (2000: 195). Robert Hampson's *Cross-Cultural Encounters in Joseph Conrad's Malay Fiction* (2000) draws on period sources and adroitly handled theoretical material to develop a detailed study of Conrad's Malay fiction which argues, with an echo of Harpham, for Conrad as a literary nomad whose radical scepticism arose from his own rootlessness and whose fiction promoted a subversively ironic representation of colonial encounters.

Politics and revolution

There are, clearly, myriad political issues at stake in Conrad's works in terms of their depiction of and engagement with debates about colonialist and imperialist activity. This section, however, follows the lead of those critics for whom the study of Conrad's politics is intimately tied up with his depiction of anarchists and revolutionaries and whose focus has been on *Nostromo, The Secret Agent,*

Under Western Eyes and the anarchist tales collected in *A Set of Six* (see Works, pp. 63–8, 69–73, 82–7, 74–81). The early contributions on this topic were produced during the Cold War when revolutionary Marxists were deemed to be a major threat to Western life, and this may have given added impetus to the early work in this field. The pioneering work was done by Irving Howe in his long essay 'Joseph Conrad, Order and Anarchy: The Political Novels' (1953 and 1954), which was later reprinted as part of *Politics and the Novel* (1957). Howe views Conrad as a conservative whose personal political convictions marred his ability to draw revolutionaries in *The Secret Agent* and *Under Western Eyes*. Howe sees Conrad's conservatism as a reaction to his father's radicalism, observing that when 'the children of revolutionaries revolt, it is against revolution' (1957: 78) and positing '[c]onservatism as the anarchism of the fortunate', the double of anarchism in that both positions promote individual resistance to the State (1957: 84).

This study was followed by Eloise Knapp Hay's *The Political Novels of Joseph Conrad* (1963) which sees Conrad as offering an essentially Polish personal politics that were 'characteristically jealous of the privilege of anarchy but conscientiously hopeful of preserving each man's rights against his neighbour' (1963: 26). Hay offers contextualised readings of *The Rescue*, 'Heart of Darkness', *Nostromo*, *The Secret Agent* and *Under Western Eyes* in support of her claim that '[m]ost of Conrad's best work came out of the years . . . when he had most to say about the relationship between the nonconforming individual and the social forces that hedge him in' (1963: 83). Avrom Fleishman's *Conrad's Politics: Community and Anarchy in the Fiction of Joseph Conrad* (1967) offers a counter reading to Howe and Hay in what has become the definitive starting point for later work on this topic. Fleishman provides a detailed account of Conrad's Polish background, which emphasises the role of Conrad's Uncle Bobrowski in sowing 'the seeds of change in Conrad's political attitudes' (1967: 10) and then traces the development of Conrad's political views on the nature of community via close readings of *Nostromo*, *The Secret Agent* and *Under Western Eyes*. *Nostromo* is seen as 'the fulfilment of Conrad's political imagination: it represents the history of a society as a living organism' (1967: 161).

Alan Swingewood's chapter on Conrad in his *The Novel and Revolution* (1975) largely echoes Howe's views in its account of the failure of *The Secret Agent* and *Under Western Eyes* to understand revolutionary action. John Orr's *Tragic Realism and Modern Society: Studies in the Sociology of the Novel* (1977) locates Conrad's work in the tradition of European political writing in the period 1848–1948. Carol Vanderveer Hamilton's 'Revolution from Within: Conrad's Natural Anarchists' (1994: 47) concludes that 'even the anti-anarchist characters in these texts are secret sharers, implicated in anarchy, defending their fragile, elaborate order against the violence that anarchist and capitalist share' (1994: 47). More recent investigations of Conrad's politics are available in a clutch of theoretically driven essays which appeared in *The Conradian* (22, 1/2 [spring/winter] 1997), including Gail Fincham's 'The Dialogism of *Lord Jim*' which studies Marlow's marginalisation of the politics of race and class, and Andrzej Gasiorek's examination of the interrelation of ethics and politics in his ' "To Season with a Pinch of Romance": Ethics and Politics in *Lord Jim*'.

Gender and sexuality

Thanks largely to Thomas Moser's influential study, Conrad's alleged inability to present female characters convincingly has been a critical commonplace since the late 1950s (see Criticism, **p. 144**). Since the 1960s, however, a growing body of critical work has developed more nuanced accounts of his depiction of women and alongside this there have also developed studies of Conrad's depiction of sexuality – and of his representation of homosexuality in particular. Important early studies are Gordon Thompson's 'Conrad's Women' (1978) which mounts an ultimately rather indefensible argument about the importance of stereotypes of femininity in Conrad's fiction, and Ruth Nadelhaft's 'Women as Moral and Political Alternatives in Conrad's Early Novels' (1982). Nina Pelikan Strauss's widely reprinted essay, 'The Exclusion of the Intended from Secret Sharing in "Heart of Darkness"' (1987) offers a powerful feminist critique of the novel's 'brutally sexist' (1987: 351) masculinist assumptions. This essay sparked much debate for its account of 'Heart of Darkness' as 'male self-mystification whose time is passing if not past' (1987: 362) but, despite Strauss's arguments, the novella shows little sign of being displaced from the canon. Ruth Nadelhaft's *Joseph Conrad (Feminist Readings)* (1991) builds upon her earlier essay to suggest that Conrad wrote through 'the critical eyes of women characters' and through them creates works that, ironically, were 'prized by patriarchal culture' (1991: 12). Nahdelhaft argues that it was via his female characters that Conrad 'found means to express ... a consistent and profound criticism' of the dominant culture of his epoch (1991: 12). In addition to the major novels, Nadelhaft's study offers readings of less frequently studied works such as 'Gaspar Ruiz', 'The Return' and *The Rescue*.

Andrew Michael Roberts's special issue of *The Conradian* on 'Conrad and Gender' (17 [2, spring] 1993) brings together eight essays on *Lord Jim, The Secret Agent, Chance*, and *Twixt Land and Sea*, that collectively demonstrate that 'gender in Conrad is a theme which challenges and provokes' but also 'one which illuminates' (1993: xi). Susan Jones's *Conrad and Women* (1999) provides a much-needed in-depth study of the topic. Her work begins with a chapter on 'Conrad, Women, and the Critics', which offers a useful survey of published criticism alongside a study of the marketing of his fiction for a female audience. This is followed by chapters on the influence of Polish writing on Conrad's depiction of women, a consideration of the influence of his aunt, the writer Marguerite Poradowska, and detailed readings of *Chance* and the late fiction which seek to underscore the importance of 'women's writing' and 'women readers ... in shaping Conrad's later fiction' (1999: 4).

Conrad's men have been studied implicitly and explicitly for a number of years. Thomas Moser's *Joseph Conrad: Achievement and Decline* (1957) considers Conrad's misogyny and depiction of what today would be called strongly homosocial bonds. An early study of Conrad's sexuality is Bernard Meyer's *Joseph Conrad: A Psychoanalytic Biography* (1967) which sees him as resolutely misogynist and gripped with castration anxieties. Several critics have examined Conrad's relationship with gay men such as Roger Casement and Norman Douglas and his fiction's presentation of homosexual men such as the Count in 'Il Conde' or Mr Jones in *Victory*. Early essays on the topic include Jeffrey Meyers'

'Conrad and Roger Casement' (1973) and Douglas Hughes ' "Il Conde": A "Deucedly Queer Story" ' (1975). In Jeffrey Meyers' chapter on Conrad's *Victory* in his *Homosexuality and Literature 1890–1930* (1977) he argues that 'Victory is a deliberate compromise between Conrad's desire to write openly about homosexuality and his need to suppress the theme and to surround the sexual core of the novel with reticence and irony' (1977: 77).

After a careful marshalling of the facts, Meyers suggests that the Morrison–Heyst partnership could be read as a homosexual one, and he goes on to read Ricardo as Jones' 'paid lover' (1977: 87) (see Works, **pp. 107–13**). A more subtle reading, encompassing a wide range of Conrad's works, is developed by Robert Hodges in his neglected essay 'Deep Fellowship: Homosexuality and Male Bonding in the Life and Fiction of Joseph Conrad' (1979). Hodges argued that whilst Conrad's biography revealed only peripheral, though suggestive, awareness of homosexuality, it was his fiction that 'shows a continuing concern with some underlying features of female and male homosexuality'. Hodges identifies a homosexual element in *Lord Jim*, noting that 'Jim inspires considerable affection in several older men' (1979: 384), citing both Mr Denver and Jim and Marlow and Jim as potential couples. In 'The Secret Sharer', he reads Legatt and the Captain as a homosexual pairing, and in *Chance* he notes the lesbian character of Mrs Fyne. In *Victory* (1915) he notes Jones's homosexuality and also suggests a homosexual element to the Jones and Ricardo relationship. Finally, in *The Shadow Line* (1915) he outs the Captain and Ransome and suggests – coming back to biography – that '[i]f the story is indeed completely autobiographical, then Conrad is clearly revealing a strong homosexual attraction to a former crew member' (1979: 389–90) (see Works, **pp. 114–17**).

More recently, emerging out of gender-studies approaches inspired by theorists such as Eve Sedgwick and Judith Butler, there have been a number of high-profile readings of Conrad which develop a more complex and culturally grounded account of his depiction of the instability of English masculinity in the light of the late nineteenth-century/early twentieth-century 'panic' about homosexuality. Christopher Lane's 'Fostering Subjection: Masculine Identification and Homosexual Allegory in Conrad's *Victory*' (1995) develops a subtle reading which presents Conrad's novel as 'a socio-symbolic allegory that inadvertently exposes the cultural and psychic constituents of colonial and homo/sexual identity' (1995: 101). His account looks at what he terms the marginal figures of the text and begins with a careful reading of the Heyst–Morrison relationship which, following Meyers, explores links between it and the Heyst–Lena relationship: Lane concludes that 'the text demonstrates a significant proximity between Heyst's homo and heterosexual interests' (1995: 113). Another mid-1990s text, Geoffrey Galt Harpham's *One of Us: The Mastery of Joseph Conrad* (1996), argues that whilst Conrad does not consciously engage with homosexuality, it nonetheless enters his work as a side effect of his struggle to master the English language: 'The unmentioned subject, sexual desire, and especially homosexual desire, escapes the vigilance of the artist searching after the elusive *mot juste*, concentrating on one kind of exactitude while leaving the chaotic domain of secondary meanings to itself' (1996: 177).

As examples, Harpham cites scenes and sequences from *The Nigger of the 'Narcissus', Lord Jim* and *Nostromo*, concluding that, 'Conrad . . . was surely oblivious to the systematic intimations of the homosexual embrace legible in his work' (1996: 79). The readings lack the carefully theorised justifications which were a feature of Lane's work and tend towards reliance upon assertion. In essence, Harpham gives a glimpse of a queer Conrad and then firmly puts him back into the closet.

Richard Ruppel has built on his provocative essay 'Joseph Conrad and the Ghost of Oscar Wilde' (1998) with a number of investigations into what is at stake in reading Conrad as 'an early investigator of the homosocial continuum' (1998: 35), including his study of 'potential and actual expressions of homosexual desire' in 'Heart of Darkness' (Ruppel 2003: 153). Andrew Michael Roberts's pioneering study of *Conrad and Masculinity* (2000) offers a theorised and historicised reading which examines how Conrad's representation of masculinity 'interacts with themes and techniques of Conrad's fiction' (2000: 4). Roberts argues that 'homosexuality is neither definitely present nor definitely absent in Conrad's work, but figures as an occluded part of a homosocial structure, not as the key which undoes that structure' (2000: 9). Sarah Cole's *Modernism, Male Friendship and the Great War* (2003) includes insightful discussion of the operation of homosociality – 'a whole host of intertwined masculine relations' (2003: 129) – in the Ford Madox Ford/Conrad collaboration *Romance*.

It is my personal view that if Conrad is to speak to the twenty-first century as powerfully as he did to the twentieth, then his work must be exposed more fully to the insights and issues of contemporary critical inquiry. Of course, this needs to be done without indulging in the transiently fashionable application of the latest theoretical fad but studies of Conrad which open his texts to queer rereading, to post-colonial reimagining, or to feminist re-evaluation have only just begun to shape a Conrad for the twenty-first century, and it is my hope that some of the readers of this volume will come to play their part in extending the work in this field.

4

Chronology

Bullet points denote events in Conrad's life and asterisks to denote historical and literary events.

This chronology provides concise annotated coverage of those aspects of Conrad's life which are not covered in detail in the opening section of this book. The coverage provided of his writing life is not annotated to the same extent since this aspect of his career is covered in detail in Part 2 of the present work. Attention is given, however, to the provision of information regarding historical and cultural contexts for his fiction.

Note: titles and publication dates cited are for the first English edition of a text. Serial publication is noted, but readers are referred to Part 2 for discussion of any differences between serial and book versions.

A Polish childhood

1857
- 3 December, Józef Teodor Konrad Korzeniowski born to Polish patriots Apollo and Ewa (née Bobrowska) Korzeniowski in Berdyczów in the Ukraine, part of Poland annexed by Russia since 1793
* Indian Mutiny (to 1859); E. Browning, *Aurora Leigh*; C. Brontë, *The Professor*; Eliot, *Scenes of Clerical Life*; Ruskin, *Political Economy of Art*

1859
- Korzeniowski family move to town of Zytomierz
* Franco-Austrian War (to 1861); Collins, *The Woman in White*; Eliot, *Adam Bede*; Dickens, *A Tale of Two Cities*; Mill, *On Liberty*; Smiles, *Self Help*

1861
- By spring, family moves to Warsaw, centre of anti-Russian activity; Apollo Korzeniowski arrested in October as part of general clamp-down on political dissidence
* American Civil War (to 1865); Prince Albert dies; emancipation of the serfs in Russia; Eliot, *Silas Marner*; Mill, *Utilitarianism*

1862
- Apollo Korzeniowski and family sent into exile to Vologda, *c.* 300 miles north-east of Moscow
* England cricket team tour Australia; Braddon, *Lady Audley's Secret*; Meredith, *Modern Love*; Christina Rossetti, *Goblin Market*

1863
- Family permitted to move south to Chernikhov, near Kiev; in summer, Ewa and Conrad permitted to leave Russia for three months to allow Ewa to undergo medical treatment; on return to Poland, Ewa's health continues to decline
* Huxley, *Man's Place in Nature*; Lyell, *Antiquity of Man*; Kingsley, *The Water Babies*

1865
- 18 April, death of Conrad's mother
* US President Lincoln assassinated; Carroll, *Alice's Adventures in Wonderland*; Arnold, *Essays in Criticism* (First series); Ruskin, *Sesames and Lilies*

1866
- Conrad falls ill, is sent to maternal grandmother's home in Nowochwastów; in autumn, Conrad and grandmother return to Chernikhov but his illness requires further periods of treatment in Kiev
* George Eliot, *Felix Holt*; Swinburne, *Poems and Ballads*

1867
- Summer, Conrad's uncle Tadeusz Bobrowski takes him to Odessa, where he sees sea for first time; towards end of year, Apollo Korzeniowski granted leave from exile on health grounds
* Second Reform Act (UK); typewriter invented; Marx, *Kapital* (translated 1887); Arnold, *New Poem*

1868
- January, Apollo Korzeniowski reunited with son; both travel to Lwów (in Galician region of south-east Poland), where Apollo resumes political activity, largely in form of journalism
* Public executions abolished in UK; Collins, *The Moonstone*; Browning, *The Ring and The Book*

1869
- Apollo Korzeniowski moves to Kraków to further journalistic work, but health deteriorates; 23 May Apollo dies; funeral becomes occasion for popular protest and young Conrad leads funeral procession of several thousand people; Conrad initially cared for by father's friend Stefan Buszczyński, then by maternal grandmother Teofila Bobrowska
* Suez Canal opened; Girton College, Cambridge opened; Mill, *On the Subjection of Women*; Arnold, *Culture and Anarchy*; Blackmore, *Lorna Doone*

1870

- Conrad's grandmother becomes official guardian; management of Conrad's education subject to influence of uncle Bobrowski
- Franco-Prussian War (to 1871); papal infallibility declared; Forster's Education Act; Dickens, *Edwin Drood*

1871

- Conrad attends boarding school in Kraków but lack of prior formal education puts him behind year group; family appoints personal tutor
- Trade unions legalised in UK; Stanley finds Livingstone in Africa; Darwin, *Descent of Man*; Eliot, *Middlemarch* (to 1872)

1872

- Conrad stuns family by announcing wish to have career at sea; family resists plans
- Edison's telegraph; Hardy, *Under the Greenwood Tree*

1873

- May, Conrad travels to Switzerland for medical treatment; after brief period back in Kraków with grandmother is sent to boarding school in Lwów
- Pater, *Studies in the Renaissance*; Mill, *Autobiography*

1874

- September, Conrad moved back to Kraków by uncle (perhaps because of disapproval over flirtation between Conrad and cousin Tekla); October, with uncle's approval, Conrad travels to Marseilles to begin life as sailor on French ships; December, undertakes first voyage, as passenger, aboard *Mont Blanc* from Marseilles to Martinique
- Factory Act; Hardy, *Far from the Madding Crowd*; Thomson, *City of Dreadful Night*

Sea life

1875

- May, *Mont Blanc* returns to Marseilles; June, Conrad sails with *Mont Blanc* as apprentice; December, returns to France
- Hardy, *The Hand of Ethelberta*

1876

- July, Conrad sails on *Saint Antoine* for Martinique
- Queen Victoria declared Empress of India; telephone invented; Eliot, *Daniel Deronda*; Spencer, *Principles of Sociology*

1877

- Conrad leaves shipping firm after illness and falling out with owners; uncle Bobrowski loans him 3,000 francs, allegedly to fund world voyage;

following events clouded in mystery and not clarified by Conrad's dramatic working-up of experiences in *The Arrow of Gold* (see Works, **pp. 117–20**). (In Conrad's version he joins 'syndicate' [*The Mirror of the Sea*, 157] who smuggle guns to supporters of pretender to Spanish throne, Don Carlos de Bourbon, but research suggests that many of Conrad's claims about this activity lack substance and commentators suggest that financial difficulties stemmed from losses at Monte Carlo gaming tables.)

*   Russo-Turkish war

1878

•   Mounting financial worries lead Conrad to attempt suicide by shooting self with revolver (would later present injury as result of duel); Bobrowski subsequently visits, settles bills, makes arrangements for Conrad to travel to England to begin career in English Merchant Marine; 24 April, Conrad takes passage on British steamer *Mavis* as apprentice, sailing from Marseilles to Lowestoft (east coast of England), arriving 10 June; spends short time in London; returns to Lowestoft, signs on with coaster *Skimmer of the Sea*, sails during summer, learns English during three voyages to Newcastle (CL2: 35); 15 October, sails for Australia on wool clipper *Duke of Sutherland*

*   Salvation Army founded; Hardy, *The Return of the Native*; James, *The Europeans*

1879

•   31 January, *Duke of Sutherland* arrives in Sydney after 109 days at sea; 5 July, Conrad makes return voyage to England with *Duke of Sutherland*, arriving 19 October; December, signs on steamship *Europa*, travels to Italy and Greece

*   Electric lightbulb invented; Meredith, *The Egoist*

1880

•   Late January, Conrad returns to London aboard *Europa* but had fallen out with captain; successfully studies for second mate's exam during period of shore life; August, sails as third mate on clipper *Loch Etive*, arriving 24 November in Sydney after ninety-three days (in *The Mirror of the Sea*, Conrad briefly describes experiences, suggesting that it was on *Loch Etive* that 'I completed my training' (40))

*   Tennyson, *Ballads*; James, *The Portrait of a Lady* (to 1881); Hardy, *The Trumpet Major*

1881

•   11 January, *Loch Etive* sails for England, arriving 25 April; September, Conrad signs on as second mate aboard *Palestine* (voyage later becomes basis for 'Youth' [see Works, **pp. 48–9**]); December, *Palestine* enters Falmouth harbour after springing leak in English Channel, stays eight months for repairs

*   Stevenson, *Treasure Island*; Wilde, *Poems*

1882

- Conrad remains with *Palestine* in order to build up service record prior to first mate's exam; 17 September, sails with *Palestine* to Bangkok
* Married Women's Property Act; Besant, *All Sorts and Conditions of Men*

1883

- March, en route to the East, *Palestine*'s cargo of coal spontaneously combusts, crew abandons ship and rows to safety on Bangka Island near Sumatra, then taken by SS *Sissie* to Singapore where marine court of inquiry exonerates them from blame; May, Conrad returns to UK as passenger, commences work on the chief mate's exam but turned down due to lack of service at sea; July, travels to Marienbad to meet uncle for first time in five years; September, sails for India as second mate on *Riversdale*
* Henty, *Under Drake's Flag*; Moore, *A Modern Lover*; Jeffries, *Story of my Heart*

1884

- Conrad falls out with Captain of *Riversdale*, whose drunken behaviour he reported, and is discharged at Madras, 17 April; travels to Bombay; 3 June, sails for England aboard clipper *Narcissus* as second mate; later draws on this voyage for *The Nigger of the 'Narcissus'* (see Works, **pp. 31–5**); 16 June, ship docks, Conrad signs off with sufficient service to sit first mate's exam; 17 November, fails first attempt at exam, but passes on twenty-seventh birthday (3 December)
* Third Reform Act; *Oxford English Dictionary* (to 1928); James, 'The Art of Fiction'

1885

- 27 April, Conrad sails from Hull on *Tilkhurst* as second mate (only work available despite first mate's exam); 10 June, after stop for cargo at Penarth (Wales), *Tilkhurst* sails for Singapore, arriving 22 September; *Tilkhurst* then sails for Calcutta, waits seven weeks from November until early January 1886
* Haggard, *King Solomon's Mines*; *Dictionary of National Biography*; fall of Khartoum; Pater, *Marius the Epicurean*

1886

- June, Conrad returns to England; during summer prepares for master's exam, seeks British citizenship, toys with idea of taking permanent shore-based work, possibly writes first fiction, short story 'The Black Mate' (see Works, **pp. 133–4**); 28 July fails master's certificate; 18 August, naturalised as British citizen; 10 November, successfully retakes master's exam; signs on again as second mate due to lack of commands, sails on *Falconhurst* to Penarth
* Trafalgar Square Riots; Haggard, *She*; Stevenson, *Dr Jekyll and Mr Hyde*; Hardy, *The Mayor of Casterbridge*; Tennyson, *Locksley Hall Sixty Years After*

1887

- January, Conrad takes up post as first mate of *Highland Forrest*; is hurt during voyage; June, arrives in Samarang and advised to seek medical attention in Singapore; enters European Hospital as patient and convalesces in Sailor's Home – experiences were drawn upon in *The Shadow Line* and *Lord Jim* (see Works, **pp. 114–17, 43–7**); August, joins *Vidar* as first mate on trading runs to Borneo and Celebes, meets Charles William Olmeijer (original for Almayer, see Works, **pp. 22–7**) at Malay settlement of Berau in eastern Borneo – later draws upon experiences of trading in Malay Archipelago in first two novels and in *Lord Jim*, *Victory* and *The Rescue*
- * Queen Victoria's Golden Jubilee; Independent Labour Party formed; Haggard, *Allan Quartermain*; Doyle, *A Study in Scarlet*

1888

- January, Conrad takes up command of *Otago*, a role he was to fulfil for fourteen months – would draw on this for *The Shadow Line*, 'The Secret Sharer' and 'A Smile of Fortune' (see Works, **pp. 114–17, 94–5, 93–4**); 9 February to 7 May, first voyage as captain, from Bangkok to Sydney, with illness amongst crew and calms in Gulf of Siam; May to July, *Otago* makes round trip to Melbourne; 7 August to end September, voyage to Mauritius; ship spends two months at Mauritius, makes social contacts amongst French-speaking inhabitants, becomes romantically involved with Eugénie Renouf but discovers she is already engaged (later draws upon experiences on Mauritius in 'A Smile of Fortune'); 21 November, *Otago* leaves for Australia
- * Kipling, *Plain Tales from the Hills*; Ward, *Robert Elsemere*; Arnold, *Essays in Criticism* (second series)

1889

- Early January, *Otago* arrives in Australia; few months later, Conrad resigns command, returns to Europe as passenger aboard SS *Nürnberg*; in England takes lodgings in Pimlico district of London, works in shipping firm of Barr and Moering in which he has financial stake; 2 July, learns he has been officially released from his Russian citizenship, freeing way for return to Poland; autumn, after several months of shore life, begins writing novel that, over course of five years, would evolve into *Almayer's Folly*
- * London Dock Strike; Eiffel Tower; C. Booth, *Life and Labour in London*, *Vol. 1* (to 1903); Gissing, *The Netherworld*

1890

- Conrad travels to Poland for first time in sixteen years; en route to Poland visits terminally ill distant cousin in Brussels, begins intense friendship and infatuation with cousin's wife, novelist Marguerite Poradowska, whom he playfully calls 'aunt'; June, travels to Africa to take up post as captain of riverboat in Belgian controlled Congo; experiences severe illness in Africa, returns to Europe at the end of the year (later draws upon African experience in 'An Outpost of Progress' and 'Heart of Darkness', see Works, **pp. 38, 49–52**).

*   London slum clearances; W. Booth, *In Darkest England*; Stanley, *In Darkest Africa*; W. James, *Principles of Psychology*

1891

• Conrad returns from Africa with broken mental and physical health; May, travels to Geneva for period of convalescence and hydrotherapy at Champel Les Bains spa where he works on *Almayer's Folly*; 16 June, returns to England, spends summer resting, seeking work, experiencing further bouts of ill health, and makes two trips on river Thames with friend G. F. W. Hope aboard yawl *Nellie* (experience upon which he later draws for frame narration of 'Heart of Darkness', see Works, **pp. 49–52**); takes on work as manager of warehouse for Barr, Moering Shipping Company but employment interrupted by illness; continues to work intermittently on *Almayer's Folly*; 21 November, sails for Adelaide on *Torrens* as first mate

*   Trans-Siberian railway begun; Hardy, *Tess of the D'Urbervilles*; Mahler's First Symphony; Wilde, *The Picture of Dorian Gray*

1892

• 28 February, *Torrens* arrives in Australia; 2 September, *Torrens* returns to England; 25 October, Conrad sails with *Torrens* again, befriends passenger W. H. Jacques and allows him to read incomplete draft of *Almayer's Folly*, Jacques encourages Conrad to complete book

*   Kipling, *Barrack Room Ballads*; Doyle, *The Adventures of Sherlock Holmes*

1893

• 30 January, *Torrens* arrives in Australia; during passage Conrad becomes friendly with further passengers – landowner Ted Sanderson and future novelist John Galsworthy (see Life and Contexts, **pp. 11, 13**); 26 July, *Torrens* returns to London; early August to end September, Conrad visits uncle in Poland; back in London frequently visits offices of London Shipmasters' Society, may be introduced to future wife Jessie George at this time; late November, signs up as second mate on steamer *Adowa*, bound for Canada from Rouen, takes up post but shipowner's plans do not reach fruition, Conrad remains in dock writing Chapter 10 of *Almayer's Folly*

*   Franco-Russian Alliance; Dvorak's 'New World' symphony; Gissing, *The Odd Woman*

1894

• Conrad returns to London; 17 January, signed off from *Adowa* (not knowing this would be end of sea career); 10 February, Uncle Bobrowski dies, a father figure by turns loving and admonishing and leaving more than financial legacy to Conrad; 4 July, Conrad submits manuscript of *Almayer's Folly* to publishers T. Fisher Unwin; 4 October, hears news that book accepted for publication

*   Dreyfus trial begins in Paris (1894–9); Kipling, *Jungle Book*; Moore, *Esther Waters*; G. and W. Grossmith, *The Diary of a Nobody*; Wilde, *A Woman of No Importance*; Yeats, *Land of Heart's Desire*; launch of the *Yellow Book*;

Mark Twain, *The Tragedy of Pudd'n'head Wilson*; S. Webb and B. Webb, *The History of Trade Unionism*

Writing life

Note: given the detailed coverage of each work's composition and reception in Part 2, this part of the chronology intentionally offers a more abbreviated account of Conrad's career than those which precede it.

1895
- April, *Almayer's Folly* published (see Works, **pp. 22–7**).
* Crane, *The Red Badge of Courage*; Hardy, *Jude the Obscure*; Symons, *London Nights*; Yeats, *Poems*; Cézanne exhibition in Paris; Lumière brothers invent cinematograph; Röntgen discovers X-rays; Marconi invents wireless telegraph

1896
- March, *An Outcast of the Islands* published (see Works, **pp. 28–31**); October, 'The Idiots' serialised in *The Savoy* (see Works, **p. 38**); Conrad marries Jessie George, they honeymoon in Brittany then set up home in Victoria Road, Stanford le Hope, Essex
* *Daily Mail* launched; Puccini, *La Bohème*; Housman, *A Shropshire Lad*

1897
- January, 'The Lagoon' serialised in *Cornhill Magazine* (see Works, **pp. 39–40**); March, Conrads move to 'Ivy Walls', Stanford le Hope, Essex; June–July, 'An Outpost of Progress' serialised in *Cosmopolis* (see Works, **p. 38**); July, *The Nigger of The 'Narcissus'* published in volume format; August–December, *The Nigger of The 'Narcissus'* serialised in the *New Review* (see Works, **pp. 31–5**); December, 'Karain' published in *Blackwood's Magazine* (see Works, **pp. 36–7**).
* Hardy, *The Well Beloved*; James, *What Maisie Knew, The Spoils of Poynton*; Kipling, *Captains Courageous*; Wells, *Invisible Man*; Yeats, *Secret Rose*; Queen Victoria's Diamond Jubilee; Thompson discovers the electron; Klondike gold rush; *Yellow Book* ceases publication

1898
- Birth of son, Borys; meets Ford Madox Ford; Conrads move to 'The Pent', Postling, Kent; September, 'Youth' appears in *Blackwood's Magazine* (see Works, **pp. 48–9**)
* Curie discovers radium; death of Mallarmé; Wells, *The War of the Worlds*; Hardy, *Wessex Poems*; Wilde, *Ballad of Reading Gaol*

1899
- February–April, 'The Heart of Darkness' appears in serial form in *Blackwood's Magazine* (see Works, **pp. 49–52**)
* Boer War begins; Havelock Ellis, *Studies in the Psychology of Sex*; Dreyfus

pardoned; Wilde, *The Importance of Being Earnest, An Ideal Husband*; Symons, *The Symbolist Movement in Literature*; Kipling, *Stalky and Co*; Yeats, *The Wind among the Reeds*

1900

- October, *Lord Jim* published (see Works, **pp. 43–7**); October–November, *Lord Jim* appears in serial form in *Blackwood's Magazine*; J. B. Pinker becomes Conrad's literary agent (see Life and Contexts, **pp. 13–14**)
* Death of Stephen Crane; death of Oscar Wilde; death of Nietzsche; Planck announces quantum theory; British Labour Party founded; Nietzsche, *Ecce Homo*; Dreiser, *Sister Carrie*; Freud, *Interpretation of Dreams*; Yeats, 'The Symbolism of Poetry'

1901

- December, 'Amy Foster' appears in the *Illustrated London News* (see Works, **pp. 58–9**)
* Death of Victoria, accession of Edward VII; assassination of US President McKinley, Roosevelt appointed president; Marconi broadcasts first radio message across Atlantic; Planck's law of radiation; Kipling, *Kim*; Wells, *First Men in the Moon*; Hardy, *Poems of the Past and of the Present*; Chekhov, *Three Sisters*

1902

- July–December, 'The End of the Tether' serialised in *Blackwood's Magazine* (see Works, **pp. 52–3**); November, *Youth: A Narrative: and two other Stories* ('Heart of Darkness', 'The End of the Tether') published (see Works, **pp. 48–56**); January–March, 'Typhoon' appears in *Pall Mall Magazine* (see Works, **pp. 57–8**); August, 'To-morrow' appears in *Pall Mall Magazine* (see Works, **p. 60**)
* Boer War ends; death of Zola; Bennett, *Anna of the Five Towns*; Hobson, *Imperialism*; James, *The Wings of the Dove*; Kipling, *Just So Stories*

1903

- April, *Typhoon, and Others Stories* ('Amy Foster', 'Falk', 'To-morrow') published (see Works, **pp. 57–62**)
* Wright Brothers make first powered flight; *Daily Mirror* launched; Lenin and Bolsheviks split from Russian SDP; death of Gissing; Butler, *Way of all Flesh*; Shaw, *Man and Superman*; James, *The Ambassadors*

1904

- January–October, *Nostromo* serialised in *T.P.'s Weekly* (see Works, **pp. 63–8**); October, *Nostromo* published; Jessie Conrad becomes partially disabled following a fall
* Weber, *The Protestant Ethic and the Spirit of Capitalism*; Barrie, *Peter Pan*; James, *The Golden Bowl*; Symons, *Studies in Prose and Verse*

1905

- Conrads visit Capri to aid Jessie's recuperation; 25 June, play 'One Day More' premiers at the Royal Theatre, London (see Works, **p. 134**)
* Foundation of Sinn Féin; Einstein's Special Theory of Relativity; attempted revolution in Russia, Tsar makes concessions to remain in power; Fauvist movement in art begins; Forster, *Where Angels Fear to Tread*; Wells, *Kipps*; Synge, *Riders to the Sea*; Wharton, *House of Mirth*; Wilde, *De Profundis*

1906

- August, 'An Anarchist' appears in *Harper's Magazine* (see Works, **pp. 76–7**); October, *The Mirror of the Sea* published; July–October, 'Gaspar Ruiz' serialised in *Pall Mall Magazine* (see Works, **pp. 74–5**); December, 'The Informer' appears in *Harper's Magazine* (see Works, **pp. 75–6**); December, 'The Brute' appears in the *Daily Chronicle* (see Works, **p. 76**); October–December, *The Secret Agent* serialised in *Ridgways: A Militant Weekly for God and Country* (see Works, **pp. 69–73**); son John born; Conrads visit Montpellier
* Labour Party makes significant electoral gains in General Election; start of suffragette campaign; death of Ibsen; Sinclair, *The Jungle*; Kipling, *Puck of Pook's Hill*; Galsworthy, *A Man of Property* (first volume of *Forsyte Saga*); Edward Thomas, *The Heart of England*

1907

- September, *The Secret Agent* published (see Works, **pp. 69–73**); Conrads visit Montpellier and Geneva; Conrads move to 'Someries', Luton Hoo, Bedfordshire
* Hampstead Garden Suburb established; Boy Scout Movement founded by Baden Powell; Kipling awarded Nobel Prize for Literature; Gosse, *Father and Son*; Joyce, *Chamber Music*; Synge, *Playboy of the Western World*; Ford, *The Spirit of the People*

1908

- August, 'Il Conde' appears in *Cassell's Magazine* (see Works, **p. 78**); January–May, 'The Duel' serialised in *Pall Mall Magazine* (see Works, **pp. 77–8**); April, revised and expanded version of 'The Black Mate' published in *London Magazine* (April) (see Works, **pp. 133–4**); August, *A Set of Six* ('Gaspar Ruiz', 'The Informer', 'The Brute', 'An Anarchist', 'The Duel', 'Il Conde') published (see Works, **pp. 74–81**); December 1908–June 1909, 'Some Reminiscences', the serial and first UK title for *A Personal Record*, appears in the *English Review* (see Works, **pp. 88–92**)
* Ford Madox Ford founds the *English Review*; Old Age Pensions introduced; Cubist art movement begins; Ford Motor Company's Model T production line ushers in modern factory working methods; Bennett, *Old Wives' Tales*; Forster, *A Room with a View*; Stein, *Three Lives*; Yeats, *Collected Works I and II*; Grahame, *The Wind in the Willows*; Cubist exhibition in Paris

1909

- Break down in Conrad's friendship with Ford Madox Ford (see Life and Contexts, **pp. 12–13**); Conrads move to Aldington, Kent

*   Bleriot flies across English Channel; Labour Exchanges Act; Lloyd George's People's Budget; Wells, *Tono Bungay*; Marinetti, *Manifeste du futurisme*; Pound, *Personae and Exultations*; Masterman, *The Condition of England*

1910

• January, Conrad quarrels with agent J. B. Pinker, leading to a two-year estrangement (see Life and Contexts, **pp. 13–14**), and suffers nervous breakdown; June, Conrads move to 'Capel House', Orlestone, Kent; August–September, 'The Secret Sharer' appears in *Harper's Magazine* (see Works, **pp. 94–5**)

*   Death of Edward VII, George V succeeds; Post-Impressionist exhibition in London; Forster, *Howards End*; Wells, *The History of Mr Polly*; Yeats, *Poems II*

1911

• October, 'Prince Roman' appears in the *Oxford and Cambridge Review* (see Works, **pp. 131–2**) and *Under Western Eyes* published (see Works, **pp. 82–7**); November, 'The Partner' appears in *Harper's Magazine* (see Works, **p. 105**)

*   Increased suffragette activity; Agadir Crisis; National Insurance Act; Copyright Act; Rutherford's fundamental work on the atom; Amundsen and Scott reach South Pole; *Rhythm* founded; Beerbohm, *Zuleika Dobson*; Brooke, *Poems*; Lawrence, *The White Peacock*; Pound, *Canzoni*; S. and B. Webb, *Poverty*

1912

• January, *Some Reminiscences* published (see Works, **pp. 88–92**); April, 'Freya of the Seven Isles' appears in *Metropolitan Magazine* (see Works, **pp. 95–6**); January–June, *Chance* appears in *the New York Herald* (see Works, **pp. 98–103**); October, *'Twixt Land and Sea* ('A Smile of Fortune', 'The Secret Sharer', and 'Freya of the Seven Isles') published (see Works, **pp. 92–7**)

*   Home Rule for Ireland voted by House of Commons; serious strikes and social unrest in UK (1912–13); loss of *Titanic*; Futurist exhibition in Paris; Russian Futurist Manifesto; *Poetry* (Chicago) founded; *Georgian Poetry* founded; death of Strindberg; Wells, *Marriage*; Pound, *Ripostes*; de la Mare, *The Listeners*; Lawrence, *The Trespasser*; Freud, *Totem and Taboo*; Hulme's poems appear in *New Age*

1913

• March, 'The Inn of Two Witches' appears in *Pall Mall Magazine* (see Works, **pp. 105–6**)

*   Balkan Wars; Einstein's General Theory of Relativity; Stravinsky, *The Rite of Spring*; Lawrence, *Sons and Lovers*

1914

• January, *Chance* published, bringing first public success (see Works, **pp. 98–103**); June–July, 'The Planter of Malata' appears in *Metropolitan*

Magazine (see Works, **pp. 104–5**); September, 'Because of the Dollars' appears in *Metropolitan Magazine* (see Works, **p. 106**); July, Conrads visit Poland and are trapped there until October by outbreak of war

*   Germany invades Belgium, Britain joins the First World War; threat of civil war in Ireland; Panama Canal opened; Wyndham Lewis founds Vorticist movement; *Blast* begins publication (until 1915); *Egoist* begins publication; Joyce, *Dubliners*; Lawrence, *The Prussian Officer*; Pound, *Des Imagistes*; Buchan, *The Thirty-Nine Steps*

1915

•   February, *Within the Tides* ('The Planter of Malata', 'The Partner', 'The Inn of Two Witches', and 'Because of the Dollars') published (see Works, **pp. 104–7**) and *Victory* appears in *Munsey's Magazine*; September, *Victory* published; Borys Conrad enlists in the Army

*   Battles at Ypres, Loos; Gallipoli campaign; SS *Lusitania* sunk; Coalition Government; shop-stewards' movement; Lawrence, *The Rainbow*; Ford, *The Good Soldier*; Brooke, *1914 and Other Poems*; Pound, *Cathay*; Stein, *Tender Buttons*; Woolf, *The Voyage Out*

1916

•   November, Conrad participates as an observer in a ten-day mission of the Q ship HMS *Ready*; September 1916–March 1917, *The Shadow Line* serialised in the *English Review* (see Works, **pp. 114–17**)

*   Battle of the Somme; conscription introduced; Easter Rising in Dublin; death of Henry James; Dada launched in Zurich with Cabaret Voltaire; Joyce, *Portrait of the Artist as a Young Man*; Lawrence, *Twilight in Italy*; H.D., *Sea Garden*; Shaw, *Pygmalion*

1917

•   March, *The Shadow Line* published (see Works, **pp. 114–17**) and 'The Warrior's Soul' appears in *Land and Water* (see Works, **pp. 130–1**); October, 'The Tale' appears in *Strand Magazine* (see Works, **pp. 132–3**)

*   Russian Revolution (Bolshevik Revolution); USA enters First World War; death of Edward Thomas; Eliot, *Prufrock*; Lawrence, *Look! We have Come Through*; Edward Thomas, *Poems*; Yeats, *The Wild Swans at Coole*

1918

•   Borys Conrad suffers shell-shock, is invalided out of army; December 1918–February 1920, *The Arrow of Gold* serialised in *Lloyd's Magazine* (see Works, **pp. 117–20**)

*   Armistice; representation of the People Act, all adult men given vote, women over thirty enfranchised; death of Wilfred Owen; Joyce, *Exiles*; Lawrence, *New Poems*; Lewis, *Tarr*; Strachey, *Eminent Victorians*

1919

•   August, *The Arrow of Gold* published (see Works, **pp. 117–20**); January–July, *The Rescue* serialised in *Land and Water* (see Works, **pp. 121–6**);

March, Conrads move to 'Spring Grove', Wye, Kent; October, move to 'Oswalds', Bishopsbourne, Nr. Canterbury, Kent

* Treaty of Versailles formally ends First World War; League of Nations founded; widespread strikes and rioting in UK; 'Red Clydeside': troops and tanks used to break up demonstrations; continued civil war in Russia, Allied intervention; Alcock and Brown's first transatlantic flight; the Bauhaus founded; Keynes, *The Economic Consequences of the Peace*; Anderson, *Winesburg, Ohio*; Eliot, *Poems*; Sassoon, *War Poems*; Woolf, *Night and Day*

1920

• June, *The Rescue* published (see Works, **pp. 121–6**)

* Dada 'exhibition' in Cologne; prohibition in USA; Eliot, *The Sacred Wood*; Weston, *From Ritual to Romance*; Mansfield, *Bliss*; Pound, *Hugh Selwyn Mauberley*; Jung, *Psychological Types*; Ford, *Thus to Revisit*

1921

• Conrads visit Corsica; initial volumes of Collected Editions published in UK and USA

* Independence and partition of Ireland; economic crisis, 2 million unemployed in UK; Communist Party of Great Britain founded; Huxley, *Crome Yellow*; Lubbock, *The Craft of Fiction*; Lawrence, *Women in Love, Sea and Sardinia, Tortoises*; Pirandello, *Six Characters in Search of an Author*

1922

• February, death of J. B. Pinker, Conrad's agent (see Life and Contexts, **pp. 13–14**); 2 November, stage adaptation of *The Secret Agent* premiers at the Ambassadors Theatre, London

* Mussolini forms Fascist government in Italy; Gandhi imprisoned; Irish Civil War; death of Proust; Joyce, *Ulysses*; Eliot, *The Waste Land*; Galsworthy, *The Forsyte Saga*; Lawrence, *Aaron's Rod, Fantasia of the Unconscious*; Mansfield, *The Garden Party*; Woolf, *Jacob's Room*

1923

• Conrad visits the USA and is lionised; September–December, *The Rover* serialised in *Pictorial Review*; December, *The Rover* published (see Works, **pp. 127–9**)

* End of Irish civil war; USSR established; Yeats awarded Nobel Prize; Huxley, *Antic Hay*; Lawrence, *Birds, Beasts and Flowers, Studies in Classic American Literature, Kangaroo*; Wodehouse, *The Inimitable Jeeves*

1924

• May, Conrad declines knighthood; 3 August, dies of heart attack

* January–October, first Labour Government; death of Lenin; foundation of Imperial Airways; Forster, *A Passage to India*; Lawrence, *England my England*; Hemingway, *In Our Time*; Woolf, 'Mr Bennett and Mrs Brown';

Melville, *Billy Budd*; Richards, *Principles of Literary Criticism*; Breton, *Surrealist Manifesto*

1925

- January, *Tales of Hearsay* ('The Warrior's Soul', 'Prince Roman', 'The Tale', and 'The Black Mate') posthumously published (see Works, **pp. 130–3**); September, incomplete novel *Suspense* posthumously published (see Works, **p. 135**)
* Baird displays first television; Locarno Pact; Shaw wins Nobel Prize; Woolf, *Mrs Dalloway*, *The Common Reader*; Eliot, *Poems 1905–25*; Dreiser, *An American Tragedy*; Dos Passos, *Manhattan Transfer*; Yeats, *A Vision*; Hitler, *Mein Kampf* (Vol. I); Kafka, *The Trial* (posth.)

Bibliography

Note: all quotations from and references to the works of Joseph Conrad are keyed to the texts of Dent's Uniform Edition (London, Dent, 1923–8). The majority of quotations from Conrad's letters are taken from the texts given in the Cambridge *Collected Letters*. These are attributed by the abbreviation CL and the number of the volume, followed by page reference(s).

Achebe, C. (1977) 'An Image of Africa', *The Massachusetts Review* 18 (4, winter): 782–94. Reprinted in Carabine, K. (ed.) (1992) *Joseph Conrad: Critical Assessment: Volume 2*. Robertsbridge: Helm Information, pp. 393–404.

Acheraïou, A. (2004) 'Floating Words: Sea as Metaphor of Style in "Typhoon"', *The Conradian* 29 (1, spring): 27–38.

Adams, D. (2001) ' "Remorse and Power": Conrad's "Karain" and the Queen', *Modern Fiction Studies* 47 (4): 723–52.

Andreach, R. (1965) 'The Two Narrators of "Amy Foster"', *Studies in Short Fiction* 2 (spring): 262–69.

Aubry, G. Jean (ed.) (1927) *Joseph Conrad: Life and Letters*. 2 vols. New York: Doubleday, Page and Co.

—— (1957) *The Sea Dreamer: A Definitive Biography of Joseph Conrad*. London: Novello.

Baines, J. (1971) *Joseph Conrad: A Critical Biography*. Harmondsworth: Penguin. First published in 1960, London: Weidenfeld and Nicolson.

Batchelor, J. (1992) 'Conrad and Shakespeare', *L'Époque Conradienne* 18: 125–51.

—— (1994) *The Life of Joseph Conrad*. Oxford: Blackwell.

Berman, J. (1977) 'Introduction to Conrad and the Russians', *Conradiana* 9 (3): 269–74.

Berthoud, Jacques (1978) *Joseph Conrad: The Major Phase*. Cambridge: Cambridge University Press.

—— (1984) 'The Preface to *The Nigger of the "Narcissus"'*, in J. Berthoud (ed.) *Joseph Conrad, The Nigger of the 'Narcissus'*. Oxford: Oxford University Press, pp. 175–82.

—— (1985) 'Narrative and Ideology: A Critique of Fredric Jameson's *The Political Unconscious*', in *Narrative: From Malory to Motion Pictures*, edited by J. Hawthorn. London: Edward Arnold, pp. 101–15.

—— (1996) 'The Secret Agent', in The Cambridge Companion to Joseph Conrad, edited by J. Stape. Cambridge: Cambridge University Press, pp. 100–21.

Bhabha, Homi (1994) The Location of Culture. London: Routledge.

Bickley, P. and Hampson, R. (1988) ' "Lips that Have Been Kissed": Boccaccio, Verdi, Rossetti and The Arrow of Gold', L'Époque Conradienne: 77–91.

Biddiss, Michael (1977) The Age of the Masses: Ideas and Society in Europe since 1870. Harmondsworth: Penguin.

Billy, Ted (1997) A Wilderness of Words: Closure and Disclosure in Conrad's Short Fiction. Lubbock, Tex.: Texas Tech University Press.

Blackburn, W. (ed.) (1958) Joseph Conrad: Letters to William Blackwood and David Meldrum. Durham, NC: Duke University Press.

Bloom, Harold (ed.) (1987a) Joseph Conrad's Nostromo. New York: Chelsea House.

—— (1987b) Joseph Conrad's Heart of Darkness. New York: Chelsea House.

—— (1992) Marlow. New York: Chelsea House.

Bock, Martin (2002) Joseph Conrad and Psychological Medicine. Lubbock, Tex.: Texas Tech University Press.

Bode, R. (1994) ' "They . . . Should Be out of It": The Women of "Heart of Darkness" ', Conradiana 26 (1): 20–34.

Boehmer, Elleke (1995) Colonial and Postcolonial Literature. Oxford: Oxford University Press.

Bonney, William (1980) Thorns and Arabesques: Contexts for Conrad's Fiction. Baltimore, Md.: Johns Hopkins University Press.

—— (1996) 'Contextualizing and Comprehending Joseph Conrad's "The Return" ', Studies in Short Fiction 33: 77–90.

Bradbrook, Muriel (1941) Joseph Conrad: England's Polish Genius. Cambridge: Cambridge University Press.

Brantlinger, Patrick (1988) Rule of Darkness British Literature and Imperialism: 1830–1914. Ithaca, NY: Cornell University Press.

Brebach, Raymond (1985) Joseph Conrad, Ford Madox Ford, and the Making of "Romance". Ann Arbor, Mich.: UMI Research Press.

—— (1996) 'Conrad and Curle', The Conradian 21 (1, spring): 5–14.

Bristow, Joseph (1995) Effeminate England: Homoerotic Writing after 1885. Buckingham: Open University Press.

Brodsky, G. W. S. (2001) ' "What Manners!": Contra-Diction and Conrad's Use of History in "The Warrior's Soul" ', Conradiana 33 (3): 189–229.

Bross, A. (1975) 'A Set of Six: Variations on a Theme', Conradiana 7 (1): 27–44.

Brown, Spencer Curtis (1906) 'The Commercialisation of Literature and the Literary Agent', Fortnightly Review, NS, 80 (1 August): 359.

Burden, Robert (1991) Heart of Darkness: An Introduction to the Variety of Criticism. London: Macmillan.

Busza, A. (1966) 'Conrad's Polish Literary Background and Some Illustrations of the Influence of Polish Literature on his Work', Antemurale 10: 109–225.

—— (1976) 'Rhetoric and Ideology in Under Western Eyes', in Joseph Conrad: A Commemoration, edited by N. Sherry. London: Macmillan, pp. 105–18.

—— (1980) 'St Flaubert and Prince Roman', L'Époque Conradienne, 19: 23–9.

Carabine, K. (1984) 'Introduction', Nostromo by Joseph Conrad. Oxford: World's Classics, pp. vii–xxxii.

—— (1987) ' "The Secret Sharer": A Note on the Dates of its Composition', *Conradiana* 19: 209–13.

—— (1988) ' "The Black Mate": June–July 1886; January 1908', *The Conradian* 13: 128–48.

—— (1989) ' "Irreconcilable Differences": England as an "Undiscovered Country" in Conrad's "Amy Foster" ', in *The Ends of The Earth*, edited by S. Gaterell. London: Ashfield Press, pp. 187–217.

—— (ed.) (1992) *Joseph Conrad: Critical Assessment*. 4 vols. Robertsbridge: Helm Information.

—— (1996a) *The Life and the Art: A Study of Conrad's under Western Eyes*. Amsterdam: Rodopi.

—— (1996b) '*Under Western Eyes*', in *The Cambridge Companion to Joseph Conrad*, edited by J. Stape. Cambridge: Cambridge University Press, pp. 122–39.

—— (1997) 'Introduction', to *Joseph Conrad: Selected Short Stories* Ware: Wordsworth Editions, pp. vii–xvii.

—— (1999) ' "Gestures" and "The Moral Satirical Idea" in Conrad's "The Informer" ', *Conradiana* 31 (1, spring): 26–41.

Chaikin, M. (1955) 'Zola and Conrad's "The Idiots" ', *Studies in Philology* 2 (July): 502–7.

Chon, S. (1990) ' "Typhoon": Silver Dollars and Stars', *Conradiana* 22 (1): 25–43.

Clifford, H. (1902) 'The Art of Mr. Joseph Conrad', *Spectator* 89 (29 November): 827–28.

Cole, Sarah (2003) *Modernism, Male Friendship, and the First World War*. Cambridge: Cambridge University Press.

Collits, T. (1989) 'Imperialism, Marxism, Conrad: A Political Reading of *Victory*', *Textual Practice* 3 (3): 303–22.

Colls, Robert (1986) 'Englishness and the Political Culture', in *Englishness: Politics and Culture 1880–1920*, edited by R. Colls and P. Dodd. London: Croom Helm, pp. 29–61.

Conrad, Borys (1970) *My Father: Joseph Conrad*. London: Calder and Boyars.

Conrad, Jessie (1926) *Joseph Conrad as I Knew Him*. London: William Heinemann.

—— (1935) *Joseph Conrad and His Circle*. London: Jarrolds.

Conrad, John (1981) *Joseph Conrad: Times Remembered*. Cambridge: Cambridge University Press.

Conroy, Mark (1985) *Modernism and Authority: Strategies of Legitimation in Flaubert and Conrad*. Baltimore, Md.: Johns Hopkins University Press.

—— (1994) 'Ghostwriting (in) "Karain" ', *The Conradian* 18 (2): 1–16.

Coroneos, Con (2002) *Space, Conrad and Modernity*. Oxford: Oxford University Press.

Cox, C. B. (1977) *Joseph Conrad*. Harlow: Longman/The British Council.

—— (ed.) (1981) *Conrad: Heart of Darkness, Nostromo and Under Western Eyes: A Casebook*. London: Macmillan.

Crankshaw, Edward (1936) *Joseph Conrad: Some Aspects of the Art of the Novel*. London: John Lane.

Curle, Richard (1914) *Joseph Conrad: A Study*. London: Kegan Paul.

Cuthbertson, D. (1974) ' "The Informer": Conrad's Little Joke', *Studies in Short Fiction* 11 (fall): 69–90.

Cuthbertson, G. M. (1974) 'Freedom, Absurdity, and Destruction: The Political Theory of Conrad's *A Set of Six*', *Conradiana* 6 (1): 46–52.

Daiches, D. (1960) *The Novels and the Modern World*. Chicago, Ill.: University of Chicago Press.

Daleski, H. M. (1977) *Joseph Conrad: The Way of Dispossession*. London: Faber.

Darras, Jacques (1982) *Joseph Conrad and the West: Signs of Empire*. London, Macmillan.

Davies, L. (1993) 'Conrad, *Chance*, and Women Readers', *The Conradian* 17 (2): 75–88.

Davies, L. and Stape, J. (eds) (2005) *The Collected Letters of Joseph Conrad*, Vol. VII. Cambridge: Cambridge University Press.

Davis, H. (1969) 'Shifting Rents in a Thick Fog: Point of View in the Novels of Joseph Conrad', *Conradiana* 2 (2, winter): 23–38.

Davis, K. and Rude, D. (1973) 'The Transmission of the Text of *The Nigger of The "Narcissus"* ', *Conradiana* 5 (2): 20–45.

Dobrée, Bonamy (1967) *Rudyard Kipling: Realist and Fabulist*. Oxford: Oxford University Press.

Donovan, S. (2003) 'Magic Letters and Mental Degradation: Advertising in "An Anarchist" and "The Partner" ', *The Conradian* 28 (2, autumn): 72–95.

Dryden, Linda (2000) *Joseph Conrad and the Imperial Romance*. London: Macmillan.

Eddlemann F. F. and Higdon, D. L. (eds) (1994) *Almayer's Folly: Cambridge Edition of the Works of Joseph Conrad*. Cambridge: Cambridge University Press.

Eliot, George (1988) *Middlemarch*. Oxford: World's Classics.

Epstein, H. (1991) ' "Where He Is Not Wanted": Impression and Articulation in "The Idiots" and "Amy Foster" ', *Conradiana* 23 (3): 217–32.

—— (1992) 'A Pier Glass in the Cavern: London in *The Secret Agent*', in Gene Moore (ed.) *Conrad's Cities*. Amsterdam: Rodopi, pp. 175–96.

—— (1996) 'The Duality of "Youth": Some Literary Contexts', *The Conradian* 21 (2): 1–14.

—— (1997) 'The Presence of Dickens in Conrad's Writing', in G. Moore, J. Stape and O. Knowles (eds) *Conrad: Intertexts and Appropriations*. Amsterdam: Rodopi.

Erdinast-Vulcan, Daphna (1988) 'Conrad's Double Edged Arrow', *Conradiana* 20 (3): 215–28.

—— (1991) *Joseph Conrad and the Modern Temper*. Oxford: Clarendon Press.

—— (1999) *The Strange Short Fiction of Joseph Conrad*. Oxford: Oxford University Press.

Erdinast-Vulcan, D., Simmons, A. H. and Stape, J. H. (eds) (2004) *Joseph Conrad: The Shorter Fiction*. Amsterdam: Rodopi.

Fincham, Gail and Mrtyle Hooper (eds) (1996) *Under Postcolonial Eyes: Joseph Conrad after Empire*. Cape Town: University of Cape Town Press.

—— (1997) 'The Dialogism of *Lord Jim*', *The Conradian* 22 (1/2, spring/winter): 58–74.

Fleishman, Avrom (1967) *Conrad's Politics: Community and Anarchy in the Fiction of Joseph Conrad*. Baltimore, Md.: Johns Hopkins University Press.

—— (1992) 'Conrad's Last Novel', in K. Carabine (ed.) *Joseph Conrad: Critical Assessment*, Vol. III. Robertsbridge: Helm Information, pp. 633–40. First published 1969, *English Literature in Transition* 12 (4): 189–94.

Fletcher, C. (1999) *Joseph Conrad: Writer's Lives*. London: British Library.

Fogel, Aaron (1985) *Coercion to Speak: Conrad's Poetics of Dialogue*. Cambridge, Mass.: Harvard University Press.

Follett, Wilson (1915) *Joseph Conrad: A Short Study of his Intellectual and Emotional Attitude towards his Work and of the Chief Characteristics of his Work*. Garden City, NY: Doubleday, Page.

Ford, Ford Madox (1924) *Joseph Conrad: A Personal Remembrance*. London: Duckworth.

Ford, J. (1995) 'An African Encounter: A British Traitor and *Heart of Darkness*', *Conradiana* 27: 123–34.

Fraser, Gail (1992) 'Conrad's Revisions to "Amy Foster"', in K. Carabine (ed.) *Joseph Conrad: Critical Assessments*. Robertsbridge: Helm Information, pp. 514–26.

Freidman, A. (1974) 'Conrad's Picaresque Narrator: Marlow's Journey from "Youth" through *Chance*', in *Joseph Conrad: Theory and World Fiction*, edited by Wolomyr, et al. Lubbock, Tex.: Texas Tech University Press, pp. 17–39.

Galen, G. (1983) 'Stephen Crane as a Source for Conrad's Jim', *Nineteenth Century Fiction* 38: 78–96.

Garnett, E. (1902) 'Mr. Conrad's New Book: *Youth: A Narrative; and Two Other Stories*', *Academy* 63 (6 December): 606–7.

—— (ed.) (1928) *Letters from Conrad: 1895–1924*. London: NoneSuch Press.

Gasiorek, A. (1997) ' "To Season with a Pinch of Romance": Ethics and Politics in *Lord Jim*', *The Conradian* 22 (1/2, spring/winter): 75–112.

Geddes, Gary (1980) *Conrad's Later Novels*. Montreal: McGill-Queen's University Press.

Gekoski, R. (1969) '*An Outcast of the Islands*: A New Reading', *Conradiana* 2 (3, spring): 47–58.

Gikandi, Simon (1996) *Maps of Englishness: Writing Identity in the Culture of Colonialism*. New York: Columbia University Press.

Giles, Judy and Middleton Tim, (eds) (1995) *Writing Englishness: 1900–1950*. London: Routledge.

Gill, D. (1999) 'The Fascination of the Abomination: Conrad and Cannibalism', *The Conradian* 24 (2, autumn): 1–30.

Gillon, Adam (1960) *The Eternal Solitary: A Study of Joseph Conrad*. New York: Bookman Associates.

—— (1966) 'Some Polish Literary Motifs in the Works of Joseph Conrad', *Slavic and East European Journal* 10 (winter): 424–39.

Gillon, Adams and Krzyzanowski, Ludwik (eds) (1975) *Joseph Conrad: Commemorative Essays*. New York: Astra Books.

GoGwilt, Christopher (1995) *The Invention of the West: Joseph Conrad and the Double-Mapping of Europe and Empire*. Stanford, Calif.: Stanford University Press.

Goonetilleke, D. C. R. A. (1971) 'Conrad's African Tales: Ironies of Progress', *Ceylon Journal of the Humanities* 2 (January): 64–97.

—— (1977) *Developing Countries in British Fiction*. London: Macmillan.

Gordan, J. D. (1940) *Joseph Conrad: The Making of a Novelist*. Cambridge, Mass.: Harvard University Press.

Graham, Kenneth (1990) *Indirections of the Novel: James, Conrad and Forster*. Cambridge: Cambridge University Press.

Graham, K. (1996) 'Conrad and Modernism', in *The Cambridge Companion to Joseph Conrad*, edited by J. Stape. Cambridge: Cambridge University Press, pp. 203–22.

Graver, Lawrence (1969) *Conrad's Short Fiction*. Berkeley, Calif.: University of California Press.

Green, Martin (1980) *Dreams of Adventure: Deeds of Empire*. London: Routledge and Kegan Paul.

Gross, John (1973) *The Rise and Fall of the Man of Letters: English Literary Life since 1800*. Harmondsworth: Penguin. First published in 1969, London: Weidenfeld & Nicolson.

Guerard, A. (1947) 'Joseph Conrad', *Direction* I: 7–92.

—— (1958) *Conrad: The Novelist*. Cambridge, Mass.: Harvard University Press.

—— (1963) 'Conrad's "The Lagoon"', in M. Maitlaw and L. Leif (eds) *Story and Critic*. London: Harper and Row, pp. 271–3.

Gurko, Leo (1965) *Joseph Conrad: Giant in Exile*. London: Frederick Muller.

Hagopian, J. V. (1964) 'The Informer', in J. V. Hagopian and M. Dolch (eds) *Insight II: Analyses of Modern British Literature*. Frankfurt Am Main: Hirschgraben-Verlag, pp. 58–62.

—— (1965) 'The Pathos of "Il Conde"', *Studies in Short Fiction* 3 (fall): 31–8.

Hammer, Robert (ed.) (1990) *Joseph Conrad: Third World Perspectives*. Washington DC: Three Continents Press.

Hampson, Robert (1980) 'The Affair of the Purloined Brother', *The Conradian*, 6 (2): 5–15.

—— (1992) *Joseph Conrad: Betrayal and Identity*. London: Macmillan.

—— (1995) 'Introduction', *Heart of Darkness*. London: Penguin.

—— (2000) *Cross-Cultural Encounters in Joseph Conrad's Malay Fiction*. Basingstoke: Palgrave.

Hand, R. (2002) 'Producing *Laughing Anne*', *Conradiana* 34 (1/2, spring/summer): 43–62.

Harkness, Bruce (ed.) (1960) *Conrad's "Heart of Darkness" and the Critics*. Belmont, Calif.: Wadsworth.

—— (ed.) (1962) *Conrad's Secret Sharer and the Critics*. Belmont, Calif.: Wadsworth.

Harkness, Bruce and Reid, S. (eds) (1990) *The Secret Agent: Cambridge Edition of the Works of Joseph Conrad*. Cambridge: Cambridge University Press.

Harpham, Geoffrey Galt (1996) *One of Us: The Mastery of Joseph Conrad*. Chicago, Ill.: University of Chicago Press.

Harrington, D. and Estness, C. (1964) 'Aesthetic Criteria and Conrad's "The Tale"', *Discourse* 7 (autumn): 437–45.

Harris, José (1993) *Private Lives, Public Spirit: Britain 1870–1914*. London: Penguin.

Harris, W. (1968) 'English Short Fiction in the Nineteenth Century', *Studies in Short Fiction* 6 (fall): 82–3.

Hawthorn, Jeremy (1979) *Joseph Conrad: Language and Fictional Self-Consciousness*. London: Edward Arnold.

—— (1990) *Joseph Conrad: Narrative Technique and Ideological Commitment*. London: Edward Arnold.

—— (2003a) 'Conrad and the Erotic: "A Smile of Fortune" and "The Planter of Malata"', *The Conradian* 28 (2, autumn): 111–41.

—— (2003b) 'Introduction', *Under Western Eyes*. Oxford: World's Classics, pp. vii–xxii.

Hay, Eloise Knapp (1963) *The Political Novels of Joseph Conrad*. Chicago, Ill.: University of Chicago Press.

—— (1975) 'Conrad's Self-Portraiture', in *Joseph Conrad Colloquy in Poland*, edited by Roza Jablkowska. Warsaw: Polish Academy of Sciences, pp. 57–71.

—— (1996) '*Nostromo*', in *The Cambridge Companion to Joseph Conrad*, edited by J. Stape. Cambridge: Cambridge University Press, pp. 81–99.

Hays, P. (1978) 'Joseph Conrad and Stephen Crane', *Études Anglaises*, 31: 26–37.

Henricksen, Bruce (1992) *Nomadic Voices: Conrad and the Subject of Narrative*. Urbana, Ill.: University of Illinois Press.

Herndon, R. (1960) 'The Genesis of "Amy Foster"', *Studies in Philology* 57 (July): 549–66.

Hervouet, Yves (1990) *The French Face of Joseph Conrad*. Cambridge: Cambridge University Press.

Hicks, J. (1964) 'Conrad's *Almayer's Folly*: Structure, Theme and Critics', *Nineteenth Century Fiction* 19 (June): 17–31.

Higdon, D. L. (1975) 'The Text and Context of Conrad's First Critical Essay', *Polish Review* 20 (2/3): 78–66.

—— (1992) 'Conrad's *The Rover*: The Grammar of Myth', in K. Carabine (ed.) *Joseph Conrad: Critical Assessment*, Vol. III, pp. 624–32. First published in 1965, *Studies in the Novel* 1 (spring): 17–26.

Hillis-Miller J. (1985) *Poets of Reality*. Cambridge, Mass.: Harvard University Press.

Hodges, R. (1979) 'Deep Fellowship: Homosexuality and Male Bonding in the Life and Fiction of Joseph Conrad', *Journal of Homosexuality* 5: 379–93.

Holden, Philip and Richard Ruppel (eds) (2003) *Imperial Desire: Dissident Sexualities and Colonial Literature*. London and Minneapolis, Minn.: University of Minnesota Press.

Holt, Henry (1905) 'The Commercialisation of Literature', *Atlantic Monthly* 96 (5, November): 600.

Howe, Irving (1953) 'Joseph Conrad, Order and Anarchy: The Political Novels' Part 1, *Kenyon Review* 15 (4): 505–21.

—— (1954) 'Joseph Conrad, Order and Anarchy: The Political Novels' Part 2, *Kenyon Review* 16 (1): 1–19.

—— (1957) *Politics and the Novel*. New York: Meridan Books.

Hughes, D. (1975) 'Conrad's "Il Conde": A "Deucedly Queer Story"', *Conradiana* 7 (1): 17–25.

Hunter, J. (1982) 'Conrad and Adventure', in *Edwardian Fiction*. Cambridge, Mass.: Harvard University Press, pp. 124–52.

Hussey, W. R. (1971) 'He Was Spared that Annoyance', *Conradiana* 3 (2): 17–25.

Hyland, P. (1988) 'The Little Woman in *Heart of Darkness*', *Conradiana* 20: 1–11.

James, H. (1963) 'The New Novel', in *Henry James: Selected Literary Criticism*, edited by M. Shapira. London: Hutchinson, pp. 358–92. First published in the *Times Literary Supplement* 635 (10 March, 1914): 133–4 and 637 (2 April, 1914): 157–158.

Jameson, Fredric (1981) *The Political Unconscious: Narrative as a Socially Symbolic Act*. London: Methuen.

Johnson, B. (1963) 'Conrad's "Karain" and *Lord Jim*', *Modern Language Quarterly* 24 (March): 13–20.

—— (1965) 'Conrad's "Falk": Manuscript and Meaning', *Modern Language Quarterly* 16 (June): 267–84.

—— (1971) *Conrad's Models of Mind*. Minneapolis, Minn.: University of Minnesota Press.

Johnson, Barbara and Garber, Marjorie (1987) 'Secret Sharing: Reading Conrad Psychoanalytically', *College English* 49: 628–40.

Johnson, James M. (2001) 'The "Unnatural Rigidity" of Almayer's Ethnocentrism', *The Conradian* 26 (2): 71–8.

Jones, Susan (1999) *Conrad and Women*. Oxford: Clarendon Press.

Kaehle, Sharon and German, Howard (1964) 'Conrad's Victory: A Reassessment' *Modern Fiction Studies*, 10: 55–72.

Kaplan, Carola (1997) 'No Refuge: The Duplicity of Domestic Safety in Conrad's Fiction', *The Conradian*, 22 (1/2, spring/winter): 138–46.

Karl, Frederic (1960) *A Reader's Guide to Joseph Conrad*. New York: Noonday Press.

—— (1973) 'Conrad, Wells, and the Two Voices', *Publication of the Modern Language Association* 88: 1049–65.

—— (ed.) (1975) *Joseph Conrad: A Collection of Criticism*. New York: McGraw Hill.

—— (1976) 'Conrad and Pinker', in N. Sherry (ed.) *Joseph Conrad: A Commemoration*. London: Macmillan, pp. 56–73.

—— (1979) *Joseph Conrad: The Three Lives*. London: Faber and Faber.

—— (1983) '*Victory*: Its Origins and Development', *Conradiana* 15: 23–51.

Karl, Frederic and Davies, L. (eds) (1983–96) *The Collected Letters of Joseph Conrad*, Volumes 1–5. Cambridge: Cambridge University Press.

—— (1985) *Modern and Modernism*. New York: Athenaeum.

Karl, Frederic, Davies, L., and Knowles, O. (eds) (2002) *The Collected Letters of Joseph Conrad*, Volume 6. Cambridge: Cambridge University Press.

Kehler, Joe (1974) 'The Centrality of the Narrator in Conrad's "Falk"', *Conradiana* 6 (1): 19–30.

Kerr, Douglas (1998) 'Conrad and the "Three Ages of Man": "Youth", *The Shadow Line*, "The End of the Tether"', *The Conradian* 23 (2, autumn): 27–44.

Kertzer, J. M. (1974–5) Conrad's Personal Record. *University of Toronto Quarterly* 44: 290–303.

Kimborough, R. (ed.) (1979) *The Nigger of the "Narcissus" (Norton Critical Edition)*. New York and London: W. W. Norton.

—— (ed.) (1988) *Heart of Darkness (Norton Critical Edition)*. New York and London: W. W. Norton.

Kinney, Arthur (1965) 'Jimmy Wait: Joseph Conrad's Kaleidoscope', *College English* 26 (March): 475–8.

Kirschner, Paul (1964) 'Conrad's Strong Man', *Modern Fiction Studies* 10 (spring): 31–6.

—— (1965) 'Conrad and Maupassant', *Review of English Literature* 6 (October): 37–5.

—— (1968) *Conrad: The Psychologist as Artist*. Edinburgh: Oliver and Boyd.

—— (1996) 'Introduction', *Under Western Eyes*. London: Penguin, pp. i–xx.

Knowles, O. (1990) *A Conrad Chronology*. London: Macmillan.

—— (1992) *An Annotated Critical Bibliography of Joseph Conrad*. London, Macmillan.

Knowles, O. and Moore, G. (eds) (2000) *The Oxford Reader's Companion*. Oxford: Oxford University Press.

Kolupke, Joseph (1988) 'Elephants, Empires, and Blind Men: A Reading of the Figurative Language in Conrad's "Typhoon"', *Conradiana* 20 (1): 71–85.

Kramer, Dale (1983) 'The Maturity of Conrad's First Tale', *Studies in Short Fiction* 20: 45–9.

—— (1988) 'Conrad's Experiments with Language and Narrative in "The Return"', *Studies in Short Fiction* 25: 1–12.

Kramer, Jurgen (2003) 'What the Country Doctor "Did Not See": The Limits of the Imagination in "Amy Foster"', *The Conradian* 28, 2 (autumn): 1–11.

Krenn, Heliéna (1990) *Conrad's Lingard Trilogy: Empire, Race, and Women in the Malay Novels*. New York: Garland.

Krzyzanowski, Ludwik (ed.) (1960) *Joseph Conrad: Centennial Essays*. New York: Polish Institute of Arts and Sciences in America.

Lafferty, William (1965) 'Conrad's "A Smile of Fortune": The Moral Threat of Commerce', *Conradiana* 7: 63–74.

Lane, Christopher (1995) 'Fostering Subjection: Masculine Identification and Homosexual Allegory in Conrad's *Victory*', in *The Ruling Passion: British Colonial Allegory and the Paradox of Homosexual Desire*. Durham, NC: Duke University Press, pp. 99–125.

Larabee, Mark D. (2003) 'Territorial Vision and Revision in "Freya of the Seven Isles"', *The Conradian* 28 (2, autumn): 96–110.

Leavis, F. R. (1980) *The Great Tradition*. London: Pelican. First published 1948. London: Chatto and Windus.

Ledger, Sally and McCracken, Scott (eds) (1995) *Cultural Politics at the Fin de Siècle*. Cambridge: Cambridge University Press.

Levenson, Michael (1984) *A Genealogy of Modernism*. Cambridge: Cambridge University Press.

—— (1991) *Modernism and the Fate of Individuality*. Cambridge: Cambridge University Press.

Levine, Paul (1964) 'Joseph Conrad's Blackness', *South Atlantic Quarterly* 63 (spring): 198–206.

Lodge, David (1964) 'Conrad's *Victory* and *The Tempest*: An Amplification', *Modern Language Review* 59: 195–9.

Lothe, Jakob (1989) *Conrad's Narrative Method*. Oxford: Clarendon Press.

Lucas, Michael (2003) 'Rehabilitating "The Brute"', *The Conradian* 28 (2, autumn): 61–71.

McClure, John (1981) *Kipling and Conrad: The Colonial Fiction*. Cambridge, Mass.: Harvard University Press.

McCracken, Scott (1995) 'Postmodernism, a *Chance* to Reread?' in S. Ledger and S. McCracken (eds) *Cultural Politics at the Fin de Siècle*. Cambridge: Cambridge University Press, pp. 267–89.

McDonald, Peter (1996) 'Men of Letters and Children of the Sea: Conrad and the Henley Circle Revisited', *The Conradian* 21 (1): 15–56.

McLauchlan, Juliet (1975) 'Conrad's "Three Ages of Man": The *Youth* Volume', in A. Gillon and L. Krzyzanowski (eds) *Joseph Conrad: Commemorative Essays*. New York: Astar Books, pp. 188–201.

—— (1977) *Conrad: Nostromo*. London: Edward Arnold.

Macleod, Glen (1999) 'The Visual Arts', in M. Levenson (ed.) *The Cambridge Companion to Modernism*. Cambridge: Cambridge University Press, pp. 194–216.

Mahood, Molly (1977) *The Colonial Encounter: A Reading of Six Novels*. London: Rex Collings.

Manicom, David (1986) 'True Lies/False Truths: Narrative Perspective and the Control of Ambiguity in *The Nigger of the "Narcissus"* ', *Conradiana* 18 (2): 105–18.

Marcus, Miriam (1998) 'Writing, Race, and Illness in *The Nigger of The "Narcissus"* ', *The Conradian* 23 (1): 37–50.

Marle, Hans van (1991) 'A Novelist's Dukedom: From Joseph Conrad's Library', *The Conradian* 16 (1): 55–78.

Marle, Hans van and Moore, Gene (1997) 'The Sources of Conrad's *Suspense*', in O. Knowles et al. (eds) *Conrad: Intertexts and Appropriations*, Amsterdam: Rodopi, pp. 141–63.

Martin, W. R. (1971–2). 'Gaspar Ruiz: A Conradian Hero', *Conradiana* 3 (3): 46–8.

Matthews, James (1974) 'Ironic Symbolism in Conrad's "Youth"', *Studies in Short Fiction* 11 (spring): 117–23.

Meixner, J. (1974) Ford and Conrad, *Conradiana* 6: 157–69.

Melchiori, Barbara (1985) *Terrorism in the Late Victorian Novel*. Beckenham: Croom Helm.

Meyer, B. (1967) *Joseph Conrad: A Psychoanalytic Biography*. Princeton, NJ: Princeton University Press.

Meyers, Jeffrey (1973) *Fiction and the Colonial Experience*. Ipswich: Boydell Press.

—— (1973) 'Conrad and Roger Casement', *Conradiana* 5 (3): 64–9.

—— (1977) *Homosexuality and Literature*. London: Athlone Press.

Middleton, Tim (1998) 'Re-reading Conrad's "Complete Man": Constructions of Masculine Subjectivity in "Heart of Darkness" and *Lord Jim*', in K. Carabine, et al. (eds) *Conrad, James and Other Relations*. New York: Columbia University Press, pp. 261–76.

—— (2000) 'From Mimicry to Menace: Conrad and Late Victorian Masculinity', in Philip Holden and Richard Ruppel (eds) *Imperial Desire*. Minneapolis, Minn.: University of Minnesota Press, pp. 135–51.

—— (ed.) (2003) *Modernism: Critical Concepts in Literary and Cultural Studies*, 5 vols, London: Routledge.

Mongia, Padmini (1993) 'Empire, Narrative and the Feminine in *Lord Jim* and

Heart of Darkness', in K. Carabine et al. (eds) *Contexts for Conrad*. Boulder, Col.: University of Colorado Press, pp. 135–50.

Moore, Carlisle (1963) 'Conrad and the Novel as Ordeal', *Philological Quarterly* 42 (January): 55–74.

Moore, Gene (ed.) (1992) *Conrad's Cities*. Amsterdam: Rodopi.

Moore, Gene, Stape, John and Knowles, Owen (eds) (1997) *Conrad: Intertexts and Appropriations*. Amsterdam: Rodopi.

—— (1997) 'Conrad's "Film-Play": *Gaspar the Strong Man*', in G. Moore (ed.) *Conrad on Film*. Cambridge: Cambridge University Press, pp. 31–47.

Morf, Gustav (1930) *The Polish Heritage of Joseph Conrad*. London: Sampson Low.

Morris, Robert (1950) 'Eliot's "Game of Chess" and Conrad's "The Return"', *Modern Language Notes* 65 (June): 422–33.

Morrison, Mark (2001) *The Public Face of Modernism: Little Magazines, Audiences and Reception, 1905–1920*. Madison, Wisc.: University of Wisconsin Press.

Morzinski, Mary (1994) *Linguistic Influence of Polish on Joseph Conrad's Style*. Lublin: Maria Curie Sklodowska University.

Moser, Thomas (1957) *Joseph Conrad: Achievement and Decline*. Cambridge, Mass.: Harvard University Press.

—— (1992) ' "The Rescuer" Manuscript: A Key to Conrad's Development and Decline', in K. Carabine (ed.) *Joseph Conrad: Critical Assessment*, Vol. III, pp. 552–76. First published 1965, *Harvard Library Bulletin* 10 (autumn): 325–55.

—— (ed.) (1996) *Lord Jim (Norton Critical Edition)*, 2nd edn. London and New York: W. W. Norton.

Moynihan, William (1958) 'Conrad's "The End of the Tether": A New Reading', *Modern Fiction Studies* 4 (summer): 173–77.

Mudrick, Marvin (1957) 'The Artist's Conscience and *The Nigger of The "Narcissus"* ', *Nineteenth Century Fiction* 11: 288–97.

—— (ed.) (1966) *Conrad: A Collection of Critical Essays*. Englewood Cliffs, NJ: Prentice-Hall.

Murfin, Ross (ed.) (1989) *Joseph Conrad: 'Heart of Darkness': A Case Study in Contemporary Criticism*. New York: Bedford St Martin's Press.

Mursia, Urgo (1992) 'Notes on Conrad's Italian Novel: *Suspense*', in G. Moore, (ed.) *Conrad's Cities*. Amsterdam: Rodopi, pp. 269–81.

Nadelhaft, Ruth (1982) 'Women as Moral and Political Alternatives in Conrad's Early Novels', in G. Mora and K. S. Van Hooft (eds) *Theory and Practice of Feminist Literary Criticism*. Ypsilanti: Bilingual Review Press, pp. 242–55.

—— (1991) *Joseph Conrad (Feminist Readings)*. Atlantic Highlands, NJ: Humanities Press International.

—— (ed.) (1997) *Nostromo*. Ontario: Broadview.

Najder, Z. (ed.) (1964) *Conrad's Polish Background: Letters to and from Polish Friends*. Oxford: Oxford University Press.

—— (ed.) (1978) *Joseph Conrad: Congo Diary and Other Uncollected Pieces*. New York: Doubleday.

—— (1983a) *Joseph Conrad: A Chronicle*. Cambridge: Cambridge University Press.

—— (1983b) *Conrad under Familial Eyes*. Cambridge: Cambridge University Press.

—— (1988) 'Introduction', *The Mirror of the Sea and A Personal Record*. Oxford: World's Classics, pp. vii–xxi.

—— (1997) *Conrad in Perspective*. Cambridge: Cambridge University Press.

—— (2003) Meditations on Conrad's Territoriality: An Essay in Four Tacks. *The Conradian* 28 (1, spring): 1–16.

Nettels, Elsa (1974) 'The Grotesque in Conrad's Fiction', *Nineteenth Century Fiction* 29 (September): 144–63.

—— (1977) *James and Conrad*. Athens, Ga.: University of Georgia Press.

—— (1978) 'Conrad and Stephen Crane', *Conradiana* (10): 267–83.

Newhouse, Neville (1966) *Joseph Conrad*. London: Evans.

Niland, Richard (2004) 'Ageing and Individual Experience in "Youth" and "Heart of Darkness"', *The Conradian* 29 (1, spring): 99–118.

O'Connor, Peter (1975) 'The Function of Nina in *Almayer's Folly*', *Conradiana* 7, (3): 225–32.

Oppenheim, Janet (1985) *The Other World: Spiritualism and Psychical Research in England, 1850–1914*. Cambridge: Cambridge University Press.

Orr, John (1977) *Tragic Realism and Modern Society: Studies in the Sociology of the Novel*. London: Macmillan.

Owen, Alex (1989) *The Darkened Room: Women, Power and Spiritualism in Late Victorian England*. London: Virago.

Palmer, John (ed.) (1969) *Twentieth Century Interpretation of The Nigger of The 'Narcissus': A Collection of Critical Essays*. Englewood Cliffs, NJ: Prentice Hall.

Parry, Benita (1983) *Conrad and Imperialism*. London: Macmillan.

—— (1989) 'Conrad and England', in R. Samuel (ed.) *Patriotism: The Making and Unmaking of British National Identity: Volume 3: National Fictions*. London: Routledge, pp. 189–98.

Pinsker, Sanford (1971–2) ' "The End of the Tether": Joseph Conrad's Death of A Sailsman', *Conradiana* 3 (2): 74–6.

—— (1977) ' "Amy Foster": A Reconsideration', *Conradiana*, 9: 179–86.

Postacioglu-Banon, Sema (2003) ' "Gaspar Ruiz": A Vitagraph of Desire', *The Conradian* 28 (2, autumn): 29–44.

Putnam, George Palmer (1902) 'Short Stories', *Athenaeum* 75 (20 December): 824.

—— (1902a) '*Youth; A Narrative and Two Other Stories*', *Times Literary Supplement*, 12 December: 372.

—— (1902b) '*Youth; A Narrative and Two Other Stories*', *Daily Chronicle* (20 December): 3.

Quiller-Couch, Arthur (1903) 'Recent Fiction: Some Stories by Joseph Conrad', *New York Times Saturday Review* (4 April): 224.

Raban, Jonathan (1992) 'Introduction', *The Oxford Book of the Sea*. Oxford: Oxford University Press, pp. 1–35.

Raval, Suresh (1980) 'Conrad's *Victory*; Skepticism and Experience', *Nineteenth Century Fiction*: 414–33.

—— (1986) *The Art of Failure: Conrad's Fiction*. London: Allen and Unwin.

Reilly, Jim (1993) *Shadowtime: History and Representation in Hardy, Conrad and George Eliot*. London: Routledge.

Rice, Thomas J. (1975) ' "Typhoon": Conrad's Christmas Story', *Cithara* 14 (2): 19–35.

Rimmon-Kennan, Shlomith (1983) *Narrative Fiction: Contemporary Poetics*. London: Methuen.

Roberts, Andrew Michael (1993) 'Secret Agents and Secret Objects: Action, Passivity, and Gender in *Chance*', *The Conradian* 17 (2): 89–104.

—— (ed.) (1998) *Joseph Conrad (Longman Critical Readers)*. London: Longman.

—— (2000) *Conrad and Masculinity*. London: Macmillan.

Rosenfield, C. (1967) *Paradise of Snakes: An Archetypal Analysis of Conrad's Political Novels*. Chicago, Ill.: University of Chicago Press.

Roussel, Royal (1971) *The Metaphysics of Darkness: A Study in the Unity and Development of Conrad's Fiction*. Baltimore, Md.: Johns Hopkins University Press.

Rundle, Vivian (1992) ' "The Tale" and the Ethics of Interpretation', *The Conradian* 17 (1, autumn): 17–36.

Ruppel, Richard (1996) 'Yanko Goorall in the Heart of Darkness: "Amy Foster" as Colonialist Text', *Conradiana* 28 (2): 126–32.

—— (1998) 'Joseph Conrad and the Ghost of Oscar Wilde', *The Conradian* 23 (1, spring): 19–36.

—— (2003) ' "Girl! What? Did I Mention a Girl?": The Economy of Desire in *Heart of Darkness*', in P. Holden and R. J. Ruppel (eds) *Imperial Desire: Dissident Sexualities and Colonial Literature*. London and Minneapolis, Minn.: University of Minnesota Press, pp. 152–71.

Russell-March, P. A. (2003) 'The Anarchy of Love: "The Informer" ', *The Conradian* 28 (2, autumn): 45–59.

Said, Edward (1966) *Joseph Conrad and the Fiction of Autobiography*. Cambridge, Mass.: Harvard University Press.

—— (1983) *The World, the Text and the Critic*. Cambridge, Mass.: Harvard University Press.

—— (1993) *Culture and Imperialism*. London: Chatto and Windus.

Sandison, Alan (1967) *The Wheel of Empire*. London: Macmillan.

Saunders, Max (1996) *Ford Madox Ford: A Dual Life*, 2 vols. Oxford: Oxford University Press.

Saveson, John (1972) *Joseph Conrad: The Making of a Novelist*. Amsterdam: Rodopi.

—— (1974) *Conrad the Later Moralist*. Amsterdam: Rodopi.

Schneider, Lissa (2003) *Conrad's Narratives of Difference*. London: Routledge.

Schuster, Charles (1984) 'Comedy and the Limits of Language in Conrad's "Typhoon" ', *Conradiana* 16 (1): 55–71.

Schwarz, Bill (1996) 'Night Battles: Hooligan and Citizen', in Mica Nava and Alan O'Shea (eds) *Modern Times: Reflections on a Century of English Modernity*. London: Routledge, pp. 101–28.

Schwarz, Daniel (1969) 'Moral Bankruptcy in Ploumar Parish: A Study of Conrad's "The Idiots" ', *Conradiana* 1 (3, summer): 113–17.

—— (1971a) 'The Lepidopterist's Revenge: Theme and Structure in Conrad's "An Anarchist" ', *Studies in Short Fiction* 8 (spring): 330–4.

—— (1971b) 'The Significance of the Narrator in Conrad's "Falk" ', *Tennessee Studies in Literature* 16: 103–10.

—— (1975) ' "A Lonely Figure Walking Purposefully": The Significance of Captain Whalley in Conrad's "The End of the Tether" ', *Conradiana* 7 (2): 165–73.

—— (1980) *Conrad: Almayer's Folly to Under Western Eyes*. Ithaca, NY: Cornell University Press.

—— (1982) *Conrad: The Later Fiction*. Ithaca, NY: Cornell University Press.

Secor, Robert (1971) *The Rhetoric of Shifting Perspectives: Conrad's Victory*. University Park, Pa.: Pennsylvania University Press.

Seigle, Robert (1984) 'The Two Texts of *Chance*', *Conradiana* 16 (2): 83–101.

Shaddock, Jennifer (1994) 'Hanging a Dog: The Politics of Naming in "An Anarchist" ', *Conradiana* 26 (1): 56–69.

Sherry, N. (1966) *Conrad's Eastern World*. Cambridge: Cambridge University Press.

—— (1971) *Conrad's Western World*. Cambridge: Cambridge University Press.

—— (1972) *Conrad and his World*. Cambridge: Cambridge University Press.

—— (ed.) (1973) *Conrad: The Critical Heritage*. London: Routledge and Kegan Paul.

—— (ed.) (1976) *Joseph Conrad: A Commemoration*. London: Macmillan.

Simmons, Allan (1989) 'Ambiguity as Meaning: The Subversion of Suspense in *Almayer's Folly*', *The Conradian* 14: 1–18.

—— (1997a) ' "Conflicting Impulses": Focalization and the Presentation of Culture in *Almayer's Folly*', *Conradiana* 29 (3): 63–172.

—— (1997b) 'Cinematic Fidelities in *The Rover* and *The Duellists*', in G. Moore, (ed.) *Conrad on Film*. Cambridge: Cambridge University Press, pp. 120–34.

—— (2000) 'England', in O. Knowles and G. Moore (eds) *The Oxford Reader's Companion to Conrad*. Oxford: Oxford University Press, pp. 100–1.

—— (2004) 'The Art of Englishness: Identity and Representation in Conrad's Early Career', *The Conradian* 29 (1, spring): 1–26.

Simons, Kenneth (1985) *The Ludic Imagination: A Reading of Joseph Conrad*. Ann Arbor, Mich.: UMI Research Press.

Simmons, Allan and Stape John, (eds) (2000) *Lord Jim: Centennial Essays*. Amsterdam: Rodopi.

Slight, William (1980) 'Anagram, Myth, and Structure of *Almayer's Folly*', *Ariel* 11 (3): 23–38.

Smith, David R. (1991a) 'Dostoevsky and Conrad', *The Conradian* 15 (2) (January): 1–11.

—— (ed.) (1991b) *Joseph Conrad's Under Western Eyes: Beginnings, Revisions, Final Forms: Five Essays*. Hamden, Conn.: Archon Books.

Smith, Joanna (1989) ' "Too Beautiful Altogether": Patriarchal Ideology in "Heart of Darkness" ', in R. Murfin (ed.) *Heart of Darkness: A Case Study in Contemporary Criticism*. New York: St Martin's Press, pp. 179–95.

Spatt, Hartley S. (1976) '*Nostromo*'s Chronology: the Shaping of History', *Conradiana* 8: 37–48.

Spittles, Brian (1992) *Joseph Conrad: Text and Context*. London: Macmillan.

Stallman, R. W. (ed.) (1960) *The Art of Joseph Conrad: A Critical Symposium*. East Lansing, Mich.: Michigan State University Press.

Stape, John (1992) 'Conrad's "The Duel": A Reconsideration', in K. Carabine (ed.) *Joseph Conrad: Critical Assessment*, Vol. III. Robertsbridge: Helm Information, pp. 122–6. First published in 1986, *The Conradian* 11 (1): 42–6.

—— (ed.) (1996) *The Cambridge Companion to Joseph Conrad*. Cambridge: Cambridge University Press.

—— (ed.) (2004) *Notes on Life and Letters: Cambridge Edition of the Works of Joseph Conrad*. Cambridge: Cambridge University Press.

Stape, John and Knowles, O. (eds) (1996) *A Portrait in Letters: Correspondence to and about Joseph Conrad*. Amsterdam: Rodopi.

Stauffer, Ruth (1922) *Joseph Conrad: His Romantic-Realism*. Boston, Mass.: Four Seas.

Steinmann, Theo (1974) 'The Perverted Pattern of *Billy Budd* in *The Nigger of The "Narcissus"*', *English Studies* 55: 239–46.

Stott, Rebecca (1993) 'The Woman in Black: Race and Gender in *The Secret Agent*', *The Conradian* 17 (2): 38–58.

Strauss, Nina Pelikan (1987) 'The Exclusion of the Intended from Secret Sharing in "Heart of Darkness"', *Novel* 20 (2, winter): 123–7.

Sullivan, E. W. (no date). 'The Several Endings of Joseph Conrad's *Lord Jim*', London: The Joseph Conrad Society.

Swingewood, Alan (1975) *The Novel and Revolution*. London: Macmillan.

Tagge, Anne (1997) ' "A Glimpse of Paradise": Feminine Impulse and Ego in Conrad's Malay World', *Conradiana* 29 (2): 101–12.

Tanner, Tony (1976) ' "Gnawed Bones" and "Artless Tales": Eating and Narrative in Conrad', in N. Sherry (ed.) *Joseph Conrad: A Commemoration*. London: Macmillan, pp. 17–36.

—— (1981) 'Gentlemen and Gossip: Aspects of Evolution and Language in Conrad's *Victory*', *L'Époque Conradienne* (May): 1–56.

—— (1986) 'Joseph Conrad and the Last Gentleman', *Critical Quarterly* 28 (1/2): 109–42.

Teets, B. E. (1990) *Joseph Conrad: An Annotated Bibliography*. New York: Garland.

Teets, B. E. and Gerber, H. E. (1971) *Joseph Conrad: An Annotated Bibliography of Writings About Him*. De Kalb, Ill.: University of Northern Illinois Press.

Thomas, Claude (ed.) (1975) *Studies in Joseph Conrad: Number 2*. Montpellier: Université Paul Valéry.

Thompson, Gordon (1978) 'Conrad's Women', *Nineteenth Century Fiction* 32 (4): 442–63.

Thorburn, David (1974) *Conrad's Romanticism*. New Haven, Conn.: Yale University Press.

Tredell, Nicolas (1998) *Joseph Conrad: Heart of Darkness*. Cambridge: Icon Books.

Tutien, D. (1990) *Joseph Conrad's Reading: An Annotated Bibliography*. West Cornwall, Conn.: Locust Hill Press.

Tyley, Sue (1983) 'Time and Space in The Secret Agent', *The Conradian* 8 (2, summer): 32–8.

Vanderveer Hamilton, Carol (1994) 'Revolution from Within: Conrad's Natural Anarchists', *The Conradian* 18 (2, autumn): 31–48.

Vitoux, Pierre (1975) 'Marlow: The Changing Narrator of Conrad's Fiction', in Claude Thomas (ed.) *Studies in Joseph Conrad: Number 2*. Montpellier: Université Paul Valéry, pp. 83–102.

Voytovich, Edward (1974) 'The Problems of Identity for Conrad's Women', *Essays in Literature* 2 (March): 51–68.

Walsh, Dennis (1974) 'Conrad's "Typhoon" and the Book of Genesis', *Studies in Short Fiction* 11 (winter): 99–101.

Watt, Ian (1960) 'Story and Idea in Conrad's "The Shadow Line"', *Critical Quarterly* 2: 133–48.

—— (ed.) (1973a) *Conrad: The Secret Agent (A Casebook)*. London: Macmillan.

—— (1973b) 'The Versions of *The Secret Agent*', in I. Watt (ed.) *Conrad: The Secret Agent (A Casebook)*. London: Macmillan, pp. 81–8.

—— (1973c) 'The Political and Social Background of *The Secret Agent*', in I. Watt (ed.) *Conrad: the Secret Agent* (A Casebook). London: Macmillan: 229–250.

—— (1974) '*Almayer's Folly*: Memories and Models', *Mosaic* 8 (fall): 165–82.

—— (1979) *Conrad in the Nineteenth Century*. Berkeley, Calif.: University of California Press.

—— (1988) *Joseph Conrad: Nostromo*. Cambridge: Cambridge University Press.

Watts, Cedric (1978) *Conrad and Cunninghame Graham*. London: The Joseph Conrad Society.

—— (1985) 'The Narrative Enigma of Conrad's "A Smile of Fortune"', *Conradiana* 17: 131–6.

—— (1989) *Joseph Conrad: A Literary Life*. London: Macmillan.

—— (1990) *Joseph Conrad: Nostromo*. London: Penguin.

—— (1993) *A Preface to Conrad*. London: Longman.

—— (1994) *Joseph Conrad: Writers and their Work*. Plymouth: Northcote House.

—— (1996) 'Edward Garnett's Influence on Conrad', *The Conradian* 21 (1): 79–91.

—— (1997) 'Introduction', *The Secret Agent*. London: Everyman, pp. xvii–xxvi.

—— (2002) 'Introduction' *Typhoon and Other Tales*. Oxford: World's Classics, pp. xi–xxxiii.

—— (2004) 'Fraudulent Signifiers: Saussure and the Sixpence in "Karain"', in D. Erdinast-Vulcan et al. (eds) *Joseph Conrad: The Short Fiction*. Amsterdam: Rodopi, pp. 12–27.

Weston, John Howard (1974) ' "Youth": Conrad's Irony and Time's Darkness', *Studies in Short Fiction* 11 (fall): 399–407.

Wexler, Joyce P. (1997) *Who Paid for Modernism? Art, Money and the Fiction of Conrad, Joyce and Lawrence*. Fayetteville, Ark.: University of Arkansas Press.

Wheatley, Alison (1999) 'Conrad's *One Day More*: Challenging Social and Dramatic Convention', *The Conradian* 24 (1, spring): 1–17.

—— (2002) '*Laughing Anne*: "An almost unbearable spectacle"', *Conradiana*, 34 (1/2, spring/summer): 63–76.

White, Allon (1981) *The Uses of Obscurity: The Fictions of Early Modernism*. London: Routledge and Kegan Paul.

White, Andrea (1993) *Joseph Conrad and the Adventure Tradition: Constructing and Deconstructing the Imperial Subject*. Cambridge: Cambridge University Press.

Wiley, Paul (1954) *Conrad's Measure of Man*. Madison, Wisc.: University of Wisconsin Press.

Willcocks, Tim (1998) 'Introduction and Screenplay' *Amy Foster*. London: Hodder and Stoughton, pp. vii–xiii, 1–112.

Williams, Porter (1968) 'Story and Frame in Conrad's "The Tale"', *Studies in Short Fiction* (winter): 179–85.

Willis, John Howard (1955) 'Adam, Axel, and "Il Conde"', *Modern Fiction Studies* 1: 22–5.

—— (1963) 'A Neglected Masterpiece: Conrad's "Youth"', *Texas Studies in Literature and Language* 4 (spring): 591–601.

Willy, Todd (1980) 'The Call to Imperialism in Conrad's "Youth": An Historical Reconstruction', *Journal of Modern Literature* 8: 39–50.

—— (1985) 'The Conquest of the Commodore: Conrad's Rigging of "The Nigger" for the Henley Regatta', *Conradiana* 17 (3): 163–85.

Wollaeger, Mark (1990) *Joseph Conrad and the Fictions of Skepticism*. Stanford, Calif.: Stanford University Press.

Wolodymyr, T. Z. and Aycock, W. M. (eds) (1974) *Joseph Conrad: Theory and World Fiction*. Lubbock, Tex.: Texas Technical University Press.

Woolf, Virginia (1938) 'Modern Fiction', in *The Common Reader*. London: Pelican, pp. 145–53. First published, *Times Literary Supplement* 1918, amended version, *The Common Reader* 1925.

Wright, Walter F. (1949) *Romance and Tragedy in Joseph Conrad*. Lincoln, Nebr.: University of Nebraska Press.

Young, Vernon (1971) 'Lingard's Folly: The Lost Subject', in B. E. Teets and H. E. Gerber, *Joseph Conrad: An Annotated Bibliography of Writings about Him*. De Kalb, Ill.: University of Northern Illinois Press, pp. 340–1. First published 1953, *Kenyon Review* 15 (autumn): 522–39.

Zable, Morton (ed.) (1947) *The Portable Conrad*. New York: Viking.

Index

Related titles from Routledge

Jane Austen

Robert P. Irvine

Routledge Guides to Literature

Jane Austen is one of England's most enduringly popular authors, renowned for her subtle observations of the provincial middle classes of late eighteenth- and early nineteenth-century England.

This guide to Austen's much-loved work offers:

- an accessible introduction to the contexts and many interpretations of Austen's texts, from publication to the present

- an introduction to key critical texts and perspectives on Austen's life and work, situated within a broader critical history

- cross-references between sections of the guide, in order to suggest links between texts, contexts and criticism

- suggestions for further reading.

Part of the *Routledge Guides to Literature* series, this volume is essential reading for all those beginning detailed study of Jane Austen and seeking not only a guide to her works, but a way through the wealth of contextual and critical material that surrounds them.

Hb: 0–415–31434–8
Pb: 0–415–31435–6

Available at all good bookshops
For ordering and further information please visit:

www.routledge.com

Related titles from Routledge

Jane Austen's *Pride & Prejudice*:
A Sourcebook
Edited by Robert Morrison
Routledge Guides to Literature

Jane Austen's *Pride and Prejudice* (1813) is perhaps her most popular novel. A work of comedy, wit, romance, it is also haunted by ironic shadows and dark anxieties as Austen traces the fortunes of central character Elizabeth Bennet.

Taking the form of a sourcebook, this guide to Austen's classic novel offers:

- extensive introductory comment on the contexts and many interpretations of the text, from publication to the present
- annotated extracts from key contextual documents, reviews, critical works and the text itself
- cross-references between documents and sections of the guide, in order to suggest links between texts, contexts and criticism
- suggestions for further reading.

Part of the *Routledge Guides to Literature* series, this volume is essential reading for all those beginning detailed study of *Pride and Prejudice* and seeking not only a guide to the novel, but a way through the wealth of contextual and critical material that surrounds Austen's text.

Hb: 0–415–26849–4
Pb: 0–415–26850–8

Available at all good bookshops
For ordering and further information please visit:
www.routledge.com

Related titles from Routledge

William Shakespeare's *Hamlet*
Edited by Sean McEvoy
Routledge Guides to Literature

William Shakespeare's *Hamlet* (c.1600) is possibly his most famous play, in which the motives of revenge and love are entangled with the moral dilemmas of integrity and corruption.

Taking the form of a sourcebook, this guide to Shakespeare's remarkable play offers:

- extensive introductory comment on the contexts, critical history and many interpretations of the text, from first performance to the present
- annotated extracts from key contextual documents, reviews, critical works and the text itself
- cross-references between documents and sections of the guide, in order to suggest links between texts, contexts and criticism
- suggestions for further reading.

Part of the *Routledge Guides to Literature* series, this volume is essential reading for all those beginning detailed study of *Hamlet* and seeking not only a guide to the play, but a way through the wealth of contextual and critical material that surrounds Shakespeare's text.

Hb: 0–415–31432–1
Pb: 0–415–31433–X

Available at all good bookshops
For ordering and further information please visit:
www.routledge.com

Related titles from Routledge

Macbeth
A Sourcebook
Alexander Leggatt

William Shakespeare's *Macbeth* (c.1606) is a timeless tale of murder, love and power, which has given rise to heated debates around such issues as the representation of gender roles, political violence and the dramatisation of evil.

Taking the form of a sourcebook, this guide to Shakespeare's play offers:

- extensive introductory comment on the contexts, critical history and performance of the text, from publication to the present
- annotated extracts from key contextual documents, reviews, critical works and the text itself
- cross-references between documents and sections of the guide, in order to suggest links between texts, contexts and criticism
- suggestions for further reading.

Part of the *Routledge Guides to Literature* series, this volume is essential reading for all those beginning detailed study of *Macbeth* and seeking not only a guide to the play, but a way through the wealth of contextual and critical material that surrounds Shakespeare's text.

0-415-23824-2 (hbk)
0-415-23825-0 (pbk)

978-0-415-23824-3 (hbk)
978-0-415-23825-0 (pbk)

Available at all good bookshops
For ordering and further information please visit:
www.routledge.com

Related titles from Routledge

Thomas Hardy
Geoffrey Harvey
Routledge Guides to Literature

Thomas Hardy found fame as both a major novelist and a supreme poet, whose work reflected the many revolutionary social and intellectual changes of the nineteenth and early-twentieth centuries. One of England's most popular writers, his work is still widely read and enjoyed.

This guide to Hardy's memorable work offers:

- an accessible introduction to the contexts and many interpretations of Hardy's texts, from publication to the present

- an introduction to key critical texts and perspectives on Hardy's life and work, situated within a broader critical history

- cross-references between sections of the guide, in order to suggest links between texts, contexts and criticism

- suggestions for further reading.

Part of the *Routledge Guides to Literature* series, this volume is essential reading for all those beginning detailed study of Hardy and seeking not only a guide to his works, but a way through the wealth of contextual and critical material that surrounds them.

Hb: 0–415–23491–3
Pb: 0–415–23492–1

Available at all good bookshops
For ordering and further information please visit:
www.routledge.com

Related titles from Routledge

Routledge Dictionary of Literary Terms

Peter Childs and Roger Fowler

The *Routledge Dictionary of Literary Terms* is a twenty-first century update of Roger Fowler's seminal *Dictionary of Modern Critical Terms*. Bringing together original entries written by such celebrated theorists as Terry Eagleton and Malcolm Bradbury with new definitions of current terms and controversies, this is the essential reference book for students of literature at all levels. This book includes:

- New definitions of contemporary critical issues such as 'Cybercriticism' and 'Globalization'.

- An exhaustive range of entries, covering numerous aspects to such topics as genre, form, cultural theory and literary technique.

- Complete coverage of traditional and radical approaches to the study and production of literature.

- Thorough account of critical terminology and analyses of key academic debates.

- Full cross-referencing throughout and suggestions for further reading.

0–415–34017–9

Available at all good bookshops
For ordering and further information please visit:
www.routledge.com